LISTENING IN ON MUSEUM CONVERSATIONS

GAEA LEINHARDT AND KAREN KNUTSON

ALTAMIRA PRESS
A Division of Rowman & Littlefield Publishers, Inc.
Walnut Creek • Lanham • New York • Toronto • Oxford

To our special and unique
conversational companions
Saki and Moonsoup

ALTAMIRA PRESS
A division of Rowman & Littlefield Publishers, Inc.
1630 North Main Street, #367
Walnut Creek, CA 94596
www.altamirapress.com

Rowman & Littlefield Publishers, Inc.
A wholly owned subsidary of The Rowman & Littlefield Publishing Group, Inc.
4501 Forbes Boulevard, Suite 200
Lanham, MD 20706

PO Box 317
Oxford
OX2 9RU, UK

British Library Cataloguing in Publication Information Available

Library of Congress Cataloging-in-Publication Data

Leinhardt, Gaea, 1944–
  Listening in on museum conversations / Gaea Leinhardt and Karen
Knutson.
    p. cm.
Includes bibliographical references and index.
  ISBN 0-7591-0441-7 (hardcover : alk. paper) — ISBN 0-7591-0442-5
(pbk. : alk. paper)
  1. Museums—Educational aspects. 2. Museum exhibits. I. Knutson,
Karen, 1969– II. Title.

  AM7.L45 2004
  069—dc22

                          2003026629

Printed in the United States of America

♾™ The paper used in this publication meets the minimum requirements of American
National Standard for Information Sciences—Permanence of Paper for Printed Library
Materials, ANSI/NISO Z39.48-1992.

LISTENING IN ON MUSEUM CONVERSATIONS

CULTURAL RESOURCE MANAGEMENT PROGRAM
Division of Continuing Studies
University of Victoria
PO Box 3030 STN CSC
Victoria, BC V8W 3N6 Canada

CONTENTS

Preface

F OR BOTH OF US, museums are fascinating and enchanting places. They are places of enormous beauty, places of transport, and places that reflect both the most conservative views of the status quo and the most provocative new ideas of our time. Our own connections to museums press us to want to share the good features with friends, families, and children and researchers. We want to share the fascination and mystery we find in places that lift a curtain on objects of beauty, objects of history, objects of our modern world, and ideas and concepts that weave through our everyday life. By way of an introduction we share here our own personal identification with the museums of our childhood and adolescence.

Gaea Leinhardt

To me there is only one museum, the museum uptown on the edge of the park, the temple-like, cool, cavernous one, the Met. The Metropolitan Museum of Art was a mid-distance walk from my family's apartment, about twenty minutes. I was allowed to go there by myself as far back as I can remember; as shocking as it may seem today, I know I was visiting on my own by the age of eight or nine. In my memory, the broad, flat staircases are always brightly lit with sunshine (meaning a morning visit because the steps face east); the interior is always dark and cool and enormously inviting. I drift past marbles and carvings to wonderful, glorious men in metal and, most of all, men on horseback. Medieval armor is not usually a fascination for young girls, but I was not really looking at the armor— I was loving the horses. For a horse lover in Manhattan, there were three opportunities to see horses: the mounted police, the carriages in the park, and the Met. Granted, the horses in the Met were not alive, but they were up on platforms, and the detail of their tack and armament was simply fascinating to me. I did not see

medieval knights; I did not see warriors or jousters. I saw intricate designs, delicate carvings, amazing levers and supports. And therein lies the complication of
museums for me, as an educator, today. Museums are co-constructed by the eyes,
memories, and identities of the visitors. In spite of the most artful intentions of
the curatorial and design teams, in spite of hours of argument and passion behind the design of the scenes, I saw no historical progression, no cultural distinctions between France, Spain, and the Holy Roman Empire; I saw decorated
horses—horses in fabulous costumes. I failed to see what I was intended to see
and instead saw something totally different. I still love the Met; no museum has
its light, sound, or intensity of memories for me. But I have come to know other
museums, and I have come to watch how others move through and engage with
exhibitions in other museums. I have come to listen in on museum conversations.
This book is about what my colleagues and I have seen and heard that may be of
special use for museum educators, curators who have begun to consider the visitor in a new way, evaluators who having counted seconds and stops are ready for
more, and educators who want to go beyond the walls of a school.

Karen Knutson

My first summer job was at a small local history museum in Bertie Township,
Ridgeway, Ontario. I loved to wander through the storage areas looking at some of
the more bizarre parts of the collection, marveling at a "petrified pear found at a
nearby farm" and little curio whimsies such as a satin-lined jewelry container fash-
ioned out of a goat hoof. I wondered about the people who had originally made,
used, or found these strange objects, and I wondered why they kept them. What
memories did these cherished objects hold for their original owners? And how did
they wind up in a museum collection? As a part of my work, I carefully numbered
and preserved collections of household materials such as lace collars, spools of
thread, photographs, and kitchen utensils that came mostly from local farmsteads.
The local place names were vaguely recognizable to me, and the household objects
seemed similar to the odd kinds of detritus found around my own home. Perhaps
for these reasons, I found that the museum storage area was a place of lingering
souls, stories and time preserved, and evidence of lives lived, witnessed in shreds
and whispers. Some objects in the museum were created for the specific purpose of
memorializing family members, such as intricately woven memorial wreaths, their
delicate flowers and leaves spun with collected human hair of deceased family
members. But to me, traces of human lives were witnessed more poignantly some-
how through the indirectness of christening gowns, utensils, and baskets of sewing
notions—objects that reflect the active lives these people had lived. In the public
area of the museum, I found it fascinating to see how these same objects were used

to stand in for a broader category representing typical farm life in the region in the nineteenth century. I was curious about this process of musealization—the selecting, organizing, and conferring of meaning to these objects; the choices and trade-offs made to create a coherent curatorial story. In museum practice there are endless possibilities, and complex decisions to make. I continue to be fascinated by the questions: Who decides which story to tell? And how do they tell it?

Our combined memories of museums point toward the complexity of museum communication. No doubt such memories or ones similar to them are shared by others who spend time working in and around the museum world. We take Karen's memories to be evocative of the vastness of the interpretive venture of museums and the potentially rich evocative histories that are contained within them. We all need to remember that what we see in museums is the combination of hundreds of small and large decisions. We take Gaea's memories to suggest the other side of the interpretive venture, the role of visitors' identities and the impossibility of controlling the constructed meanings that arise from this informal learning environment. We all need to be aware that the identities and agendas of the visitors shape their experiences in powerful ways.

Our personal connections to museums mirror those of society at large. Questions about the changing nature of what should constitute a museum experience have emerged, as museums have become a central cultural and leisure activity in an increasingly information-centered world. Are museums for entertainment or for education? Questions about representation have also occupied society, as diverse publics have found in the museum their vision of the world depicted and supported or challenged and denied. Should museums support the status quo, or should they speak for diverse points of view? Are they sites for reverence and recognition, or are they sites to encourage dialogue and debate? We have watched with excitement as museums have moved from the dusty sidelines of the storehouse to become key players in our very definition of culture.

This book is an account of the results of a program of research envisioned by a team of government officials and their advisors to study how learning occurred in a broad variety of museums. The government team consisted of four professionals from the Institute of Museum Services (now the Institute of Museum and Library Services), the National Endowment for the Humanities, the National Endowment for the Arts, and the National Science Foundation. The specific story of how they came together—how they developed the request for proposals (RFP—a published invitation for scholars to submit ideas for research that, if chosen, the committee would then fund), how they managed the selection and research processes, and how others disagreed intensely with one or another of their decisions—is a good story in and of itself, but it is not the one being shared here.

The original RFP had a response due date of August 2, 1996. As a cooperative agreement, it requested a design of research that would cover a variety of types of museums (e.g., art, history, natural history, science, historical houses, children's centers and museums, planetariums, zoos, and aquariums). The RFP also requested that a range of visiting populations be represented (excluding organized groups such as school tours and elderhostels). One reason behind the effort to study museums as places of learning was the fact that support for museums had been sought by making the argument that they were places where learning took place and where future scientists, artists, archeologists, and historians might well get the first spark of inspiration that would direct them to their future careers. The original RFP had a two-stage plan. In the first portion of the effort, some means of coordinating the vast and often fugitive literature of the field was to be mounted. In the second phase, research on learning in museums was to be carried out. The review of the proposals was to be conducted by a team of peer reviewers, with the final decision residing with the four funding agencies. The evaluation criteria were standard (impact, balance, research, management, dissemination, budget, personnel, cooperative relationships, and in-kind contributions). No weighting of the criteria was provided. After an initial round of reviewing, the team from the Learning Research and Development Center at the University of Pittsburgh received a request for revisions and clarifications for the Museum Learning Collaborative (MLC) proposal on October 25, 1996. The response was submitted on November 14, 1996, and we received notification of the award on January 16, 1997, with an effective start date of March 1997.

While the MLC was the largest funded project to study learning in museums at the time, it was by no means an isolated foray. The work we conducted was built upon a foundation of research from a variety of scholars. Among the most significant contributions was Falk and Dierking's interactive experience model, which called attention to the importance of context in considering museum learning. They suggested a holistic model that included aspects of visitor background and expectations (the personal context), the impact of the museum environment (the physical context), and mediation within social groups (the social-cultural context). Zahava Doering and her colleagues have focused on the importance of visitor motivation and agenda to museum experiences, and her work has also brought the finely honed tools of social science investigation and analysis to the field. Beverley Serrell's work using the notion of time as an organizer and indicator that predicts and defines learning has been deeply influential in content and approach. Howard Gardner has moved the field of museum education to consider varieties of modes of visitor experience that museums might support. George Hein has voiced the need for the role of theory in learning and interpreting experiences. Hein's theory of choice is constructivism, and he has discussed how that theory might help in the design and interpretation of museum experiences. While Hein has focused on the constructivist features of Piagetian theory, others, such as Abigail Housen and Anna Kindler, have emphasized developmental aspects of Piaget's work. These scholars have guided the field of museum education by moving the conception of what constitutes a museum learning experience from a simplistic outcome-based assessment to a description of development, to considering the museum learning experience as a rich and complex layering of causes, factors, and supports.

In this book we are certainly aware of and connect to the work of these scholars; but here we are primarily giving an account that, while influenced by many of these ideas, also departs from them. In the chapters that follow, we develop and use a model of learning in the museum setting that owes much to sociocultural theory as interpreted by James Wertsch and his reflection of Vygotsky. We also try to exemplify a style of thinking about specific features of the museum experience in order to understand and define learning. In this aspect of the effort, we are trying not only to expand what learning means in museums or other informal environments but also to challenge conceptions of learning in the more formal environment of schooling. The book is not intended as a recipe or how-to guide, nor is it intended as a stand-alone scholarly element in a debate; rather we hope readers will see it as a voice in an extended conversation among thoughtful practitioners from the formal and informal worlds of learning in museums.

We have enormous debts to many people. The work could not have been done without the funding and initial intellectual support of the Institute for Museum and Library Services (Diane Frankel and Rebecca Danvers), the National Science Foundation (Barbara Butler), the National Endowment for the Humanities (Nancy Rogers), and the National Endowment for the Arts. The work could not have been finished without the careful and consistent management of Rebecca Danvers at the Institute for Museum and Library Services. The first design was greatly aided in its conceptualization by Kirsten Ellenbogen, Leona Schauble, and Laura Martin. Phase I research included wonderful collaborators who jointly produced the first book, *Learning Conversations in Museums*: Mary Abu-Shumays (who also acted as project director for the first three years), Sue Allen, Doris Ash, Jane Blankman-Hetrick, Kevin Crowley, Kirsten Ellenbogen, Joyce Fienberg, Mary Gleason, Madeleine Gregg, Melanie Jacobs, Melissa Mercer, Scott Paris, Ellen Rosenthal, Leona Schauble, Catherine Stainton, and Carol Tittle.

None of this research could have taken place without the extremely generous and open support of the collaborating museums and their staff. The Carnegie Museums of Art (CMA) and Natural History (CMNH) helped us at all levels. On a daily basis we were supported by Louise Lippincott, Sarah Nichols, Marilyn Russell, and Lucy Stewart at the CMA. At the CMNH we are indebted to James Richardson III, Cathy Andreychek, and Deborah Mack. The work was facilitated by the support of the directors of the museums, Richard Armstrong and Jay Apt, as well as the president, Ellsworth Brown. At Conner Prairie we were helped immeasurably by Ellen Rosenthal and Jane Blankman-Hetrick. At the Exploratorium, Sue Allen, Alice Krasniski, and Rochelle Slovin (from the American Museum of the Moving Image) were very helpful. At the Henry Ford Museum and Greenfield Village, Randy Mason and Donna Braden were immensely supportive.

The home team included enormous technical support from Chien-Fu Chang. Chien-Fu created the structure for the second version of our web page (www .museumlearning.com), which included an important and highly used searchable database of annotated references for museum research (that portion of the web page is now located at www.informalscience.org). Our invaluable team of researchers included Joyce Fienberg and Catherine Stainton. They both continue to help us find specific examples we search for and work to help clarify and simplify our prose. Joyce has gone far beyond any call of duty, going so far as taking manuscripts with her on transatlantic flights to try to clean up garbled prose (what is left is our responsibility). Joshua Space provided drawings for the appendix. For intellectual, collegial, and computational support, our partner Kevin Crowley was central. He has collaborated directly with us on other written products and will do so on future ones—time commitments alone have kept him from being a coauthor on this volume.

Many people in the museum community have been enormously helpful and gracious in talking with us, pointing out previous research or simply sending emails to correct unintended errors or to offer words of encouragement. These people include Randi Korn, Beverley Serrell, Jessica Luke, Minda Borun, Danielle Rice, Cheryl Meszaros, Zahava Doering, and Lois Silverman. In the very earliest days of the project, Lynn Dierking and John Falk were supportive and inclusive. Countless others came for visits, either virtually or face-to-face, to discuss ideas and share experiences. We thank them for including us in their world.

Introduction

THIS VOLUME REPRESENTS the central report of phase 2 of the Museum Learning Collaborative's efforts. We have organized the book around the core elements of a model of museum learning that we developed to act as a theoretical guide for our data collection and analysis. Each chapter presents one element of the model and our findings from the research that we conducted on that element. In briefest terms, our model takes seriously from the sociocultural perspective the multiple levels at which all activity takes place: the personal, the interactional, the historical, and the social. The model considers learning to be a form of conversational elaboration among participants. Learning is influenced by three clusters of factors: the cumulative personal historical identities of the visiting group; the designed features of the environment with which the group interacts; and the explanatory engagement of the group with objects, ideas, and concepts in an exhibition. Each cluster of factors has a set of measures attached to it. In discussing each construct we try to share with the reader not only the decisions and trade-offs that we made but also the rationales behind those decisions. Throughout the book we have used extensive quotes of visitor conversations in museums. As we discuss how we have quantified visitor learning across museum types using a conceptual, theoretically based model, we hope that these visitors' voices will help to remind readers of our subjects and the richness of the experiences that museums provide. We hope that these voices, and this model of learning, will help to improve museum practice and to encourage continued research on museum environments and their visitors.

Chapter I: *Learning* starts with an account of a first difficult set of decisions— how should learning be considered? We explain our decision to use conversation as the primary focus of learning and consider it in light of other discussions. We introduce the underlying model of learning that emerged. In this chapter we also introduce the format of other chapters that follow: a consideration of the conceptual issues; what we found in the studies of the MLC; how the ideas under consideration play out in different kinds of exhibitions (art, living history, hands-on science, natural history); and finally how museum educators, evaluators and curators, might make use of the ideas.

Chapter 2: *Exhibition* lays out the foundation for the discussion of our work by describing the different exhibitions and museums in which the research was conducted. Although the exhibitions and museums themselves are not an independent part of the model, these descriptions help to anchor the interpretations in the rest of the volume. We emphasize the interplay between curatorial intentions and visitors' agendas and lay bare our conceptually driven and pragmatically guided processes of decision making. We try to give the rich flavor of each show as well as provide a sense of the objectives and purposes of each venue. The details of how the work was conducted are presented in order to understand each exhibition through its curator, setting, wall text, and catalogue. The voice of the curator is included by emphasizing the hopes and aspirations for the show. Finally, the challenges that existed for the visitor are indicated.

Chapter 3: *Identity* examines the first of four critical components of the model of learning. Identity is that aspect of the visiting experience that is brought in through the door with the visiting group. The most problematic issue in considering identity is that there are many aspects of it. Identity, as we considered it, does not refer to the social-demographic categories of the group members (age, gender, race, income) but rather to the collective knowledge, dispositions, motivations, stances, and experiences that bring the group to a particular place at a particular time. Is this a chance for a grandparent to revisit experiences with cars in their life in front of, and for the benefit of, a grandchild? Is it a moment for a wife to listen in as her husband and a friend trade stories of design success and failure at the local aluminum plant? Is it a moment for three children to adjust their imagination as they confront the uniqueness and individuality of American Indian groups? Is it a time for two women to share what one knows deeply about the construction of art and the other knows about supporting and listening carefully to a good friend? Identity in this chapter reflects the motivations and intentions of visitors as they come in and experience the particulars of an exhibition. Identity filters and shapes the experiences of visitors, but it is one of the dimensions that is changed as a result of an experience with a museum.

Chapter 4: *Conversation* traces visitors through the various exhibitions. We listen in as visitors connect and disconnect from objects, themes, and each other in the various settings, and we explore the problem of what and how one listens in and how one decides to account for the language that is produced. This aspect of the model of learning—conversation, particularly explanatory engagement—

explores the interface and expressed interaction between the visitor and the curatorial team. Conversation is the real moment of co-construction of meaning; this
is where the short traces of the day are set in place to be remembered later; and
this is where the longer, carefully revisited, and reshaped memories first come into
being. Conversational discourse both mediates and contributes to learning. In this
chapter, examples of the discourse that surrounds specific exhibition themes are
presented, and we share the ways in which discourse reflects connections to other
familiar objects or ideas (syntheses), looks closely at and pulls apart the specifics
of a unique presentation (analyses), or poses a question and seeks an answer (explanations). We explore the pattern of the depth and shallowness of engagement
and the challenges reflected in the language of the visitors. Findings about the
composition of groups and how group composition plays out in the conversations
are developed. Finally, we consider the ways in which some groups practice their
"groupness" in these settings—families as families, couples as couples, and friends
as friends.

Chapter 5: *Learning Environment* focuses on the designs and manipulations of
the exhibitions that go beyond specific objects or interactive exhibit stations. Here
the museum's counterpart to visitor identity is explored. What aspects of the exhibition environment should be considered as part of a model of learning, and
how? We examine the disconnect between existing theories and debates within the
field of museum design and research and what we people actually do. What the
designers, curators, and educators brought, and in some sense left, for the visitors
to experience is shown—the intellectual guidance afforded the visitor. This guidance quite frequently exists within larger, more general text panels; within specific
juxtapositions and alignments of objects and experiences in the exhibition; and by
establishing some sense of coherence (chronological, thematic, expanding, or focusing) throughout the course of an exhibition.

Chapter 6: *Results* presents the ways that learning in museums is influenced by
the constructs of connection to environmental design and display, the identity of
the visiting group, and the activities visitors engage in as they move through the
designed space as a self-aware and established group. We consider the limitations
that are inherent in trying to move across the boundaries of different contents
(science and art), purposes (spending the day with a grandparent or fulfilling a
school assignment), and groupings (a couple on a date or a multigenerational family). This chapter is the conclusion of our work and points to the analyses and
work that are yet to come.

The appendix describes the methodology used in this program of research.
While this information is presented as an appendix, because the book can be read
without it, it is also meant as a contribution to the field and a way of opening a
dialogue about how research might be done and why. (Readers who would like

more details about the research methodology may write to either author and request a copy of the Museum Learning Collaborative Research Manual, Leinhardt, Knutson, Fienberg, and Stainton 2002.) The appendix begins with a discussion of what is meant by methodology and examines some of the assumptions about methodology that seem to be present in the research world. It first addresses some broad methodological issues, such as securing cooperation from visitors, designing interviews and developing themes, probing the curatorial premise and message, transforming talk into records and segments, and developing and using codes and statistical analyses. Then details about the methods as they pertain to each of the preceding chapters in the book are detailed. The final part of the appendix suggests ways in which a more qualitative approach to the existing data has been developed and further discusses other techniques used in the early stages of this work.

Learning

> I came because it's a time-limited show, and I wanted to get
> here before it finished because it sounded good.
> I came because I was going to lunch with a friend and we're
> both members and she suggested it and we decided it would
> be a great way to spend the afternoon.

—VISITOR CONVERSATION AT THE *ALUMINUM BY DESIGN* EXHIBITION

The Problem

HOW SHOULD WE CONSIDER learning in the museum? Most writers in the museum field, such as Hein, have emphasized that the informality of the museum learning experience refers to the environment and the curriculum and not to the kinds of learning that can and should go on.[1] Many museum educators also stress the nonfactoidal aspects of museum learning and the uniqueness of the free-choice environment. A successful experience might be represented by visitors having an "aha" or "wow" experience, or a successful experience might be one that provokes curiosity. These experiences may be memorable, and they may form the foundation for events many years later. Certainly the biographies of many famous figures would have us believe that one of the most meaningful experiences that set the budding genius on his or her path was an early trips to the planetarium or to the natural history museum.[2] And, as the opening quotes from two women who planned to see an exhibition together illustrate, museum visiting provides an opportunity for learning but is also a social activity. Clearly, learning in the museum has something to do with intense and active engagement, looking at and appreciating objects (or manipulatives), and the sheer

Museum educators themselves have also reflected common psychological views of learning, including a conception of learning in museums as a process of stage-like development and construction. It is the museum version of Piaget, in which the organism—the learner—has a tightly defined set of steps through which he or she naturally proceeds;[7] when an individual goes through these steps, or stages, in conjunction with a set of museum experiences, learning follows.[8] This developmental view of learning emphasizes the individual and the consistency of the individual's development in the museum along with his or her development in other arenas of life—such as learning science, mathematics, or art. Like developmentalists, constructivists emphasize the role of the learner in learning. Rather than seeing learners as empty vessels, they believe in the process of individual discovery, and they emphasize the role of the learner in actively seeking and building knowledge upon his or her prior knowledge and beliefs.[9]

The insight concerning the active role of the learner has been an extremely valuable contribution to the field, resulting in exhibitions reflective of visitors' prior knowledge and approaches to learning. In the most extreme view of the position, however, it is almost pointless to "teach" the learner because so much of the learning is an inherent discovery process within the individual as he or she interacts with the environment. Two important ideas emerge from these traditions that are still strongly held today: first, that the sequence of stages is immutable, and, second, that it is the individual alone who constructs his or her own understandings. One of the most eloquent and complete statements of this consideration of learning as it relates to the museum is found in the writings of Hein.[10] The risk with this view is taking it to be the *only* right way to understand learning in museums. Just as some aspect of museum learning is captured by the idea of refinement of the senses, so is some aspect of museum learning captured by the constructivist developmental view. It cannot be argued that learning is *not* a process of accommodation of new information and ideas. But it *can* be argued that there may be more to the story and more that is of interest to educators to be considered.

Traditionally, in both the cognitive and constructivist views, *learning* has been defined by psychologists and educators as some level of cognitive change: *reorganization* of familiar ideas, concepts, facts, and procedures; *acquisition* of new ideas; and *abandonment* of false or faulty ideas. The process by which this change takes place is one of adding on to existing understandings or radically readjusting such understandings, in which case learners feel out of balance for a time until they have rearranged their understandings to some level of stability again. Colloquially this tends to mean that individuals can *do* something that they could not do before—swim or read, for example; can *understand* and *appreciate* something they did not understand before—a piece of music, for example; or can *interpret* and *apply* concepts in a way that they could not previously—evolution, for example. In this cognitive way of looking at learning, it becomes important to distinguish between types of knowledge because the types are believed to be acquired and used somewhat differently. Psychologists have found it useful to distinguish declarative or coherent fact-based knowledge (e.g., knowing that impressionism differs from surrealism in specific ways, or knowing that Newtonian physics is different from Aristotelian with respect to the location of forces) from procedural or systemically organized action knowledge (e.g., knowing how to critique a school of painting or an artifact, or knowing how to design and conduct an experiment) and to distinguish both of those from conceptual or principled knowledge (e.g., knowing the principles that define a field in a way that allows one to detect violations to the knowledge structures in that discipline). All of these types of knowledge have different properties, and they tend to interact and overlap. One common feature of these conceptions of learning is that when an individual has learned something, we tend to see them as *possessing* a piece of knowledge.

However, recently a rather different perspective on learning has emerged: learning has been seen as a system of participatory competencies and activities. This view has a decidedly social feel to it. In the sociocultural way of looking at things, learning means less that an individual "owns" certain knowledge—in the sense of having a valuable possession—and more that an individual can participate in a particular group or world in an active way.[11] Thus, a doctor is knowledgeable not just because she or he has a set of skills but because the doctor can interact with a patient, support staff, other doctors, and documented sets of information in a way that allows significant flow of activity to take place. Similarly, groups often have the task of coordinating their actions and activities to meet some common set of goals. Group members "learn" to participate in increasingly complex and significant activities that are of value and importance to the group.[12] The boundaries between procedural, declarative, and conceptual knowledge, so significant in the strictly cognitive view of learning, are less of an issue for the sociocultural perspective, while the gradual emergence of shared meanings across language and representations are of more concern. Communication, emergent goals, and coordination become paramount. The tools of this participation in an intellectual framework, as Greeno and others point out, are tools of communication such as language and discourse more broadly construed.[13] So what would this conceptualization mean to the consideration of group learning in a museum?

By considering learning in a more sociocultural way, as Falk and Dierking point out in their clear summary of sociocultural theory, we can move beyond the idea of counting how many facts or concepts an individual "picks up" during a visit and we can also acknowledge the fundamentally cultural and social nature of the museum environment.[14] We can be less concerned with the dichotomous formal/informal distinction and can ask, rather, which activities are being supported in a given situation; and we can examine visitor groups to see which kinds of groups are able to take advantage of particular opportunities in the setting.[15]

Many in the museum community (writ large) seem to want learning in museums to be regarded as something special, more valuable and quite distinct from school-type learning. This is in part due to the increased role of public funding that requires museums to prove their educational value. This desire reflects much more than a wish to justify museum existence by demonstrating success over and above that of schooling (and museums are not schools); rather, it reflects a genuine belief about the nature of learning itself. In museum research, learning is often discussed in terms of meaning making, focusing not only on the acquisition of factual knowledge, but also, importantly, on the diverse and personal ways in which visitors' prior knowledge and experiences are divulged, shared, and reinforced during a museum visit and in interaction with authentic objects.[16] It is clear that most members of the museum community, ourselves included, value such intellectual activities as attention, curiosity arousal, and imaginative expansion more than they value naming scientific terms or painters' styles. Finally, it is clear that the museum community believes in the power of museum experiences for long-term memory.[17] But realistically we cannot expect that each and every object, in each and every exhibition, will arouse the individual and inspire him or her on a life course of learning. Neither is it reasonable to assume that while playing with water in a children's museum the child is necessarily laying down a bedrock foundation of examples from which to draw at a later point in time.

We can assume that on occasion visitors will be sparked in a way that has them following up on a spiral of curiosity and interest or that over extended periods of time and repeated visits a child may lay down a set of indexed examples to be accessed under different conditions.[18] Searching for the unusual moment of arousal or the repeated moments of concept development would be a completely legitimate and even exciting approach to understanding learning in museums. We, however, were in search of something that was less spectacular and more common, on the one hand, and more immediate, on the other. We wanted to consider learning as it took place in a group context and as it happened generally (perhaps not always) for most groups, most of the time.

The Concept

One of the most difficult parts of making a research decision and sticking with it is that as soon as it is done one must wave goodbye to all the other paths one might have chosen. In taking the first tentative steps toward a decision about how to examine museum learning—that it should be a group event and that it should be relatively common—we lost the solitary visitor; and while we did not lose the spectacular, we could not guarantee its presence. Some elements of the specific had to be sacrificed in order to create a research study that would work across museum settings and with different visitor types.[19] (Throughout this book we present examples that suggest some of the complexities of individual cases and how they fit into our larger picture of museum learning.)

We began to think of learning as an elaboration of what was already known and understood—as an extension in detail and refinement of what the visitors already appreciated. We also considered learning to be a modification of assumptions or presumptions from one given perspective to another. But how, we wondered, could you observe such a thing? We return here to our original sense of learning. We can think of learning as the ways in which individuals can participate in a group activity as well as the ways in which a group can coordinate its goals and meanings in increasingly sophisticated ways. So what does that mean for a museum visit? It means that we would expect a visiting group to talk about what they were experiencing in a variety of ways, some of which might be quite trivial, some of which would bind the group together and remind them of their shared or individual pasts, and some of which would clearly be informed by the details of what they were seeing and experiencing. This way of considering the group activity of learning in a museum through conversational mediation is quite different from the way in which Lois Silverman approaches both conversation and individual learning. We treat the group as the unit of study and development, and we treat conversation as a mediating process for group activity and learning.

We could expect that the conversations of a small group at a museum would show variation in the level of elaboration throughout the duration of their visit. By conversational elaboration we mean the gradual enrichment of talk that adds to the skeletal form of a typical museum exchange with details of observation, comparisons, attachments to memories, and evaluations. We mean that the experience of the museum becomes a situation remembered in its detail and in its specificity and that this experience and set of examples enrich and expand future conversations. These enrichments, these elaborated and memorable examples, become things remembered and revisited beyond the time frame of the visit. This is not true for every observation, but for some. We expect that occasionally visitors' values and views will be sufficiently challenged by experiences that shared assumptions will be altered and that these alterations will be marked by conversational utterances such as "I didn't know that aluminum was developed so early, and that it was so rare and valuable." The group visiting a museum does not necessarily have a set of explicit goals aimed at enhancing their conversations with exhibit content; rather, a group might establish emergent goals of learning and enjoyment, and their conversations are a product of such engagement.

We believe that the details of a knowledge system about, say, designs in aluminum, the meaning of light in art and science, the ways in which film and video are constructed, the aesthetics and technology of cars, the lives of modern American Indians, or the collectives of African peoples (all content areas in our data set) become extended and embedded in the visiting groups' awareness when they visit exhibitions that display and discuss such topics. We believed that we could detect these changes by asking visitors to participate in a few fairly simple tasks and by monitoring their conversations as they went through a museum.

Why, one might well ask, this emphasis on groups? Doesn't the solitary visitor matter? Doesn't the quiet couple who chooses not to talk in a museum, but rather saves discussions for coffee afterward, also learn? Our answer here is "of course!" We chose groups because conversation is far more likely to occur in situ in groups than by the solitary visitor; so it is observable. Other researchers have selected different methods of observing visitors. Minda Borun, working at the exhibit level, searched for specific preidentified behaviors and tracked their occurrence in an effort to assess learning.[20] Lois Silverman, in careful examinations of language, categorized the particular collection of activities of a visitor and his or her conversation as representing a totality, such as "personalizer" or "recognizer."[21] Beverley Serrell used time, understanding its limitations, as a central part of her method of gauging learning.[22] Time can be an indicator of learning, and we use it as a part of our measure. From the early 1970s to the end of the 1980s, time was considered to be an extremely significant educational issue; but the questions always remained: What is inside time? What is it about time that is meaningful in a given set of activities or experiences?[23] Collecting time data is physically unobtrusive, and time provides an objective and readily comparable measure. But time itself is not learning. As an indicator, time has the problem that it does not account for a trade-off between short but intensive moments of looking at some part of an exhibition but not talking, and spells of long detached pauses where nothing related to learning appears to be going on. As John Carroll pointed out as early as 1962, it is the percentage of time needed that should be measured, not simply time spent or allocated.[24]

Choosing conversational elaboration as the focus of learning in museums still leaves us with the question of how to categorize or think about the talk. Should we look at the average length of the utterance? Should we count the total number of words? Should we reassign talk produced in a group back to the individual to determine who talked the most and about what? In the fields of sociolinguistics, there are many models of how to approach this issue, especially those models that focus on discourse.[25] Some approaches require accurate recordings of utterances at a fine-grained level that allows for distinctions between "um" and "uhh,"[26] while others focus more on the overall gist of the conversation. In her dissertation,

Lois Silverman examined talk for consistent patterns that related to the identity and relationship of the visitors, putting forward the compelling finding that visitors' meaning-making processes are personal, complex, and not necessarily related to the content provided in the exhibition.[27] Minda Borun's work on family learning looked for behavioral criteria in visitor interactions—including questioning, reading, and explaining—to indicate learning in family talk.[28]

We considered the conversation itself as an entity; the total conversation was in some sense assumed to be the property or understanding of the entire group. This way of looking at the shared discussion among visitors is quite distinct from other uses of conversation in museums. We took this approach because of what has been learned in recent years about the co-construction of joint tasks and the talk that supports such tasks, most notably in the work of Clark.[29] It turns out that in many conversations where ideas and or actions must be coordinated, both parties (or all members of the group for more than dyads) are engaged in important work, not just the speaker. Through gesture, and well-placed "uh-huhs" and "okays," the listener—not just the speaker—is investing in and supporting the task. If the task is to make sense of, make meaningful, or make enjoyable a visit to a museum exhibition, then it is all participants that contribute in multiple ways (speaking at the same informed level, playing dumb, acting bored, or enthusiastically responding). It is also the case that in these socially constructed situations, people practice both being themselves and being a member of a particular social group, be that a family group, a friendship group, or a couple.

Examples

Let us turn now to a few examples of conversations in museums. We intend to provide many examples of visitor conversations in museums throughout this book because we want to share extended examples of real visitors' conversations to illustrate both the rewards and the challenges of using conversational analysis as a methodology. Here we provide five examples that we believe illuminate the different levels and textures of learning conversations. The first example involves a quotation that directly reflects learning. Here, in the simplest terms, we provide an example that shows visitors gaining knowledge from an exhibit. The subsequent examples illustrate different levels of conversational experience. First, we want to show what it sounds like when a group starts a visit unfocused and unsure and near the end has more confidence, has established a "way in," and is elaborating on their ideas and reactions. Second, we want to share a conversation where the rhythm changes from a deep, engaged explanation somewhere in the tour to a trivial, superficial connection—almost as a relief from their intense engagement. Finally, we want to share a real problem that remains for informal learning environments.

Hearing Learning

This excerpt seems like the sound of knowledge being "poured in" and accepted, a direct communication, sender-message-receiver. This family group was touring through an exhibit about American Indians, and the mother noticed a display about the role of American Indians in World War II. She absorbed the content and called her son over to see the display.

> *Mother:*   You have to read this—I didn't know this. Read that about the war. How they transmitted, relayed messages to one another.
> *Son:*   [reading label silently]
> *Mother:*   The Japanese were never able to break this code. (IN 08/19)[30]

The quotation is about as direct and directive an instance of learning from a museum exhibition as we have found. The mother read, absorbed, and pointed out a small factoid, but one of unique interest to her young son. We know that visitors read labels, we know that visitors gain some factual knowledge, and we can test them for that. This is not how most of us in the museum world think conversation might support deep, meaningful learning. It would be more interesting if we saw this small factoid reappear if they later went to see the movie *Windtalkers*, a movie about Navajo code talkers during World War II, and there was an echo of this brief encounter that would give strong evidence of learning. However, in our studied museum conversations, in most cases the process of making meaning is more subtle, personal, and complex, and in the next four examples we explore such situations.

Hearing Rhythms of Connection

Visitors' conversations have their own unique and personal rhythms. Routes through exhibits vary as visitors shop around for sights that appeal to them and pass by those that do not strike their fancy. In this example, a young college-aged pair of friends, a man and woman, at the *Light!* exhibition, spend nine minutes at a single exhibit object, the classic science fiction movie *A Trip to the Moon* (1902). The woman had taken a film class in which she had watched a lot of old movies, and she had seen this one before. Throughout, as they sat and watched the video, she recalled other movies and pondered why this particular video was selected to be included in the show. Below we include three segments of their lengthy conversation about the film:

> *Man:*   You know, if they're showing this as a light exhibit, I wonder why? Maybe because of the crude ways they had to light the set.

	Because you can tell—it's like light, blaring light on one side, and dark on the other.
Woman:	We watched this other movie called *Metropolis*. This really old, old, silent movie. And you could see the makeup on people in there because of the lights they had to use.
Man:	Right.
Woman:	They used really different lights. And they used this crazy make-up on people to make their faces show up. You can see some of these guys wore so much eyeliner. They wore more eyeliner than I do and that's a lot! . . . .
Man:	I wish they had a little thing saying this is how they made the movie. The crude lighting they had, whatever. Maybe it's to make you think . . . but let people think too much and they always think the wrong thing! Ha ha.
Woman:	No, I think you just think and you think what you think. Ha ha. . . .
Woman:	That was a very realistic comet that rolled by. And those are some nice stars. [long pause, watching silently] They didn't put out a lot of money on different sets or anything, did they?
Man:	They probably actually did.
Woman:	Oh, there's another one.
Man:	So when was this made, 1902? It was before the golden years.
Woman:	It was nice that they thought to bring an umbrella. [referring to characters' actions in the film] (LT 02/48)

These segments show several of the features we will be examining throughout the book: that objects in museums provide a springboard for visitors to discuss diverse and personal topics; that visitors try to figure out how objects were created or how they work; and also that spoken language is quite distinct from written language. Looking at this example, then, we see the way that the pair's engagement with an artifact serves as a springboard for them to discuss other related items not in the show (*Metropolis* as contrasted to *A Trip to the Moon*) and as a way of describing the complexity of the task of creating the object (the film). The man had the chance to explain his theory of why the movie was included in the exhibition and how the film was done. In the second segment from their conversation, we see the man wanting more information and expressing his concern that he might not get "it" (the intended message) right, while the woman saw the film as an opportunity to explore visual material in a more open-ended way. In this segment, they analyzed curatorial decisions involved in creating the exhibition and their own intentions for the museum visit. Through these statements, they both had a chance to reveal obliquely their stance toward the knowledge offered by the museum and the personal intentions inherent in visiting the museum. This second segment also illustrates that the spoken language segments we study are, in fact, very different from written or formal speech. In this book, for example, you will not likely encounter a single sentence in which we use the same verb four times, as the woman does with "think." In the final segment, they were beginning to detach from the exhibit. They watched silently and then threw out some superficial descriptive and evaluative comments about the film's narrative sequence.

After looking at the video for nine minutes the pair then spent fifteen seconds walking about and looking before settling on another exhibit to engage with. They moved from the second room of the exhibition to the third, to a section called Makers of Light. Once in the new room, they noticed a small portable theater (ca. 1750-75), a box with glass painted panels inside, lit from behind by an electrical candle. The label copy read:

> The illusion of three dimensions results from the theater's five painted glass panels, placed one behind the other. A flickering candle made the fireworks appear to sparkle.

They spent sixteen seconds looking at this object, and we include their total conversation below:

Woman: Okay, this section is called Makers of Light. Oh my gosh, my eyes are like freaked out after watching that flip-flip-flip-flip-flip. [referring to the film] Oh, look at these over here.

Man: Yeah, they look really cool.

Woman: What's this over here with the candle? Oh, that's neat.

Man: Yeah, that is.

Woman: That is cool! (LT 02/50-51)

The same couple who put forth so much effort less than a minute earlier now passes with the most trivial of list-like comments. This segment illustrates the individual rhythms of museum visits, as choice and interest and fatigue direct the attention of the group. By studying the conversations throughout an entire exhibition, we are able to capture the ebbing and flowing of attention that illustrates the complexities of a free-choice learning environment and the personal meaning making that takes place within it.

Hearing Lives

In our third example, we show another group's meandering and varied attention to elements in an exhibition. This example comes from an exhibition about the making of movies and television, *Behind the Screen*. Unlike the previous example, these two twenty-year-old friends did not have extensive prior knowledge of the element with which they chose to engage, but they were drawn to it out of sheer curiosity. Their conversation first concerned a group trip they were thinking about planning to Napa, California. This remained the topic of conversation as they moved past various exhibits, from a display of optical toys (a thaumatrope, a pheakistoscope, and a zoetrope) to a station where visitors can record their own animation to a video that explains cinematography and editing, until they were distracted by a display that showed how baseball games are edited live for viewing on television. They were drawn in by the display of different video screens that showed different camera angles on a baseball game. A screen in the middle of the display showed the edited version that is seen by TV viewers around the world. Visitors can hear the director calling out camera operator numbers and giving them quick orders, in shorthand, to focus in on different events in the game and in the stands. The whole enterprise is a high-wire act, requiring intense concentration on the part of the operators and highly tuned skills of anticipation, timing, and flow on the part of the editor. The display was surrounded by text that, among other things, explained the codes used by the editor to his team. The group's route and excerpts of their conversation in areas leading up to the baseball exhibit are shown below. First they spend ten seconds glancing at the exhibit called Optical Toys, where an oblique connection to Napa is made, starting a longer conversational thread:

Man 1: That's cool. That was Coppola's first film production company, Zoetrope.
Man 2: Oh, yeah.
Man 1: There's something on that up in Napa.
Man 2: Oh, cool.
Man 1: We gotta go there, dude.
Man 2: Yeah, I know. I kinda wanted to go yesterday, but I'm really trying to rally people. (EX 23/5)

They spend nineteen seconds wandering past the animation exhibit:

Man 1: I would have been dead yesterday.
Man 2: Do you think Alex[31] would want to go there? You guys wanna do Tahoe, don't you?

Man 1:   He's up for anything. He wants to see you and me, you know
what I mean?

Man 2:   Yeah.

Man 1:   He's already been up there.

Man 2:   Where, to Napa?

Man 1:   Yeah. (EX 23/6)

They spend twelve seconds walking past the Getting the Picture station:

Man 2:   I haven't been to Tahoe, but I don't think I'll ski there, or board,
and I don't want to come across a party pooper if I don't do that.
(EX 23/7)

Finally, they stop at an exhibit of a television control room and watch the editing
of a baseball game. This exhibit engaged them for five minutes and forty-one seconds. Here's the first part of their conversation:

Man 1:   Oh, let's do this.

Man 2:   Dude, this is fucking cool! Can you hear the director?

Man 1:   Oh!

Man 2:   That's what people see. But here are all the different camera angles.
So we're seeing that one, and then we just cut to which one, that one.

Man 1:   Oh, and it's lit up which one it's on.

Man 2:   So he just says it. I was wondering how this worked. It's the director.
. . . Wow, this is great. [hear the director calling shots]

Man 1:   Wow. [director calls]

Man 2:   This is hard. . . . How much do you think they enjoy the game when
they're doing this? He does a lot of "3-5."

Man 1:   Yeah. This reminds me of *Daryl*, the movie. He's in a room playing twenty video games at once and he's watching TV too. It's a
whole room with like twenty screens on it or something.

Man 2:   Wow.

Man 1:   Imagine doing this for a hockey game? I have a hard enough time
knowing what the fuck is going on on one screen! Ha ha!

Man 2:   I know . . . there are so many jobs out there I have no idea about. You
know?

Man 2:   Yeah.

Man 1:   "What do you do for a living?" "Oh, I shoot second base." [speaking
in an acting voice]

Man 2:   Ha ha!

Man 1: This is so different from being a movie director.

Man 2: Oh yeah. You've got to be "on" for three hours, right? (EX 23/8)

In addition to the in-and-out feel to this conversation, this example illustrates the challenge of the informal free-choice environment. One has the distinct sense of how the exhibition has interrupted and flowed into the historical strand of the lives of these two friends. The exhibition is not the major point of focus for the two. They take trips together, they both like sports, and they have shared experiences like movies, and into the current of that conversation they incorporate the museum experience, not as a separate topic but rather as an aspect of what they are already engaged in—a social experience. We imagine that this is exactly how museum experiences become a part of the group activity and shared histories.

Hearing Memories

The following is an example of conversation that begins with the museum object but takes a personal route. This pair of forty-something girlfriends toured through an exhibition on the history of aluminum called *Aluminum by Design: From Jewelry to Jets*. Their tour included lots of personal anecdotes. Looking at a shiny Brancusi-like airplane propeller and a large photo of a man building the inside of an airplane wing, one of friends recalled a moment in her past.

Woman 1: Aluminum propellers. Look at that old TWA thing. Did you know that all stewardesses used to have to be nurses and they had to wear their white nursing uniforms?

Woman 2: Hmm?

Woman 1: It's true.

Woman 2: How did you know that?

Woman 1: I spent a summer doing a research project on nurses and aviation.

Woman 2: What? Are you kidding me?!

Woman 1: No, I'm not kidding.

Woman 2: Why did you put those two together?

Woman 1: I got hired by these nursing profs. And they had tons of money and they had me researching the images of nurses for society. And they had tons of documents and they handed me all this stuff and said that nurses were the first stewardesses. And I did. . . . It was very interesting actually. . . .

Woman 2: And how are nurses?

Woman 1:   They had a bad image in pop culture. Now they're seen as sexy, trying to meet doctors, and they're on the covers of romance novels with their uniforms bursting open. (AL 23/13)

This example provides insight into the power of visitors' prior knowledge and the influence of the group composition on the resulting conversation and learning that take place. These longtime friends are visiting the exhibition as an opportunity to share their interests and have a fun time together. The content of the show provides a spark for a memory that one visitor shares with the other. Clearly there is learning going on here, but in this case, the learning that takes place focuses less on the exhibition content and more on the visitors' background interests and histories. It is quite amazing throughout our study of museum visitors to see the trajectories of conversations that begin with an object and end up in the recounting of a long-forgotten anecdote or personal memory. These personal moments, we feel, are just as important to the value of a museum experience as learning about the content of the exhibition per se.

Hearing Misconceptions

In our final example, three teenagers are visiting the *Africa: One Continent, Many Worlds* exhibition at the Carnegie Museum of Natural History. They evidently have been asked to go to the exhibition by their teacher. They have seen and loosely commented on just about everything in the show and have been reasonably attentive if not captivated. Just as Isabel Beck and her colleagues have described fifth graders' serious misconceptions about American history, in which the children develop a sort of holiday soup of factoids,[32] here, too, we see soup in the making. Misconceptions and inappropriate connections abound: African items are mistaken for dream catchers—Southwest Indian objects available in many tourist shops; they express an interesting belief that Africa is one country; they claim that Africans, very far away from the European experience, "don't get a lot of wars . . . you think about it, you know how we had all those world wars . . . Africa never took part in any of them"; Ethiopia, Rommel, El Alimein, and South Africa melt into some vague notion of the pastoral African herder and people carrying spears; finally, "They have no major government."

Girl 1:   Pipe. That's a long pipe.
Girl 3:   What's this?
Girl 2:   What are those dream catcher things?
Girl 1:   Yeah?
Girl 2:   Is that from Africa?

Girl 1: That's from the Indians.

Boy: [at same time] I thought that was Indian culture.

Girl 3: Yeah, Native American. [——] my grandma . . .

Girl 1: What's this? Are those daggers? Knife? Dagger? Oh, either way, that looks like it would hurt so bad.

Girl 2: Yeah.

Girl 1: Do they fight with them?

Girl 2: What's this?

Girl 1: Africans don't get a lot of wars, though, do they? [pause] Africa's like, isolated.

Girl 2: 2000 B.C. [reading label]

Girl 1: If you think about it, you know how we all had those world wars?

Girl 2: Yeah.

Girl 1: Africa never took part in any of them.

Girl 3: That's because they don't have any like . . . like the army and stuff like that. They're all separated.

Boy: They have no like, major government. It's just like, little societies.

Girl 3: Little tribes.

Girl 2: Well I know in some war . . .

Boy: They take care of each other.

Girl 2: We just learned about it. It was Ethiopia. And we like, it wasn't us, it was some another country and they, like, dominated them. They had no technology; they were fighting them with spears. (AF 10/23)

Here we have conscientious students getting it just about as wrong as they can get it. The exhibition has not been able to address their misconceptions, and where it has they have not attended to the information. This example points out that informal learning environments, in and of themselves, have no greater claim on solid, conceptually accurate, deeply meaningful interpretations than any other form of learning environment. We should not expect too much. Instead, we need to examine how informal settings fit into a larger picture of how we expand knowledge and wisdom over time.

We use this last example as a segue into the other underlying issue of learning in museums. What influences it? Does every group that goes to an exhibition have the same experience and the same result? Of course not. But do we want to think about every single group as being so totally unique that we cannot or should not make any generalizations about a set of experiences? To this too, we say, of course not. In the rest of this book, we examine several critical components that we think influence the learning that takes place in a museum when learning is defined as elaboration of meanings and details by a group around a set of thematically linked ideas that are prompted and supported by a specific museum experience.

The Message

Our sense of learning as conversational elaboration is more than a behaviorist pattern of reinforcement and includes, but is distinct from, a purely constructivist discussion of meaning making. Instead it reflects the museum situation and cultural role as being part and parcel of the learning that takes place. We developed a fairly complex measure of learning, one that reflected both conversational depth and engaged time at the museum. (The definition appears in the appendix and is discussed as we go through the various chapters.)

Our model of learning conceives of the group activity and conversation at a museum as being influenced by several factors: the identity of the group with respect to the content of the exhibition; the explanatory engagement of the group through conversation about the objects, activities, and experiences of the exhibition; and the design and crafting of the learning environment and its use by the group. In each of the ovals in figure 1.1, we can imagine a system of specific measures, observations, or characterizations that describe any one group as it visits a particular exhibition. Each of these constructs—identity, conversation, learning environment—reflects a complex and intricate dimension that is only *partially* measured by the specific indicators that we are working with. By identity we mean the entire cluster of characteristics that contribute to the positioning and enactments of an individual or group in a particular setting and activity. We had a considerable amount of information about the identities of the groups that we followed; the aspects of identity that were both measurable and reflective—but not exhaustive—were the motivation and connection that the group members have to the exhibition. We explore in more detail

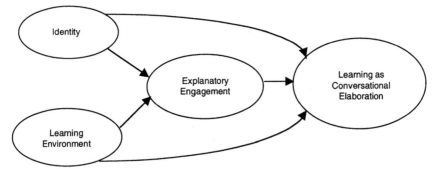

Figure 1.1.   Model of museum learning.

what we mean by identity in chapter 3, but here it is important to realize that our model assumes that identity influences what people experience in a museum, what they do, and what they take from that experience. We have tried to explain what we mean by conversation in terms of learning with some examples in this chapter. In the model we also have explanatory engagement, which represents the ongoing conversation in the museum, particularly that devoted to explanation of exhibition themes. Explanatory engagement is assumed to be influenced by two other clusters of variables and to influence conversational elaboration. In chapter 4, we go into greater depth, exploring the various aspects of conversation that we used and posing questions about those we chose not to use. The cluster of issues surrounding the learning environment included various layers of text and design features in the museums. In the model, the learning environment is shown as influencing both the explanatory engagement and the conversational elaboration. The exhibitions that we studied were all carefully designed; they were not random collections of objects thrown together but were conceptually driven thematic displays, and we therefore chose to study them in their entirety. We describe the specific exhibitions in our study in chapter 2. The cluster of the learning environment in our model was designed to reflect these many features. In chapter 5 we explore the aspects of exhibition design that we included in the learning environment category.

The model we have designed suggests that learning is a form of conversational elaboration, which we measured by combining the scores a group attained on their posttour conversation (based on the coding scheme we devised) together with a calculation of time spent on their tour (as opposed to nontour activities, such as the pre- and posttour conversations). Learning is influenced by conversation, especially conversation that provides explanatory engagement in the exhibition. Both learning and explanatory engagement are influenced by the design features of the environment and by the identities of the visiting groups.

Questions

We took a particular stance on what it means to learn in a museum. The stance constrains not only who we can look at but what it is that we might follow. Consider a very different meaning of learning, but one that is direct (time is indirect because one assumes the real learning is what one does with the time). Imagine what you might need to do to capture that different meaning of learning and how you might actually go about it. Other than the technical issues of sampling and representation, what are some issues or problems with your way of considering learning? Now reconsider what we have chosen to do and think of museum settings that might make it quite a challenge to use conversational elaboration as a way to consider learning and think through how those challenges might be overcome.

Notes

1. Hein 1998, 7.
2. Poundstone 2000; Schleier 1998.
3. Becker, MacAndrew, and Fiez 1999; Fiez 2001.
4. Montessori 1964; Weil 2002.
5. Schauble et al. 2002.
6. Blühm and Lippincott 2000.
7. Piaget 1955, 1967.
8. Gardner 1983, 1993; Housen 1992. See also Kindler 1997.
9. Fosnot 1993; Hein 1998.
10. Hein 1998.
11. Sfard 1998; Vygotsky 1978; Wells 1999.
12. Lave and Wenger 1991.
13. Greeno 1998.
14. Falk and Dierking 2000.
15. Matusov and Rogoff 1995.
16. Silverman 1995; Falk and Dierking 2000.
17. Falk and Dierking 1990; McManus 1993; Stevenson 1991.
18. Leinhardt and Crowley 2002.
19. In earlier work we tried to make up for this by doing special smaller studies about these situations. See Abu-Shumays and Leinhardt 2002; Ash 2002; Ellenbogen 2002; Leinhardt, Tittle, and Knutson 2002; Stainton 2002.
20. Borun, Chambers, and Cleghorn 1996.
21. Silverman 1990.
22. Serrell 1995, 1997.
23. Fisher and Berliner 1985.
24. Carroll 1963.
25. See, for example, Gee 1999; Grice 1989; Wells 1999.
26. Clark 1996.
27. Silverman 1990.
28. Borun, Chambers, and Cleghorn 1996.
29. Clark 1996.
30. The reference that follows each example of visitor conversation notes the exhibition (IN), the group number (08), and the track number (19). More information about the exhibitions is provided in chapter 2. Information about segmenting and tracking is provided in the appendix.
31. All names used in conversation excerpts are pseudonyms.
32. See Sinatra, Beck, and McKeown 1992.

Exhibitions 2

Oh, I've seen pictures of it, but I've never seen it.

—VISITOR CONVERSATION AT THE *LIGHT!* EXHIBITION

"Possibly Swedish."
What?
It says, "possibly Swedish." (laughs) We're not quite sure.
Hi, my name is Carl. I'm possibly Swedish.

—VISITOR CONVERSATION AT THE *LIGHT!* EXHIBITION

The Problem

AT THE SAME TIME that we were thinking through what we meant by learning in museums, we were addressing a second complex task: Which museums should we study, and what should we study within them? Should we study a whole museum visit, focus on single objects, or select whole exhibitions? How could we ensure comparability across museum types and locales? In this chapter we discuss the issues we encountered and our solutions to them, as we provide an overview of the selected museums and exhibitions to give background information that helps to situate the rest of the book. Although the findings of our research apply to other museums and exhibitions, the unique situation of each museum and exhibition critically defines and affects what people actually experience and how they react, as the visitor comments that open this chapter suggest.

The funders of the Museum Learning Collaborative study specified that a wide range of museum types be included. The funders also asked that the museums have some geographical distribution. Within these broad parameters of museum type and geographical dispersion we selected specific exhibitions and museums to be included. Pragmatism helped to shape our decisions. The most important feature in selecting a site was the type of museum and content of the exhibition, although another important feature was the availability and cost of doing research at the site. The project was conducted in two phases. The work of the first phase involved a year and a half of methodological and exploratory studies;[1] the second phase was designed as a single, comprehensive, coherent study that included two years of data collection.

The two years were structured to accommodate data collection at museums while specific exhibitions were on view. The coordination of sometimes overlapping or simultaneous data collection activities across different exhibitions required iterative planning. We studied seven exhibitions and worked with five museums: the Carnegie Museum of Art and the Carnegie Museum of Natural History in Pittsburgh, PA; Conner Prairie (a living history museum) in Fishers, IN; the Henry Ford Museum and Greenfield Village in Dearborn, MI; and the Exploratorium in San Francisco, CA.

While deciding whether to include a museum, we contacted members of the museum staff and arranged the first in a series of meetings. Over the course of a site study we developed relationships with educational, curatorial, and design staff. We worked with these staff members to choose exhibitions that would be appealing to a wide cross section of visitors and that would also represent the museum's best work. We tried to select exhibitions that were roughly equivalent in size and scope and that included a strong thematic focus. We selected primarily temporary exhibitions, but we also included permanent installations if staff considered them to be important examples of their best work. Finally, we studied exhibitions at five different types of museums: art, science, history, natural history, and living history. As we discuss each exhibition and museum, we hope to provide the reader with a sense of the range of experiences that are provided by these varied institutions that all call themselves museums. There is not a dusty attic among them.

The decision to study exhibitions and to include different kinds of museums required careful thinking about methodology; these issues are explored in depth in the appendix. Research is an emergent and fluid process. Trade-offs must be made in order to create a holistically sensible research design. For example, a question we confronted early on was the size of the thing we were going to study. Should we trace visitors from the moment they entered a museum until they left? If we did that, should we consider what we saw as the visitors' experience at the museum as a whole? Or should we trace visitors from their entrance to the museum until they had seen a specific number or types of exhibitions? And, if that were the case, was it important that the exhibitions seen were of comparable size? Should we perhaps simply take a chunk of time, say an hour, and examine that? Our concern focused on issues of comparability and the depth of analysis that would be possible. At some museums it would be nearly impossible for our team to undertake the depth of analysis of the exhibitions themselves that we wanted to conduct if *all* of the exhibitions in a given museum were to be included. And while the decision of what to choose is largely a decision about what one wants to generalize to (a museum, an exhibition, a display, an object), it is also a question of detail. It is possible to capture every word, gesture, and reaction if only a few displays are observed. Alternatively, it is possible to get a sense of the whole museum experience only if fewer details are tracked. We decided to focus our attention at the level of the exhibition. That choice allowed us to select exhibitions of comparable size. Other analyses of visitors in museums have tended to look at a smaller grain size, for example at the object level,[2] or to look at general reflections of a whole museum visit.[3] We looked at visitors' learning at a single exhibition within a museum.

The Concept

In selecting museums and exhibitions we found ourselves juggling many goals and constraints. We wanted examples of best practice and accessible content, but we also had to gather data within a specific time frame for each museum; we wanted to reflect the true atmosphere of each museum, but we needed to have some spatial boundaries for technical reasons and to have some equivalence of size. In this section, we explore the concepts of best practice, time frame, boundedness, and size.

Best Practice

Our first guiding principle was to work with the museums to focus on exhibitions that were examples of best practice. Thus, for example, we selected *Light! The Industrial Age, 1750–1900*, an important large-scale art exhibition that was a major undertaking for the museum and was the focal point for the Carnegie Museum of Art's marketing plans. The exhibition ultimately had a large regional draw, especially after it was used as the foundation for a major Pittsburgh tourism campaign ("Pittsburgh Shines"). A second principle was to select exhibitions that had accessible content for a wide range of visitors. With this goal in mind, and given our society's love of cars, we selected the *Automobile in American Life* exhibition at the Henry Ford Museum. At the same time, however, while including exhibitions with accessible content, we did not want to shy away from exhibitions that attempt to deal with politically sensitive subject matter. To meet that goal we selected *Alcoa Foundation Hall of American Indians*, a recently recast permanent installation at the Carnegie Museum of Natural History. Exhibitions of non-European cultures, such as this one, must deal with issues of authority, representation, and otherness.[4]

We also wanted to balance our selections with both traveling and permanent exhibitions, so we selected a well-traveled exhibition that originated at Chicago's Field Museum—*Africa: One Continent, Many Worlds*, which was showing at the Carnegie Museum of Natural History during the time of our studies. Depending on the institution, it is possible that visitors to temporary shows are slightly different from those to permanent installations. The *Automobile in American Life* exhibition, for example, and the Henry Ford Museum in general, tended to attract a large number of visitors who were tourists to the area, whereas museum members and regular museum visitors were heavily represented in our sample of visitors to the temporary exhibition, *Aluminum by Design*. Not all temporary art exhibitions attract this local, member-dominated audience, however. Because of the large marketing efforts undertaken by the Carnegie Museum of Art for the *Light!* exhibition, we had a mix of locals and tourists visiting it.

Exhibitions were selected for theoretical reasons; however, practical factors were also considered. Four of the seven exhibitions studied were installed in Pittsburgh, where the research team was headquartered. However, in order to maximize the applicability of the research, we chose exhibitions with an eye to their potential for traveling to multiple venues. Three of the four exhibitions studied in Pittsburgh traveled out of the city.[5]

Timing

Timing influenced exactly which shows we looked at locally and nationally. For example, we knew we wanted to study an outdoor living history museum, so we needed to schedule this for a time when seasonal weather permitted it to be open. We also wanted to study a show at the Exploratorium, but in this case cost, not weather, was a constraint: collecting data in the San Francisco Bay area would be nearly three times as expensive as collecting data in other locales, so the work needed to be done quickly and efficiently. That, in turn, meant that the Exploratorium data collection should be scheduled nearer the end of the MLC's data-gathering period. At that point in our schedule we would be most skilled in our data collection process, and, with most of our other data collected, we would have extra team members available for backup should an unforeseen emergency arise. We targeted February 2001, a date during which we would not be able to study the excellent *Frogs* exhibition that had been on display at the Exploratorium.[6] *Frogs* was a show we knew a good deal about and had examined carefully in phase I. It would have been a perfect choice for the study (it was bounded, it had fabulous, engaging displays, it was developed by the Exploratorium, and it incorporated a complex take on controversial scientific issues). Our timing constraints, while barring us from capturing the *Frogs* exhibition, left us with two other options: *Behind the*

Screen: Making Motion Pictures and Television, a traveling exhibition from the American Museum of the Moving Image in New York; and an exhibition presented by the National Health Sciences Consortium on women's health issues, *The Changing Face of Women's Health.* We would have liked to have studied an Exploratorium-curated exhibition, as the museum is well known for its expertise in creating engaging science exhibitions; but without an Exploratorium-created option, the *Behind the Screen* exhibition was selected because it would be more accessible for a greater number of visitors than would the exhibition on women's health issues. In fact, *Behind the Screen* turned out to be an excellent choice. This traveling exhibition used state-of-the-art computer technologies to provide extensive information about the process of making movies, and it included iconic artifacts from popular movie culture as well as numerous hands-on opportunities to explore the technologies used in the industry. The choice of *Behind the Screen* reflects issues of timing, trade-offs of a highly valued and understood exhibition versus one that was less typical, and highly accessible content of general interest versus a self-curated exhibition from an institution famous for its competence in science education.

Size

In thinking about comparability of size across exhibitions we needed to understand what "size" means. Does it mean roughly comparable proportions of a total museum (if, say, a museum normally has ten exhibitions, then one exhibition would be one-tenth), or does it mean roughly equivalent numbers of objects or stations? Does it mean roughly equivalent time needed to see the exhibition? Again, the issue is: To what did one want to generalize? A specific portion of a museum? A specific number of objects? A general amount of space? We selected exhibitions that were approximately the same size in square footage and that also would take roughly the same amount of time to see. We tried to select an exhibition—or an area within a very large exhibition—that would take one to one-and-a-half hours to thoroughly explore. In the study of Conner Prairie, a living history museum, this meant that only a part of *Prairietown* was included, and at the Henry Ford Museum only a part of The *Automobile in American Life* exhibition was included, whereas at all the other museums the entire exhibition was included.

Boundedness

Another consideration that informed the selection of exhibitions to study was the situation of the exhibition within the museum space. Our pilot research from phase I showed that visitors in an exhibition with a clear entrance and exit area behaved similarly to those in less well-defined spaces. Many visitors seemed to be comfortable in terms of wayfinding when exhibitions had clearly defined boundaries.[7] The physical boundedness of the exhibition also supported visitor recruitment. For example, both *Aluminum by Design* and *Light!* were installed in the same series of galleries at the Carnegie Museum of Art. Glass doors enclosed this space, and the entrance to the galleries was strategically located at the top of the main staircase. From the top of the steps, visitors could either turn left into the galleries featuring the CMA's permanent collection or turn right into the temporary gallery space. This meant that visitors approaching the entrance to the temporary gallery space were clearly approaching the exhibition we were studying. By contrast, *Africa: One Continent, Many Worlds* was situated on the ground floor of the same museum complex. Although a glass door demarcated the entrance to the gallery space, the entrance area—and our data collection staging area—was part of the bustling central corridor of the museum; furthermore, visitors and staff routinely cut through the *Africa* exhibition space in order to reach the cafeteria and other areas of the museum. Thus, an approach to the gallery entry doorway did not always indicate that visitors were deciding to enter the *Africa* exhibition we were studying. At the *Automobile in American Life* exhibition at the Henry Ford Museum, the *Africa* show at the CMNH, and *Behind the Screen* at the Exploratorium, visitors could find themselves unintentionally wandering out of the target exhibition area and into other areas of the museum. Although the temporary exhibition space for *Behind the Screen* at the Exploratorium was clearly bounded by movable walls, which created a very obvious entranceway, the particularities of the museum—children running around and squeezing through gaps in the movable walls, everyone being very active and physically involved in one fun thing or another—created a complex and less well-bounded exhibition space.

At each museum we worked with museum staff to select the specific exhibition on which to focus our research, and after the selection was made we discussed it in greater depth with curators and staff. We were still faced with the issue of trying, in a relatively short period of time (one to four weeks), to deeply understand the messages of each exhibition. We therefore asked the curators to take us through the exhibitions while being videotaped, to point out key issues and concepts and to talk specifically about their intentions and goals for the installations. In two cases, the original head curator for an exhibition was not available; but we were able to work with curators who had participated in the development of the exhibitions and they participated in a curatorial walk-through with us. At the Henry Ford Museum, Randy Mason, an original curator for the *Automobile in American Life* exhibition, had since retired, but he was generous enough to come back to the museum and take us through the exhibition. Deborah Mack, who had worked on the *Africa* show at the Field Museum, came to the Carnegie Museum of Natural History to assist staff with the installation and, while there, gave us an in-depth tour of the exhibition.

Our data collection for each exhibition included gathering artifacts related to the production process—items such as label copy, catalogues, educational programs, and layout maps of the show. We used these artifacts to help us create a schematic guide to the exhibition's layout and to design and structure the portion of our visitor interviews that dealt with the overarching themes of the exhibition. From our discussions with museum staff and a close examination of the exhibition's content, we distilled five themes unique to each show. These themes were used to anchor the conceptual framework for our study. Our five themes did not correspond directly with the curator's thematic divisions in an exhibition; rather, our themes were created in order to capture central curatorial themes, as they could potentially cut across each and every section of the exhibition. As a rule of thumb, we tried to establish themes in a manner that allowed almost any object in the show to be realistically discussed in terms of each theme. Thus, for example, the theme of social class and gender in *Prairietown* at Conner Prairie related most strongly to certain sections of the exhibition, but in fact every section of the exhibition could be considered through that lens. We confirmed the themes we identified with the curatorial staff.

The Examples: The Exhibitions

The following section provides detailed information about the exhibitions we selected for our study. They are grouped by museum type: art (2), natural history (2), science, history, and living history. For each of the museums and exhibitions described, we present information about the museum setting; the issues that faced the design team as they worked through a design of objects and experiences that might reify the museum's vision; the environment that confronted the visitors as they moved into the space; the curatorial voice that described the show to us as a lead-in to a brief description; and finally, the challenge that confronted the visitors as they moved through the objects or stations and engaged with the curatorial premise.[8] We feel that the context in which learning takes place is an important factor to consider in our research, and we use these brief segments to remind the reader to be mindful of the larger picture—the institutional orientation, the feel of the space, and the main message of the curator—as a way of pointing toward the broad range of issues, factors, and individuals working behind the scenes. In the following chapters, we discuss how visitors connected with the curatorial premise at each exhibition while simultaneously constructing meaningful connections to their personal lives. It is in this dialogue between visitors, objects, and curator, between past vision and history and present encounter, that we see sociocultural themes played out in a way that goes beyond personal meaning making and self-constructed understandings.

The Art Museum: The Carnegie Museum of Art

The Carnegie Museum of Art in Pittsburgh, PA, is a regional museum with an excellent collection of American and European works from the sixteenth century to the present. The museum is perhaps best known for "The Carnegie International," one of the world's most venerable survey exhibitions of contemporary art, which was inaugurated by industrialist and philanthropist Andrew Carnegie in 1896. The museum includes permanent collection galleries, a small "Forum" gallery for small temporary shows, and a large-scale series of five galleries for temporary exhibitions. It also includes the Heinz Architectural Center, a center for the display of architectural drawings and ideas.

We studied two different art exhibitions at the Carnegie Museum of Art. These two exhibitions provide different types of art-viewing experiences. The first one, *Aluminum by Design: From Jewelry to Jets*, provided a visual feast of designed objects that showcased the myriad uses of the material. The second exhibition, *Light! The Industrial Age 1750–1900, Art & Science, Technology & Society*, provided a thematic look at a historical topic, using extensive labeling and juxtaposing scientific instruments and blockbuster paintings. Neither exhibition offered a strictly "traditional" art museum experience, but both exhibitions reflected some unique features that were unlikely to have been encountered in museums other than an art museum.

ALUMINUM BY DESIGN: FROM JEWELRY TO JETS October 28, 2000–February 11, 2001

The Issues. The curatorial challenge for this exhibition was to provide a harmonious context for the wide variety of objects included in it and to link all these objects thematically to several intertwining stories: a historical story of the development of the aluminum industry; a story about the evolution of product design and style; a story about the properties of aluminum; and a story about modernism, a key moment in the history of the use of aluminum.

The Environment. Two glass doors separate the modern gallery space from the hallway leading to it. Opening the doors, the visitor is greeted with a cool breeze, which is augmented by cool blue walls, shiny aluminum objects, and a gently curling aluminum banner that leads the way through the galleries. Display cases on either side of an entrance area are angled to funnel the visitor into the main exhibition space. An amazing variety of objects are on view, showcasing both the decorative and practical uses of aluminum across all the decades of the twentieth century in the United States and abroad—among them a long, sleek purple Prowler (car), French opera glasses, vacuum cleaners and a meat slicer from the

1950s, a hammered aluminum art nouveau picture frame, and a dazzling rug made from recycled pop cans.

Curatorial Voice. Curator Sarah Nichols noted that a show on aluminum as a design material had never been done before. The use of aluminum is strongly associated with modernism, and many key designers from this period used the material in their work. Pittsburgh plays a key role in the history of aluminum, and this feature made it a particularly interesting topic for the CMA to explore. The objects included exemplify the variety and versatility of the material; its properties and its uses—both successful and experimental—are explored.[9]

The Exhibition. The exhibition was divided physically into four major sections: Inventing Aluminum, The Modernist Ideal, Competition and Conflict, and Crossing Boundaries. Each one of these areas included at least two other subthematic sections. The opening paragraph of the introductory panel set the tone:

> From jewelry to jets, aluminum profoundly influenced life in the 20th century. Its wide-ranging uses and unique combination of properties are unmatched by any other modern material. Today aluminum is equally at home in industry and artists' studios.

The range of materials presented was quite breathtaking. In the first gallery visitors encountered Charles Martin Hall's globules of aluminum, created between 1886 and 1888 using an electrolytic process that marked the advent of industrial-scale production of the material. The scientific display was surrounded by early uses of the material, including an elaborate baby rattle commissioned by Napoleon III in 1856, one of the earliest known artistic uses of the material. The aluminum rattle was encrusted with emeralds and diamonds—concrete evidence of the high initial value of this once-precious material. The gallery also included such practical items as a set of surgical instruments from the 1890s, which illustrated the material's lightweight and inert properties, as well as a full-size replica of the façade of the Die Zeit building (1902), which demonstrated the important role of aluminum as epitomizing a modern-style design material at the turn of the century.

The exhibition not only explicated the developing industrial role of aluminum in the building and war industries but also provided an opportunity to examine some essential works by key designers of the modern period. Included were chairs and other housewares produced by some of the twentieth century's most well-known designers, such as Frank Lloyd Wright, le Corbusier, Russell Wright, and Ron Arad. Distinct thematic areas were suggested by hanging see-through scrims that ran from floor to ceiling. These scrims created a dramatic if somewhat challenging conceptual environment for visitors to navigate. The overall design and style of the exhibition was quite spectacular. The cool color scheme, in a range of turquoise blues, was chosen to accent the shiny cold metal. The scrims with their silvery gray color and off-white text supported the cool, slick feel of the gallery space. Cases were specially built for this exhibition with a wavy cut-out base that reflected another strong component of the design. Overhead, an undulating twelve-inch-high ribbon of aluminum wound its way through all the galleries, directing the flow of the exhibition from beginning to end. The particular look of the exhibition at the Carnegie Museum was created by a local designer; at other venues, although texts and objects traveled, this design was not repeated. Each venue had its own locally designed look.[10]

After consulting with the curator and examining the exhibition and catalogue, we decided upon five themes that could be easily attached to objects from any area in the exhibition. The themes for *Aluminum by Design* were style and aesthetics, problem solving in design, history, corporate presence, and the use of the material in transformation and recycling.

The Challenge for Visitors. The exhibition was full of varied and intriguing objects, and, while there was an inherent chronology, the visitor might easily go through in a superficial way, simply ooh-ing and aah-ing at the fabulous examples of design. The specific route through the exhibition was subtly suggested by an over-hanging ribbon of aluminum, but the intellectual route and conceptual hooks for thinking about the objects were less strongly emphasized.

LIGHT! THE INDUSTRIAL AGE, 1750–1900: ART & SCIENCE, TECHNOLOGY & SOCIETY April 7, 2001–July 29, 2001

The Issues. This exhibition included an extensive selection of blockbuster paintings (by famous artists such as Toulouse-Lautrec and Gauguin) alongside fragile scientific instruments to tell the complex story of the impact of the development of lighting theories and technologies on society and artists during the Industrial Revolution. Complex thematic goals and diverse objects were coupled with a hands-on learning experience not unlike those found in science museums. The result was rewarding but challenging, both intellectually and physically.

The Environment. Entering the galleries, visitors' eyes momentarily struggle to adjust to the low lighting levels and dark brown walls. They are then confronted by a large case of shiny, sparkling objects highlighted by boutique lighting, which sits directly in their path. A brilliantly pure colored spectrum radiates from a prism overhead, directing the visitor to the right and into the main part of the exhibition. Antique display cases were used to highlight the historic thread of the story. Gallery lighting effects change from dark to light to underscore, for example, the Impressionists' success at capturing outdoor natural daylight in their work.

Curatorial Voice. Curator Louise Lippincott characterized this exhibition as a real departure from traditional practice at the museum. She looked toward science museum exhibitions as a model for experiential learning, but she also challenged art historical practice by making object comparisons that traditional art historians would find surprising. She stretched her notion of art museum practice in order to illustrate for visitors the huge impact that these lighting developments had on artists and on society.

The Exhibition. This temporary exhibition originated at both the Van Gogh Museum in Amsterdam and the Carnegie Museum of Art in Pittsburgh. It was shown only at these two venues because of the high value and the fragility of the items included. It was a complex thematic exhibition exploring the development of lighting theory and technology during the Industrial Revolution. The exhibition combined blockbuster paintings, which showed how a broad range of artists (e.g., Monet, Van Gogh, Chardin, Turner) dealt with the new issues and ideas associated with light, alongside the scientific instruments and lighting devices that were invented during this period. Artworks, lamps, and scientific instruments and treatises were woven through the exhibitions' five major divisions: A Ray of Light, The Light of Nature, Makers of Light, Personal Lights, and Public Lighting. Each of these major sections had from two to five smaller subsections.

The curatorial goal for the exhibition was to combine hands-on learning with excellent art-viewing experiences in a dramatic venue. The design team felt strongly that this exhibition offered a prime opportunity to experiment with new ideas in their professional practice—ideas that take into account recent findings about visitor experience—to create design features they hoped would improve visitor learning. The show included didactic science displays, such as handheld camera obscuras that visitors could look through, as well as a stunning prism display that cast a large brilliant spectrum on the wall. A Rayleigh tube and a photometer were installed next to paintings that showed the science concept mediated through artistic practice. The final scientifically based station was a display that illustrated the effects of different lighting sources on a painting that was originally created to be shown in gaslight. After our conversations with the curator and an analysis of the installation and catalogue, we decided upon the following five crosscutting themes: science and technology, art and artistic techniques, spirituality, work and the Industrial Revolution, and societal changes.

The Challenge for Visitors. This exhibition was exhaustive in terms of the materials provided for the visitor. The environment was very dramatic and encouraged visitors to attend to most objects. Many visitors could (and did) spend well over an hour in the show. Occasionally, at special display areas, the visitor was faced with a difficult assessment of curatorial intention—was this sculpture a piece of art related to light, or was it merely a device to let the viewer understand how a piece of technology worked?

Taken together, *Aluminum by Design* and *Light!* highlight two very different visions of the art exhibition—the first, a more traditional, stylistic examination of a particular medium; the second, a more strongly thematic show. Both were important temporary exhibitions for the museum, and both drew large audiences.

The Natural History Museum: The Carnegie Museum of Natural History

The Carnegie Museum of Natural History in Pittsburgh is one of the six largest natural history museums in the nation, with more than 20 million specimens, objects, and artifacts. The museum is well known for its collection of dinosaur fossils, its magnificent dinosaur hall, and an excellent collection of gems and minerals. The museum is part of a large complex that includes a music hall, the Carnegie Museum of Art, and the main branch of the Carnegie Public Library. The Museum of Art and the Natural History Museum are contiguous and internally connected facilities with a combined annual attendance of over 300,000.

We studied two different exhibitions at the Carnegie Museum of Natural History; both were nominated and eventually strongly requested by the educational/curatorial team. One, the *Alcoa Foundation Hall of American Indians*, was a recently completed permanent installation at the museum. The other, *Africa: One Continent, Many Worlds*, was a well-traveled temporary exhibition that originated at the Field Museum in Chicago. Both exhibitions open a window into the complexities of curating culturally sensitive exhibitions. Both curatorial teams grappled with key ethical questions concerning the display of colonialist collections and politically unsavory histories within the museum context.[11] In developing the *Indian Hall* exhibition, curators had to deal with the particular problems of displaying a collection of historical artifacts from living cultures whose members have strong feelings about the portrayal of their traditions. The *Africa* exhibition, in addition to the above considerations, tried to deal with political issues of the African diaspora within a largely celebratory exhibition that also tried to address audience misconceptions about Africa and Africans.

ALCOA FOUNDATION HALL OF AMERICAN INDIANS Permanent collection, reinstalled 1995

The Issues. The museum wanted to reinstall their American Indian collection in a more culturally sensitive manner that would highlight the continued vitality and viability of the cultures represented by these artifacts. It had strengths in several different regional areas, so a four-culture installation was enacted. Local tribal leaders were consulted throughout the development process.

The Environment. The Carnegie Museum of Natural History is designed around an open-core, marble staircase with fabulous turn-of-the-century murals. After ascending the broad classical stairs to the third floor, visitors to the *Alcoa Foundation Hall of American Indians* first pass through a long large hall that houses *Polar World*, a display of Inuit culture. At the far end of the *Polar World* exhibition visitors approach the glass doors leading to the vestibule for *Indian Hall*. Inside, a circular path wraps around the title wall leading visitors through a gallery of large black-and-white portraits of Indian men, women, and children from different tribal nations and different eras. These photographs are head-shots of smiling or serious-countenanced American Indians, some in traditional ceremonial attire, some in military dress, and others in ordinary streetwear.

Curatorial Voice. The European-American curators felt it was important to include American Indians in the planning process. They also wanted to show the continuation of older traditions alongside contemporary life and practices. One example highlights the degree to which the curatorial staff worked with their American Indian collaborators: CMNH wanted to include a buffalo in the exhibition. Buffalo were central to the way of life of the Plains Indians and the Lakota people in particular. Curator James Richardson noted that, "When our urban Indian exhibition consultants heard this, they said that we couldn't go and kill a buffalo without first obtaining the buffalo's approval. Even though this was a sixteen-year-old buffalo from a local farm that was on its way to market for slaughter, we called up a local Lakota woman who came in and performed the ritual and chanted until the buffalo nodded its head in approval. Then we killed it and had it stuffed."

The Exhibition. The exhibition hall utilized the museum's collection, which had strengths in four different Indian cultures: Lakota, Hopi, Iroquois, and Tlingit. The cultures are treated in parallel fashion, including subsections that focus on connections to nature, local environment, and family customs. The Lakota section is the largest of the four, which perhaps reflects the fact that the head curator was a Lakota specialist. The exhibit development process made use of the museum's collection, but the team also brought in a number of local specialists and made particular reference to local Indians and to contemporary practices. Care was taken to consult local Indian groups about appropriate and respectful solutions to the display of cultural and spiritual artifacts.

Curators deal with the political challenges of exhibiting vibrant living cultures using historical collections. In this exhibit, contemporary families are featured in life-size dioramas, and videos show points of intersection between past traditions and today's society. A diorama depicting a Hopi wedding, for instance, is based on a wedding that actually took place in the 1990s. During our curatorial walk-through, the curator referred by name to the people who are depicted in the scene, recalling details of the modeling activity that resulted in such realistic representations, including the eyeglasses on one woman. A video in the Tlingit section showed a contemporary family fishing. This film illustrates how a traditional practice of using natural resources is transformed from the old techniques that used traditional tools, such as the ones on display in the museum, to the current practice, in which a family is shown using modern conveniences such as snowmobiles and a deep freezer. Other areas of the exhibition similarly depict the intersection of traditional practices and modern society. After reviewing the exhibition hall and the catalogue, and discussing the exhibition with a contributing curator, we developed the following five themes to reflect the content: the role of nature, spirituality, gender roles, cultural influences (tradition and change), and skills and techniques.

The Challenge for Visitors. The exhibition was installed in a consistent and straightforward manner, but it presented diverse geographic, cultural, and political concepts. Cases dealing with topics such as agriculture coexisted with cases dealing with tradition and change in these cultures, all presented in a coherent design that did not necessarily point toward the key concepts being presented. Visitors could become engaged with specific static or interactive installations, but they might find it difficult to connect the meanings of those interactives to the larger concepts presented in the exhibition.

AFRICA: ONE CONTINENT, MANY WORLDS Originated at the Field Museum, Chicago; shown in Pittsburgh February 10–May 13, 2000

The Issues. This exhibition represents the result of a great deal of formative evaluation. Exhibit designers worked with many focus groups to determine what the average visitor knew and did not know about Africa. The exhibition had multiple exhibit goals and a complex set of themes, including ecology, the variety and differences among African cultures, and the legacy of slavery and the diaspora.

The Environment. Along a busy hallway on the main floor of the museum, near the cloakroom and membership desk, visitors approach glass doors that mark the entrance to the *Africa* show. A floor-to-ceiling foam core replica of the façade of an African palace greets visitors, and through its archway is seen a tightly compacted group of display cases that filled the gallery. Visitors pass by a collection of market items as well as historical panels that include large-scale photos of African royalty from the turn of the century. The first of two disjointed gallery spaces, the entrance galleries have a very different feel from those in the second half of the exhibition, which can only be reached after passing through two or three noisy, crowded, intervening halls, including the ever-popular Dinosaur Hall. In the second part of the exhibition, large colorful dioramas and more interactive displays dominate the experience. There is more space between cases in the second part, and a twelve-foot-high replica of a Baobab tree in the middle of an open area suggests an open village square. For the Pittsburgh installation, all the introductory geophysical and geopolitical information was presented at the entrance to this second part of the exhibition.

Curatorial Voice. Curator Deborah Mack noted, "The curators wanted to find out where people were coming from so that they could design an exhibition that would address the most common misconceptions about Africa. This was the first exhibition they designed with such an emphasis on visitor experience. They did lots of formative evaluation. This process resulted in such things as the kiosks that ask and answer questions about the number of languages, the size, and the number of countries in Africa."

The Exhibition. This exhibition originated at the Field Museum in Chicago in 1996 as a smaller traveling version of its permanent exhibition that opened in 1993. It traveled on a five-year-long, fifteen-city tour around the country, until, as one of the last stops on its tour, it was installed at the Carnegie Museum of Natural History in Pittsburgh. The *Africa* exhibition represented a collaborative effort among African and African American scholars to create an exhibition that would celebrate African culture as it educated those with little knowledge of Africa, Africans, and the contributions of African culture to the world. As described by the Ford Motor Company, the major funder of the exhibition, "the exhibition offers visitors a deep understanding of family life, art, ecology, commerce and the Diaspora of Africa from both historical and contemporary perspectives."[12] The exhibition included African artifacts, hands-on activities, and multimedia presentations that were carefully selected and designed in order to address visitors' most common questions and misconceptions about Africa. The curator with whom we spoke talked about the lengthy process that surrounded the creation of the exhibition, noting that it was truly a ground-breaking process for the Field Museum in terms of its extensive use of formative evaluation.

The installation at the Carnegie Museum of Natural History was hampered by the constraints of available exhibition space. This large exhibition had to be split into two gallery spaces that were separated by the expanse of several other galleries, including a large dinosaur hall. Preservation issues and environmental conditions (the humidity levels) inherent in the gallery spaces required that the precious, authentic artifacts be displayed in the first, smaller gallery space, while the dioramas and hands-on activities were located in the second space. The Field Museum's original introduction, which used a question-and-answer format to address some common misconceptions about Africa, also found itself relegated to the second part of the exhibition.

The exhibition concentrated on a small number of Africa's many ethnic groups, featuring their customs and their activities as a way of showing both continuity from the past and the development and progress of modern African society and the diaspora. Differences in the lifestyles of specific groups were highlighted through videos of cooking and other domestic activities as well as through displays showing variations in African terrain and climate that support different cultural responses. For example, the nomadic Saharan lifestyle was represented by a huge Tuareg tent containing housewares and clothing and by an adjacent working well, as well as by audio recordings of songs and textual and visual information about camels. Glimpses of urban life in Dakar were shown through video clips of tea drinkers, diners, and a musician, as well as by life-size displays about hair braiding and religious holiday celebrations. Africa's different ecosystems were explored through life-sized models of hippopotami, rhinoceroses, and giraffes accompanied by explanations of the foods they eat and habitats in which they live. A section on the African diaspora was introduced by routing visitor traffic through the hold of a darkened slave ship and onto an auction block, then past displays showing different aspects of enslavement in America. The exhibition concluded with a section of displays on intellectual and artistic accomplishments of Africans who have settled around the world and brought their heritage with them.

The exhibition offered an opportunity for us to see visitors coming to terms with material that proved to be unfamiliar to many of them. As a way of making the material less abstract and more personal, many of the panels featured life-sized photographs of people engaging in activities shown in the video displays. The curator made a point of including named individuals in the exhibition and of making sure that these full-size photographic images made eye contact with visitors. The exhibition also created an environment that produced a visceral response in visitors, leading them into the dark hold of a large slave-ship reconstruction. Lighting was used to create a swaying effect, and audio added realistic sounds of coughing, mumbling, and creaking. Finally, emerging from the ship, visitors found themselves on an auction floor, where buttons underfoot triggered a recording of an auctioneer loudly describing the qualities of the slave for sale. Other hands-on elements, including question-and-answer flip labels, videos, and audio phones, were included throughout the exhibition to provide a variety of learning opportunities for visitors.

From the exhibition and our discussion with the consulting curator we developed the following five themes to reflect the content: ecosystems and natural resources; social groups and ways of living; belief systems and practices; crafts, skills, and technology; and Africans around the world.

The Challenge for Visitors. Visitors encountered a challenging conceptual layout at this exhibition. It was somewhat difficult to construct a coherent narrative passing through a space that included diverse concepts of time, history, and culture. A strong historical layer dealing with diaspora and colonialism coexisted with ongoing lives and traditions in a diverse geographical area. Physically, many of the artifacts were shown in a separate gallery space, somewhat divorced from the life-size dioramas that contextualized them. The introductory material came after the entrance galleries, leaving some visitors feeling a bit lost.

The Science Museum: The Exploratorium

Housed in facilities that occupy 110,000 square feet, and serving 600,000 visitors annually, the Exploratorium in San Francisco is a leader in the science museum field. It has 650 interactive exhibits in the areas of science, art, and human perception. Topic areas include light, color, sound and music, motion, animal behavior, electricity, heat and temperature, language, patterns, hearing, touch, vision, waves and resonance, and weather. The Exploratorium is recognized for its cutting-edge exhibition designs as well as its innovative and challenging treatment of science content. While the museum is an open space, physically and intellectually, it is more directly didactic than the other museum spaces in which we conducted studies.

In our search for a science exhibition to include in our study, we were fortunate in having made professional contact with Sue Allen and other staff members at the Exploratorium in our first phase of research. Many exhibitions in typical science museums tend to be somewhat loosely grouped around concepts or else to function as stand-alone stations. We wanted to include an exhibition that could be comparable in scope and size to the others in our study—that is, to be larger than a stand-alone station and more obviously coherent than a loose thematic connection. As we explained previously, timing and issues of boundedness resulted in the selection of a traveling exhibition that originated at the American Museum of the Moving Image (AMMI) in Astoria, New York.

BEHIND THE SCREEN: MAKING MOTION PICTURES AND TELEVISION
February 10–September 3, 2001

The Issues. The exhibition was based primarily on hands-on computer activities to illustrate the technological developments in movie and television production. It did not focus on the scientific theories of light, sound, or image construction per se. Iconic objects, photographs, and video examples were used to trigger connections with visitors' movie- and television-watching experiences. These examples illustrated and supported the didactic intentions of the exhibition.

The Environment. At the very back of the cavernous, high-ceilinged interior of the museum, past the children racing around the wind tunnel and shrieking at the soap bubble stations, just past the cafeteria and clunk-clunk of falling blocks at the bridge building station, temporary walls define the boundaries of the *Behind the Screen* exhibition. Once inside, neon titles and backlit text panel signage indicate the focus for each of the fifteen content areas of the show. Computer screens with track-ball controls are located below the signs at most of these stations, along with larger video monitors at many of them. Visitors group and regroup the small movable stools near each station.

Curatorial Voice. AMMI director Rochelle Slovin explains that this exhibition is really about the technology of making movies. The curators wanted visitors to understand the huge amount of work that is involved in making movies. The show is a traveling version of the museum's permanent collection and is all about "hands-on." There are few artifacts to get the aura of the movie industry across. Visitors really like the hands-on aspects, but Slovin wishes there was a way to include more of the resonance of Hollywood that comes from the historical artifacts available at the sister institution in New York.

The Exhibition. This exhibition was envisioned as an important moment for the newly opened AMMI. *Behind the Screen* was its first traveling exhibition, and the staff invested extensively in its development, working hard to include educational, hands-on components that would help to elucidate the complexity and technological aspects of the movie and television industries. The exhibition was divided into major sections, including From Still to Moving Images, Getting the Picture, Sound, Special Effects, Onto the Screen, The Internet and the Moving Image, a demonstration theater, and, throughout the exhibition, a database of Who Does What in Film and Television. As the director explained, the traveling exhibition represented only part of the larger exhibition that is housed at AMMI. This traveling portion included the same thematic areas as those in the permanent display; but in the traveling version, the use of authentic artifacts from the industry was scaled back in order to provide more room for the enticing, interactive, science components. In spite of the technological focus, however, many stations include pictures from key cultural moments in American film and television (photos of movie stars, advertisements on TV, clips from famous movies, artifacts from films), and these small cues were enough to create some sense of historical resonance for most visitors.

The exhibition was easily distinguishable from the rest of the museum's exhibit areas, with a high temporary wall bounding the space. Backlit signage directed visitors to different cubicle-like areas. In each area, oval-shaped track-ball pads jutted out below flat computer monitors, and small black stools offered visitors a place to sit while browsing through computer demonstrations. After interviewing the curator and viewing the exhibition, we developed the following themes: the history and the role of movies in popular culture, the technology of movie production, the assortment of job positions involved in making movies, the artistic and technical skills involved in the process, and the layering of different elements to create an illusion of reality.

The Challenge for Visitors. The challenge for visitors to this exhibition was to build up a coherent system of information across stations. Stations were experienced as engaging and complete activities within themselves, missing the thematic links between related areas. Visitors could also be distracted from the learning process by their own technical engagement with the computers or by looking for representations of their own popular cultural icons.

The History Museum: The Henry Ford Museum

The Henry Ford Museum and Greenfield Village is the nation's largest indoor/outdoor history museum, serving 1.6 million visitors annually. Henry Ford opened the museum in 1929; it now contains over 1 million artifacts, 26 million documents, and 78 historic structures, which together represent an incredible resource documenting the American experience. In addition to the cavernous building that holds artifacts of daily and industrial life, the adjacent Village includes costumed interpreters who demonstrate the processes and skills of a broad range of heavy industrial enterprises from days past.

We selected a permanent installation of the Henry Ford Museum's extensive collection of automobiles. This installation was completed in 1987, and staff felt that its conceptual organization provided a useful model for new directions in the reinstallation of other permanent display areas in the museum. The show was the product of several years of work and included input from many consultants as well as a grant from the National Endowment for the Humanities.[13]

THE AUTOMOBILE IN AMERICAN LIFE Permanent Exhibition Space

The Issues. Staff at the Henry Ford Museum wanted to change the automobile section from its former array of what they called an "indoor parking lot" into a rich thematic exploration of the role of the automobile in American life. Lengthy text panels and small object cases were added in front of the cars. A chronological, narrative picture of the development of the car was included, and diorama-like settings were created. Life-size dioramas such as a gas station, a drive-in movie, and holiday cabins and motels were designed to evoke a sense of the impact of cars.

The Environment. A broad open corridor, at least twenty feet wide, allows visitors a direct path past the Henry Ford Museum's large and varied exhibits to the entrance of the Greenfield Village outdoor living history museum beyond. Within the enormous museum space, visitors walk along the wide corridor that provides easy visual and physical access to the many exhibitions that run down a space the size of several football fields. The *Automobile* exhibition is marked by an overhead highway sign, a carpet "road" with dotted yellow lines, and lots of neon road signs for motels, fast food, and advertising cars. The cars are placed in seemingly random order, one here, one there, sometimes in a string, or even stacked up on risers, three to a row.

Curatorial Voice. Curator Randy Mason notes: "We had this great collection of cars, but they were displayed really poorly. It was like a big indoor car lot. We spent a lot of time reorganizing the collection to reflect the themes of role of the car in our lives. The focal point of the space is what we call 'the Spine.' It's a chronological history of the development of the automotive industry from bikes to the influence of the Japanese industry in the 1980s. The chronology is in reverse order, as we wanted to start with the known, the present day, and move to the unknown and unfamiliar. Other areas of the exhibition, like the gas station and the drive-in, are contextualized diorama-like settings that show how American life was influenced by the car. We thought they would be an intriguing addition to the exhibition, but we didn't have the artifacts in our collection to create them. I went out to find artifacts to support the new areas."

The Exhibition. The exhibition examined the development of modern cars, from their origin in horse-drawn carriages to the impact cars have had on society. We selected for our study an area equal to approximately half of the total automobile exhibition space, a section that was naturally set off from the remainder by a long raised ramp bordered by a bank of cars and engines; the ramp served to easily orient and constrain visitors to stay within this section. The ramp itself was divided into seven sections, each of which was devoted to a period of automotive history (e.g., Global Industry, Boom Years, Birth of the Industry).

Each section along the ramp included labels, artifacts, continuously running videos, and the display of relevant cars and engines. The rest of the exhibition space had cars arranged on plinths according to topic, such as four rare Dream Machines (concept cars that never went into production) and Family Cars (which showed the evolution of vehicles—from a carriage to a 1955 Bel Air— that were designed to carry several people as well as their gear on outings). There was also a display that focused on the emerging culture of fast food, featuring an original neon McDonald's sign, a Chevy convertible with a car-hop tray on its door, and other artifacts from the early days of the development of road food popularity. The cars on display were either representative of a particular stylistic genre (e.g., the 1959 Cadillac Eldorado with its outrageously elongated tail fins) or technological innovation (the DeSoto with its pioneering aerodynamic design), or authentic artifacts from American history (e.g., a row of presidential limousines, a race car driven by Mario Andretti). All the cars, whether ordinary or emblematic, were tied to the small or large role they played in the story of the automotive industry and the American dream. Other ancillary displays included a touchable crash-test dummy and a related crash-test computer program, a diner car complete with a living volunteer attendant and working juke boxes, and a Lego station that allowed children and adults to build and race their own cars.

The large scale of the collection and the many topics within American history covered at the Henry Ford Museum attract a broad base of visitors. Since this magnificent automotive collection is known to be among the best anywhere, we imagined that the exhibition might attract visitors with a keen interest in and deep knowledge of cars. Further, even for those visitors who might not profess any particular affinity for cars, the ubiquitous presence of cars and their centrality to the development of American society is a legitimate and potentially interesting topic for a history museum. From our curatorial walk-through and analysis of the catalogue we distilled five key thematic areas to focus on: engines and technology, aesthetics, the automotive industry, the impact of cars on society, and personal experiences with cars.

The Challenge for Visitors. Visitors faced the challenge of responding to the cars as unique instances. The exhibition asked visitors to coordinate their everyday experiences and memories of these cars with specific and deep thematic issues presented by the museum. Visitors, perhaps more highly knowledgeable about the content of this exhibition than were most visitors to the others we studied, were sometimes frustrated when they found that their specific knowledge about a car was not supported and promoted in sufficient detail by the museum-provided information.

The Living History Museum: Conner Prairie

Conner Prairie is a museum that depicts the lives, times, attitudes and values of early nineteenth-century settlers in the Old Northwest Territory, based upon the Indiana experience. The 210-acre site houses a variety of interpretive areas including a history museum, an 1836 village, and an American Indian camp. The museum has over 300,000 visitors each year, and many local families visit the museum throughout the year to experience the changing seasons as well as the special seasonal events and activities organized by the staff.

Living history museums are a special type of museum that uses human interpreters as a primary means of presenting messages to the public rather than providing a series of objects and text-based, audio or video material for interpretation. Either third-person interpretation or first-person interpretation may be used in such settings. We studied an exhibition that used first-person interpretation; that is, museum staff took on the roles of historic figures and would talk to visitors or answer questions only in those roles. At this museum we were fortunate again to have professional colleagues, Ellen Rosenthal and Jane Blankman-Hetrick, who worked with us in phase 1 and supported the efforts in phase 2 to help us thoroughly understand the thematic content of the exhibition area and the unique challenges of their museum environment.

Because such a large amount of the conversation at *Prairietown* was from the interpreter not the visitor, we felt we could not treat it in the same manner as the other exhibitions in our study. The particular problem of tracking visitors and considering their conversations in this setting is well addressed by Rosenthal and Blankman-Hetrick.[14] In this book we report only on those aspects of Conner Prairie that were unaffected by the conversational features (see chapter 3).

PRAIRIETOWN Permanent Exhibition Space

The Issues. Staff wanted to create a realistic first-person experience for visitors, where they would see what daily life might have been like for Indiana settlers. At the same time, staff wanted visitors to gain some concrete information about historical events and context.

The Environment. After following a dusty, winding, dirt path through the trees, one emerges into a little village. Smoke curls from a small log cabin, and a brown cow lifts its head and bellows. Two women in long dresses and bonnets walk by, arm in arm, talking about Mrs. Whitaker's newest quilt. An odd assortment of buildings, clapboard houses, log cabins, and barns are strung along a dirt road, in a roughly street-like array.

Curatorial Voice. Museum director Ellen Rosenthal explains that the process of determining and improving the types of conversations expected of the interpreters at Conner Prairie is ongoing and constantly changing. Each interpreter must study both autobiographical details of the character he or she will play as well as the general and specific historical events within the community and time period. To help the interpreters focus their work, curators (staff) have established a series of "post goals." These post goals are subject areas and issues that interpreters should raise during their conversations with visitors. The real trick lies in the interpreter's ability to weave these post goals into conversations about very specific or vague topics, like the weather or what work the interpreter is doing.[15]

The Exhibition. At this living history museum, we studied visitors touring a fictional but historically authentic village called *Prairietown,* set in 1836 Indiana. Created as part of Conner Prairie in 1974, the *Prairietown* village uses first-person interpretation, where costumed interpreters of all ages perform daily chores and business while maintaining the stance that they live perpetually in this historical period. As the costumed interpreters interacted with visitors, they explained their work activities and their relationships with other "residents," as well as providing in their conversation a sense of the conditions in Indiana and the pressing social, economic, or political issues of the day. Domestic tasks and skilled labor were performed daily (e.g., cooking, cleaning, blacksmithing), but each character's activities varied according to the season of the year (e.g., hog slaughtering in late fall, farming in summer) or to special events in the town (e.g., a wedding, funeral, or visit from a traveling preacher). The relationships among characters in *Prairietown* were predetermined and consistent with historical data. For example, when the character "Dr. Campbell" was in his office, he would speak at length about medications, significant cases he had treated in town, as well as any political issues of 1836 Indiana. Other members of the community, when asked, could comment on the arrival of the doctor's family or on the illnesses he had been called out to treat. "Dr. Campbell" was also able to comment on medical and political issues within the general historical period as long as these were issues that people of his status and era might have encountered.

We studied a part of this 1836 village, including a doctor's house and infirmary, a schoolhouse, a blacksmith shop, a general store, a potter's shop and kiln, and several residences. When visitors entered a building they were usually greeted by the interpreters inside and were engaged in conversation. Interpreters were trained by the museum to build on the questions received from visitors to weave specific historical issues and concepts associated with the building or character into the conversation. Most interpreters were quite forthcoming and talked readily about their chores and activities of daily life as they performed them. Although visitors were invited to look around and ask any questions they might have about any aspect of the building or its inhabitants, they were also free to enter, "enjoy the show," and move on to another building without pressure to come up with pro-found questions. The interpreters had the challenging job of imparting informa-tion without sounding forced or wooden, all while skillfully avoiding anachronism traps set by visitors. In addition to the information presented through the inter-preters, visitors had the opportunity to learn about other aspects of history pre-sented by the museum that were unspoken but all around them—they experienced firsthand nineteenth-century living conditions. The open-air buildings and grounds provided another level of realism to visitors as they were greeted with fra-grant air blue with smoke from the fire, dusty street conditions, cold and drafty or sun-baked shelters, flies buzzing around food, livestock smells, dim light from candles, the hardness of wooden benches, the feel of a crude door latch, and the generally small scale of life inside cramped, low-ceilinged quarters.

Prairietown offered visitors an unusual setting in which to engage with Ameri-can history. As a text-free environment, *Prairietown* provided a contrast case to the other museums in our study. Instead of reading label copy, visitors engaged with the material through conversation with interpreters and through their own obser-vations. They could effectively select what they wanted to learn about by visiting particular kinds of buildings and asking questions specific to their interests. And they were able to experience the time period is a multisensory way, smelling the wood smoke, feeling the temperature outside and within the different buildings, and touching the "artifacts" themselves—the furniture, clothing, and buildings. We used the following five themes for our study of this exhibition: social class and gender; family economics; values, religion, and attitudes; sense of place, settle-ment, and migration; and training and education.

The Challenge for Visitors. First-time visitors to *Prairietown* encountered an experience that was potentially foreign to them. Rather than passively viewing exhibition ma-terials, visitors walked through a village. Even if they had missed the orienting video or a map of the village, they would have no doubt that they were in an early nineteenth-century small town. Throughout the tour, visitors had to remain aware of their roles as creators of the experience and had to find ways to ask questions in a way that a nineteenth-century person would understand.

The Findings

In this chapter we have looked at the specific exhibitions that we used in our study. We shared the details of the exhibitions because they provide an essential contex-tual frame for understanding the discussions in the rest of the book. But we also shared these details because the very process of choosing which exhibition to study, and when, colors the very conclusions one can draw in any study. Even within the same museum, exhibitions differ along a number of dimensions. In this chapter we explored some of these dimensions, including size, physical access, and boundedness. Thus, for example, *Indian Hall* was very different from *Africa* because the *Africa* exhibition was divided into two sections, separated from each other by intervening galleries, with an entrance off a busy main corridor, while *Indian Hall* was housed in a single exhibition hall, yet with an entrance tucked away in back of another large exhibition. Further, the layouts of *Indian Hall* and *Africa* were quite different—*Indian Hall* had a narrow flow that circled back on itself whereas *Africa* had a more open feel, with paths that branched from the central route through the exhibition.

Even when the exhibitions in the same museum are in the same hall, as was the case with *Aluminum* and *Light!*, there are differences in the mood (color and light-ing figured quite distinctly in these two shows) and in the kinds of affordances provided for the visitor. In *Aluminum* a guiding ribbon of aluminum overhead "showed the way," while in *Light!* the angular lines of refraction marking the path were a far more subtle directional device. Instead, distinctive changes of lighting and coloring in the *Light!* exhibition marked the changes of thematic ideas quite clearly. The *Light!* show included different types of exhibition experiences, such as hands-on materials and signage geared for children and their parents, so the be-haviors and reactions supported by the two shows were quite distinct.

Each exhibition posed unique challenges for the visitors as well. These chal-lenges ranged from issues of physical navigation to making connections among the messages provided at different exhibition stations. By investigating the work that happened behind the scenes, we discovered very different objectives and assump-tions about what the museum staff thought the visiting group might be able to or want to get out of a given show. We also saw how the curator tried to convey his or her message, and we learned more precisely the intention of that message as well as how it played out through the arrangements of objects and cases.

The Message

As the visitor comments that open this chapter suggest, museums are environ-ments in which to experience the indefinable power of authentic artifacts to res-onate with us. At the same time, museums present narratives, explanations, hypotheses—interpretations—about what we know about our world. And these narratives are presented in a highly designed environment that creates a unique and powerful physical experience for visitors. As Stephen Weil and others have pointed out, it is this notion of the experience—the museum as a site for a resonant ex-perience—upon which museums should capitalize.[16] Whether engaged in plan-ning from the point of view of the museum educator, engaged in evaluation as an outside consultant, or engaged in the design of research, deep investigation into the intentionality and physicality of the exhibition is critical. Even if the focus of interest is on visitor behavior, that behavior is in figurative and literal dialogue with the design intentions of curators and educators. An exploration of the curatorial framework envisioned by museum staff reveals that exhibition narratives work in complex and multilayered ways. The degree to which elements of the exhibition are discussed and selected to support different aspects of the curatorial vision is, frankly, quite remarkable for those who see the museum by its public face alone. The fact is, exhibitions are exceedingly complex rhetorical statements. Museum staff helped us to focus upon features that they felt were crucial elements in the exhibition structure and narrative, and this information allowed us to more richly analyze visitors' reactions.

We would urge researchers from all perspectives to consider issues of size, boundedness, the level of representativeness of the exhibition for the overall museum mission, and timing. As we have discovered, and as museum professionals know, the variance among exhibitions is huge. Researchers need to understand that comparing different exhibitions within and between museums requires careful attention to content, purpose, and fit. We believed before we started, and now even more after completing the set of studies, that the museums are quite unique but the exhibitions are even more so. Finding ways for the cross-comparison of museums and exhibitions continues to be a major challenge for museum research.

Questions

If you were to study a number of museums, along what dimension would you align them? Is the key consideration that the museums should be of the same type, or would it perhaps be more telling to study the same exhibition installed at different venues? What factors should be held consistent, and what factors may fluctuate? And is the resulting study design one that you could actually implement in practice?

Notes

1. Reported in Leinhardt, Crowley, and Knutson 2002.
2. Ash 2002; Crowley and Jacobs 2002.
3. See, for example, Falk and Dierking 1990, 2000; Hood and Roberts 1994.
4. See Karp and Lavine 1991.
5. *Light!* was cocurated in the Netherlands, *Aluminum by Design* traveled internationally as well as nationally, and *Africa* traveled to Pittsburgh after several years of being shown in other venues across the country.
6. See Allen 2002.
7. Leinhardt, Crowley, and Knutson 2002.

8. One of the long-standing challenges to studying museum learning is the impact of the museum environment on learning. See Bitgood and Loomis 1993; Falk 2002; and Knutson 2002.

9. Each of the curator comments is closely paraphrased from our discussions with them and their videotaped walk-through of the exhibition.

10. For example, at the Wolfsonian-FIU Museum in Miami, a more neutral design was created, using low white platforms and wall-hung Plexiglas cases to showcase the objects.

11. Karp and Lavine 1991; Ames 1992.

12. Ford Motor Company 2002.

13. For a thorough discussion of the design process for this exhibition, see Pursell 1992.

14. Rosenthal and Blankman-Hetrick 2002.

15. Since the collection of this data, in response to the MLC study and their own studies of visitors, Conner Prairie has redesigned its interpretation mandate to focus less on post goals and more on engaging visitors in experiences and conversation.

16. Weil 2002, 68. See also Perry et al. 1997.

Identity

3

Daddy, please see this.
Whoa, this is so cool! Oh my gosh. This is really, really, cool.
Dad, look through this one.
What's that?

VISITOR CONVERSATION AT THE *BEHIND THE SCREEN* EXHIBITION

The Problem

CHAPTER 1 SUGGESTS that learning in a museum is a social process that is in part a consequence of the historical experiences of individuals and in part a consequence of the interactions with artifacts and curatorial expressions as the two connect or even collide with each other. This chapter takes on one aspect of that suggestion with greater emphasis: the identity of the visiting group. Visitors come to a museum with expectations, purposes, and past histories; they also come to the museum alone, with friends, with relatives, and with new acquaintances. The problem confronted in this chapter is: Which of the many dimensions along which people vary should be considered for the purposes of understanding museum learning? In other words, how should we most fruitfully think about the identity of a visitor group?

One way in which identity can be considered is in terms of externally visible, socially constructed, stable demographic characteristics such as age, sex, race, ethnicity, and even religion (where religious roles or affiliations are visible). These demographic features of identity are fixed and for the most part remain constant for the individual. For example, each of the two authors is female, of a particular age, and of Anglo-European ancestry, and these characteristics are easily recognized by any observer. Other somewhat stable but less visible demographic characteristics include educational background, economic status, and social position. Undoubtedly, all of these factors play a role in the experiences of the museum visitor. It is especially important to think about these characteristics when analyzing a museum's audience or "reach." Demographics can be useful tools to determine which kinds of people are visiting a museum—demographic features are static, easily measured, and independent of the specific context and situation of the museum visit. Although demographic information is useful for analyzing patterns in museum visiting, it is not the most informative tool for considering the role of the identity of a group or individual in terms of what may or may not be learned during a museum visit.

To broaden a consideration of identity, one might also include an examination of the social roles visitors play. In our case, the authors, for example, play a variety of roles, including mother, daughter, wife, close friend, guide, entertainer, and researcher. These roles are not fixed, but rather change according to the social setting, the company we keep, and the activity in which we are engaged. Thus, when taking the role of guest of an old friend or family member in a new city at a new museum, we behave and experience things quite differently than when we are a host for older family members visiting us in our city in our museums. And when we go to the museum alone for a few hours of calm contemplation, we are carrying a different identity from when we go to the museum on a first date. Since we behave differently, we may also be considered to learn differently. These different characteristics, roles, behaviors, comportments, and attitudes affect what, how, and in what ways we choose to attend to objects and exhibits within the museum environment. For this study, identity is more than demographic information—it includes these roles, relationships, positionings, and enactments within specific physical contexts.

In addition to reflecting various roles in unique situations, identity reflects the collective past of visitors. Individuals and groups have distinctive prior experiences with the content of an exhibition and even with a particular museum itself. These historical aspects of identity also influence what happens during a visit, what topics of conversation emerge, and what one member of a group wishes to share with others. The combination of roles being enacted and knowledge being shared at a specific moment works to shape the motivation and the agenda for a visit. Motivation and agenda also influence the nature of learning that takes place during a visit.[1]

By recognizing identity as the cluster of knowledge, dispositions, and activities brought with the visitor into the museum, one can answer or respond to a long-standing criticism expressed by many thinkers in the museum community[2]— that museum learning should include more than receiving wisdom from on high.[3]

In the last decade there has been a constant call for an expanded vision of museum learning, one that focuses on what visitors contribute to the process. John Falk and Lynn Dierking have suggested considering the museum experience in terms of multiple contexts, one of which is "the personal" (similar to what we call "identity" here).[4] George Hein, drawing on educational and learning theories, has emphasized the constructive nature of learning, thus requiring that at some level the visitors' background knowledge and dispositions be included in any sensible account of museum learning.[5] Eilean Hooper-Greenhill, in her disciplinarily eclectic work, looked at cultural studies, learning theory, and communication studies to create a model that emphasizes the role of the visitor in transforming the core museum message.[6] Lois Silverman in her analysis of visitor conversations pointed out how distinctive each visitor's construction of meaning was.[7] Lisa Roberts built upon Silverman's concept of personal meaning making and introduced the idea of narrative construction on the part of the visitor as each one made selective and personal interpretations of museum exhibitions.[8]

While all of these writers have expanded beyond a transmission model of learning, and while many researchers have conducted important studies of selected identity factors such as curiosity, interest, agenda, prior knowledge, and values,[9] none has collected the critical identity features of the individual or group into a set and found ways to consider measuring them in relation to a model of museum learning.

The Concept

Identity refers to an awareness of selfhood at the individual or at the group level. It is self-definitional: I am who I think I am, and we are who we think we are. For example, one visitor to the *Alcoa Foundation Hall of American Indians* made the following exclamation: "Look, young western Apache—Oh, my tribe! Navajo" (IN 16/10). But even that sense of self is powerfully shaped by how others see us, by the specific situation we find ourselves in, by the social roles we play, and by the activities in which we engage. Identity is not constructed in a vacuum. A sense of self and of activity guides what people do, what they see, and what they say in a museum. It is this very dialectic that makes the construct of identity so central to a discussion of learning in museums from a sociocultural viewpoint.

Identity as a multifaceted, situationally defined construct, however, is not unique to the sociocultural vantage point. Metacognition, or the awareness of "knowing one knows," is a central theoretical construct in cognitive psychology; but there it is conceptualized as internal and it is examined only as a property of an individual.[10] Emergent establishment of meaning through an individual's active construction of understanding is likewise a central tenet of constructivism. In constructivism, the individual, with all of his or her prior knowledge and affect, engages with objects, concepts, or events to develop meaning.[11] The ability to productively participate in valued activity is a core property of identity within the sociocultural view.[12] This participatory sense of identity is enacted in the museum in different ways depending on prior experience (glassblower, glass factory worker), the activity (parenting, guiding, flirting, nurturing), and the situation (impressionist exhibition, Gettysburg war memorial). Although we did track some demographic aspects of the visitors' identities, we decided to focus on and to measure two broad constructs—motivation and prior knowledge—to reflect a more comprehensive notion of identity.

Motivation

The motivational aspects of identity reflect the reasons that people came to a particular exhibition and what they felt they might gain from it. We considered motivation in light of several key factors. One factor is the element of choice involved in going to a museum—from the initial decision to go to an exhibition to the spontaneous decisions about what to attend to and what to skip while in the museum. A second factor in motivation deals with the influence of group expectations and social roles. Individual members of a group take on different roles in different contexts, and these roles affect the motivation in a particular context. Finally, groups vary in the way they perceive the role museums play in their lives, which indirectly contributes to the motivation for going to and engaging in an exhibition.

Choice is a major distinguishing characteristic for learning in informal versus formal environments. Although the element of choice affects learning in both formal learning environments (such as schools) and informal environments (such as museums), choice is so central to the museum experience that we need to understand why people go to a museum and what they choose to engage in while there in order to understand the learning that might take place. What is their motivation for visiting and what do they expect to do there? Motivations might include using the venues as a locale for a social experience with a friend or family member, as a place to use up time, as an educational requirement at the family level, as a way to get to know a new place, or simply as a shelter from the rain. Each of these different motivations shapes the emergent agenda, which, in turn, shapes what may or may not be learned.[13] These general orientations toward museum attendance, and the reasons for the specific visit, are further shaped by visitors' needs and goals—or strategies, as Moussouri calls them—for dealing with the specific content. In Doering and Pekarik's terms, different motivations lead to different entrance narratives, and different entrance narratives lead to both different expectations and different reactions to the museum visit.[14]

Choice is also influenced by the larger overarching beliefs that visitors have about museums and about themselves. How do they define museums as institutions? Are museums seen as a locale where the unusual, awe-inspiring experience is offered? Or where contemplative space is provided? Or as a site for learning something about the world?[15] Perhaps the visitor views museums as places that inspire curiosity or fulfill fantasies. Choice is also influenced by how people see themselves depending on the context—perhaps as critics or consumers, as participants or audience, or as amateurs or professionals.

In addition to the role of choice, agenda, and view of the museum purpose in a larger sense, once at the museum a visitor's motivation is influenced in a profound way by the experience of the museum and by the exhibition context. Aspects such as attraction, curiosity, affect, and interest vary throughout a museum experience and are deeply impacted by the features of the learning environment and the particular physical and social context in which the visit takes place. Thus, motivation is a dynamic construct that is shaped by the visit itself.

We wanted to capture in our work a sense of both the larger picture of motivation for visiting as well as the smaller-level practicalities affecting the visit. Researchers examining the effects of motivation in museums have tended to ask visitors to respond to a set of questions on a survey, or to circle on a multiple-choice form the description that best fits their motivations. In our study, as a part of the self-administered conversational prompts for the discussions among visitors before and after a tour, we worked to develop an open-ended means of getting visitors to discuss their motivation. We did not offer visitors a set selection of answers from which to choose, nor did we prompt visitors for more information during an interview, since we were not part of their conversation. We developed a series of questions that they were asked to discuss among themselves and that we recorded, one of which asked, "Why did you come to see [exhibition name] at the [museum name] today?" From the answers to this question and others in the initial interview, a motivation rating was constructed.

The rating for motivation depended upon four factors. The first factor reflected intentionality and ranged from an intentional, planned visit to a spontaneous one. One highly motivated group said, for example, that they "saw something about it on a website and at the hotel." The second factor reflected habits of museum going and ranged from those who visited museums regularly and frequently to those for whom the museum visit was an unusual event. For example, one high-scoring group said, "We were here ten years ago and wanted to come back to see the changes." The third factor reflected topical familiarity with respect to the exhibition and ranged from those who had visited the museum to see the particular exhibition to those who were wandering through the museum and happened to stop to see it. Finally, the fourth factor reflected persistence and effort. To gauge this we looked at obstacles in the path of the visit. Levels of persistence or effort ranged from visitors who traveled a long distance and overcame difficulties in order to arrive at the exhibition to those who simply walked or drove easily to the museum. For example, one of the visiting groups at the CMA was a set of elderly female friends who had planned for most of the spring and early summer in order to be able to travel the two hours to Pittsburgh to see the *Light!* exhibition; they overcame the distance and the difficulty of scheduling around each other's available time. "I saw it advertised in AAA. And of course, you and I being artists, I saw it in the Elwood City ledger, in the entertainment section. I check it to see what's happening in Pittsburgh." Visitors whose responses were scored at the low end of this scale made comments like "We were bored stiff in Windsor and had nothing else to do" and "It was raining outside and we needed something to do." The overall motivation score assigned to a visiting group represented a combination of scores on these four separate factors.

Prior Knowledge: Appreciative and Experiential

If motivation is an expression of the desire to visit an exhibition, then the cluster of knowledge and previous experiences that people have when they come to a museum is a reflection of the connection that a visiting group has to the content of an exhibition. Previous experience and information are shared resources within a group, where one member of the group often gains, albeit subtly and invisibly, the permission of the others to share his or her experiences or appreciation of the material at hand. Thus, from a sociocultural vantage point, the prior knowledge available to the visiting group is not the private possession of an individual but a public good that enhances the entire group's mission to experience and enjoy a museum visit. For constructivism, however, the paradox lies in the fact that prior knowledge is both essential, in order to interpret the new and unfamiliar, and possibly flawed. Prior knowledge shapes and affects the acquisition of new knowledge. Learners' naïve notions and understandings influence the ways in which new knowledge is built; but for real growth to occur, learners must recognize and overcome their prior misconceptions and misunderstandings.[16] These contradictions are further complicated by the informal nature of museums, where misunderstandings may well go unchallenged.[17] It is possible in some cases that group dynamics may provide challenges and counterexamples to misconceptions in a way that promotes new learning.

Prior knowledge is part of what visitors bring to the museum with them and is a part of the identity of the visiting group. Two different types of knowledge are particularly relevant to the construct of identity: we called them appreciative and experiential knowledge. Appreciative knowledge reflects the quantity and quality of direct understanding of the content of an exhibition that group members have prior to their visit; this knowledge might come from, for example, academic experiences, book reading, or viewing documentary presentations. We contrasted this type of knowledge with experiential knowledge that reflects the hands-on experience visitors might have—experience such as building cars, working in an aluminum factory, living in Africa, or working in the television industry. Experience builds participatory knowledge; study builds descriptive knowledge. We wanted to acknowledge the wisdom of both those visitors who had read about a topic or had collected objects similar to those on display and those who had physically created a similar object or engaged in an activity reflected in the exhibition, such as working on a car, beading a purse, or churning butter.[18] Both appreciative and experiential knowledge were used to form five-point scales.

With these considerations in mind, we constructed three five-point scales for identity: one for motivation, one for appreciative knowledge, and one for experiential knowledge. We ultimately combined the last two scales. Information about the demographic aspects of the visitors' identity was retained for purposes of creating particular subsections of the dataset—for example, to examine learning by social role (families, friends, couples) or other issues that will be examined in future studies.

We know that identity at the individual and group level influences the museum experience. Our colleagues in the museum world have clearly recognized this as well. The issue is how we might best study identity and include it in a model of learning. In the next section aspects of the identity construct are presented as they were revealed in the language of the museum visit.

Examples

The identity of a group of visitors comes into an exhibition with them; it may be expanded and perhaps altered, but it is definitely manifested in the course of the visit. This shared identity influences and is reflected in the conversations of various groups as they work their way through an exhibition. In this section we share several examples of conversations within groups. These conversations suggest the ways in which personal roles, motivation, and prior knowledge and disposition play themselves out during the visit. We begin with the most clear-cut examples of variation in roles, providing excerpts from conversations held by three different kinds of groups as they were near a statue of Athena in the *Light!* exhibition. This large classical marble bust, set against a black velvet curtain, was a brightly lit focal point of the first gallery of the show, where visitors were able to view the statue through one of the dozen or so hand-held camera obscuras provided for them. The camera obscura, a wooden, box-like viewing device, illustrated the principles of lenses; by holding one up to the bright statue, visitors could see a tiny, upside-down image of Athena inside the camera.

Roles

In our first example of group conversation at Athena, we see parenting in action at the *Light!* exhibition. Readers may recall an example discussed in chapter I, which showed a mother (in the *Alcoa Foundation Hall of American Indians*) directing her son to attend to the information presented about Navajo code talkers. That example focused on the direct mediation of a parent in the learning of the child. In this example, we show a different parental role—one that is more managerial.

LIGHT! ATHENA: FATHER AND YOUNG SON

Son:	Boop boop.
Father:	Wow, I wonder who this guy is?
Son:	Wow. Hey Daddy? I'm ready to go now.
Father:	You ready to go now? You've had enough light for one day?
Son:	Yeah.
Father:	I thought this was kind of interesting.
Son:	Daddy, I'm done Daddy.
Father:	You're done? Ok, we'll go.
Son:	I wanna get out. This way?
Father:	The next room is called the "Light of Nature." You wanna go see that?
Son:	Just a little . . . No, no, no. I've had enough of this. Let's just—
Father:	Enough of light for one day?
Son:	Yeah. Come back.
Father:	Oh well, that's as far as we're going to get. (LT 12/11)

In this example a father and his five-year-old son negotiated the length of time for their museum visit. The son had had enough of this exhibition and indicated unequivocally that he wanted to leave, although they were only in the first room of the exhibition, near the statue of Athena. Up until this point, the two had been looking at objects fairly closely, which is an accomplishment considering the young age of the boy. The father tried to engage the son with comments such as, "Wow, I wonder who this is?" and he later began to cajole the boy into looking at more objects: "You wanna go see that?" But the son became more and more insistent that he would like to finish with the tour. To some extent this transcript excerpt also provides evidence that, although having a pre-interview with flip cards and being wired up with a microphone for a tour is somewhat intrusive, visitors for the most part acted in the same way as they would have acted had we not been there.

That slightly humorous example of conversation between a father and his son is quite different from the next one, in which a college-aged dating couple was practicing their exchange of information as a form of display behavior that seems common among dating pairs.

LIGHT! ATHENA: YOUNG COUPLE

Girl: Ah, camera obscura.

Boy: Yeah, actually this is really. Here. [hands her a camera] [pause] Yeah, what I found really interesting about this, though, is that the, ah, statue seems to stay in the same place in the camera. I guess that makes sense; there's only one dot.

Girl: Uh-huh.

Boy: It just fades in or out, based on where, like, how directly in the front the bust is.

Girl: Pinhole cameras.

Boy: Yep.

Girl: They're pretty easy to make, I guess.

Boy: Yeah. Get a box and just put tape around the edges or something like that and poke a hole. (LT 02/48)

The boy in this duo worked hard throughout the entire tour, as he did in this example, to engage the interest of his rather cool-sounding friend and to show his "expertise" gained by an earlier visit to the exhibition. The girl gave very short answers that kept the boy talking, without requiring much energy or investment on her part, until the boy responded in a short manner himself ("Girl: Pinhole cameras. Boy: Yep."). At that point, the girl offered a new conversational direction: "They're pretty easy to make, I guess."

Throughout the young couple's tour, while the boy talked, the girl seemed to be paying scant attention to him, instead examining the exhibition and looking around. In contrast, in the next example, two older female friends engaged in a conversation that seemed to be less effortful and more co-constructed, although it was a conversation that also proceeded to some extent on parallel tracks as opposed to gradually building up an explanation.

LIGHT! ATHENA: OLDER WOMAN FRIENDS

Woman 1: It explained my question. They improved glassmaking, they improved. [pause] She doesn't look very feminine, does she? [pause—reading the label] It's Athena.

Woman 2: Okay?

Woman 1:   Is Athena the goddess of war?

Woman 2:   "Discover more, on the other side." Okay? "Each box is a simple camera obscura, what makes it work, point the end with the pinhole towards the bright light." [reading label, pick up cameras] The one with the pinhole. Yeah. "You will see a small upside-down image of the statue on the translucent paper inside the box." [reading label]

Woman 1:   I'm sure it's in there. [pause, looking at visitor guide]

Woman 2:   Okay? I don't understand that one.

Woman 1:   Nuh-uh . . .

Woman 2:   "Look here." Okay?

Woman 1:   I was looking where it said look there.

Woman 2:   I still don't see.

Woman 1:   There's a little light at the end but it doesn't uh look . . .

Woman 2:   It doesn't look any different?

Woman 1:   No.

Woman 2:   Maybe this one? I found that one difficult to understand. (LT 32/31)

These two women were intent on figuring out how the exhibit worked. Like the previous couple, this duo was attempting to use the camera obscura to look at the Athena statue. But unlike the goal operating with the previous couple, the two women focused on the task in parallel; we do not see in the women's conversation the same kind of one-sided work that the boy provided in the previous example. In the women's group, one woman read the content to the other while they both experimented with the cameras. The first woman offered commentary ("She doesn't look very feminine") and asked a question ("Is Athena the goddess of war?"). But these conversational leads about the statue provoked no reaction from her companion, since the second woman was so intent on figuring out how to make the camera obscura work. In analyzing this segment of conversation and the lack of response to the questions of woman 1, we did not presume woman 2 to be inconsiderate; rather, we saw their conversation as indicative of a certain level of social comfort between the two. After woman 1 failed to receive a response to her comments, she did not badger her friend nor did she or repeat her comments; instead she moved her attention to the goal of puzzling through the exhibit by trying to find the answer to her questions in the printed layout guide.

In these three examples of visitor conversation, the differences in social roles seemed to influence the nature of the conversation and the nature of what was understood from a single exhibit station. Three different groups with different role structures (parent-child, dating couple, and old friends) engaged in quite different kinds of conversations. Of course, it is not only their roles but also their interests and motivations that altered how the visitors interacted with the exhibit. In the next section, we look at examples from visitors who each had different motivations for their visits.

Motivation

Clearly there are different kinds of motivation and different levels of motivation. Some visitors are looking for educational enrichment, while other are merely passing the time with friends or having a quiet reflective moment. Some visitors exert considerable effort to see a particular exhibition, whereas others simply drop in. Once visitors are exploring an exhibition, their motivation may change because of the content and the way the material is presented, as well as in response to other personal attributes that affect how they feel, such as hunger, confusion, boredom, or fatigue. Within the conversations, then, one should not expect to see frequent reflections of the original motivation undergirding the museum visit, but there are often subtle indications of their original motivation both in the degree of engagement and in the depth and kinds of conversations that take place during the visit.

The following two examples illustrate the influence of high versus low motivation within a group. Each example provides the group's initial answers to the pre-tour questions about why they came to see the *Africa* exhibition and what they expected to see or do once inside it. Also provided are excerpts of their conversational engagement at a single location within the exhibition—a display case of objects representing Grassfields Art. The Grassfields case included a two-paragraph explanatory label and seven artifacts, including two masks, a pair of beaded shoes, two hats, a wooden figure, and a pipe.

The first example comes from a highly motivated group comprised of a pair of women friends in their forties who had specifically come to see the *Africa* show at the Carnegie Museum of Natural History for reasons that are revealed in their responses to the two relevant pre-tour questions:

WHY?

Woman 1: It's part of our "Faith and Health in the Africa Context" course we're going to be taking this summer when going to Ghana that we come and view this exhibit at the museum.

Woman 2: I'm looking forward to learning, seeing all the neat stuff that will be here concerning Africa and possibly introducing us to some of the cultural things before we actually get there.

EXPECT?

> Woman 1: I expect to see a great diversity in Africa, and I want to partic-
> ularly pay attention to West Africa, the area that I'll be visiting.
>
> Woman 2: I'm interested in seeing all the different clothes and the differ-
> ent things that they make, the handmade items that they do,
> and, like you, especially the Ghana area, to see what we'll be ex-
> periencing before we get there. (AF 30)

Their motivation for visiting the exhibition was audible throughout their tour.
In the following excerpts of tour conversation at the Grasslands case, the two
women were examining a map in order to situate the geographic location of the
Grasslands artifacts in relation to Ghana; then one found an artifact in the case that
she liked and wanted to bring back as a souvenir from their upcoming African trip.

AFRICA, GRASSLANDS: TWO WOMEN

> Woman 1: They live in the Grasslands of west Cameroon. [reading]
>
> Woman 2: Well, we're not going there. [pause, reading label]
>
> Woman 1: Well, not too far from where we're going.
>
> Woman 2: Oh, is that Cameroon? [looking at map]
>
> Woman 1: Yep.
>
> Woman 2: And we're going right around here. [pointing at map]
>
> Woman 1: Uh-huh. Grasslands people decorate "beaded images of frogs,
> lizards, and leopards."
>
> Woman 2: Look how colorful the clothes.
>
> Woman 1: I know, but my niece, the fashion police, would say no to all
> these stripes and plaids and everything together.
>
> Woman 2: Well, yeah. Oh, here we go. This is Africa. Look, Grassfields
> Art. That looks like something my mom would crochet. Ha ha.
>
> Woman 1: Now, do you think they would pull their hair through all those?
>
> Woman 2: I don't know. I'm reading to see if it says anything. [pause,
> reading]
>
> Woman 1: Oh these are beads. Beadwork in shoes.
>
> Woman 2: Oh yeah. [pause] That's what I want to bring home, something
> wood. Look at that, all the intricate work that goes into that.
> Must be a pipe, that thing. Aha! [finds label for the piece] (AF
> 30/6-7)

The friends' upcoming visit to Africa was a theme throughout their tour. In
the first pair of comments, for example, where woman 2 indicates, "We're not go-

ing there," she immediately joins her friend in discussion when woman 1 is able to show her that it is not too far from their own destination. Their preparation-for-the-visit-to-Africa orientation was maintained throughout, with the incorporation of personal commentary on clothing in the displays. The clothes in this exhibit were not treated by the women as quaint or distant but rather were considered as items that could be subject to the personal approval of woman 1's niece or could be compared to woman 2's mother's crocheting. Toward the end of the tour, woman 2 noted, "We're really going to have a shitload of stuff coming back!" Visit as pre-shopping tour?

This example was provided not only because the pair of women were highly motivated to see the exhibition but also because it indicated the ways in which the exhibition became the personal property and experience of the visitor—evidence of a kind of investment in or ownership of the material that is an important component of learning. In contrast, another group, a younger college-age couple, came to the *Africa* exhibition because it was simply there. This group was rated having as a relatively low motivation for seeing the exhibition. They discussed their reasons for visiting and what they expected to see:

WHY?

    Boy: Um. Because it's raining and we don't have anything else to do.
    Girl: Yeah. We were walking by and there it was.
    Boy: Yeah. We said, hey, let's go in.

EXPECT?

    Boy: I have no idea what it is.
    Girl: I bet we'll learn some more about Africa.
    Boy: Yeah, probably. (AF 24)

There is a bit of ambiguity in these responses. Perhaps they were walking by the building and came into the museum to avoid the rain, perhaps they were in the museum (having planned to come because it was raining) and noticed the *Africa* exhibition, or perhaps both. College students may attend the museum for free and the location is convenient to the campus, so the degree of effort is minimal. The other layer of ambiguity is embedded in their mutual desire to appear to be "cool" in front of each other. Neither appeared to want to admit at this stage of the visit (the beginning) that they thought the exhibition might be interesting.

Their conversation as they walked by the Grassfields Art section of the exhibition differed markedly from the previous example of the two friends who were planning a trip to Africa:

AFRICA, GRASSLANDS: TWO STUDENTS

> *Girl:* TV.
> *Boy:* We like TV a lot. Ha ha. But subtitles? Not pleasurable. Oh wow. [watching video] Know our good buddy Bill Smithfield?
> *Girl:* Uh-huh.
> *Boy:* Um, wears—I don't know what they call them.
> *Girl:* Uh-huh.
> *Boy:* Sometimes he has it on. Yesterday, it was snowing and I said to him, "How do you like this weather we're having?" And he said, "Honey, I'm from Africa, I don't like this weather." [with an exaggerated accent] Ha ha.
> *Girl:* Ha ha. "Honey, I'm from Africa."
> *Boy:* They use lots of beads. All beady.
> *Girl:* Those shoes are all beads.
> *Boy:* I don't know if I'd have the patience to do it.
> *Girl:* No, you wouldn't.
> *Boy:* What?
> *Girl:* You wouldn't. (AF 24/7)

This couple engaged in a breezy tour throughout, and they made other attempts to link in an extremely loose way to the content of the show. The connections they made were pretty superficial, touching ever so slightly on the notions of skill and patience in design that were indicated in the displays. Personal connections, where possible, were also made by the two. Later in the tour, for example, the girl commented on a video about African dancing with the rhetorical question, "Did you know that sometimes I go to African dance classes?" (AF 24/12). The *Africa* exhibition for this couple was a place to flirt, stay out of the rain, and be cool, but not a place to engage very deeply with the material.

Visitors come to museums with distinctive motivations. The motivations can change, increasing or decreasing during the course of a tour, but in most cases the entrance motivation sets up the stance toward the exhibition that echoes throughout in the visitors' conversations and subsequently influences what is learned or extracted from the visit. Whereas motivation is a characteristic that may vary during tours, prior knowledge is a more stable construct, although the opportunity to make use of or share knowledge does vary.

Prior Knowledge

In addition to having various levels of motivation, visitors vary in the level and type of background information they bring to the museum. Our core distinctions in this aspect of visitor identity are appreciative background knowledge and experiential knowledge. The following excerpts illustrate the ways in which differences in visitor background knowledge influence the nature of the discussions among visitors. Examples are provided for both types of background knowledge at each of two exhibitions—*The Automobile in American Life* (Henry Ford Museum) and *Aluminum by Design* (Carnegie Museum of Art).

In our first example at the *Automobile in American Life* exhibition, a father was talking with his preteen daughter (a grandfather was also present but was not near the twosome for this part of the tour); the father had considerable appreciative background knowledge about the ways engines work and about the history of the automobile. He was an engineering professor who was in Detroit for a convention held to test students' designs of solar-powered cars. The daughter had come to spend the weekend with him. She was quite comfortable around cars and car technology. The daughter, clearly happy to be spending time with her father at the museum, started the conversation by asking about the meaning of the word "hydromatic," which she took to be related to water.

Daughter: "General Motors hydromatic drive." [reading label] Is that supposed to go in the water?

Father: No, hydromatic, it just means fluid; so it, uh, hydromatic was one of the first automatic transmissions. I think hydromatic was the first real automatic transmission. Chrysler had something before that, but it wasn't fully automatic.

Daughter: "The Airflow DeSoto." Here it is, "the Airflow DeSoto." A door seelan- seelon- sedan. The two-door sedan, first modern car for modern life." [reading label aloud]

Father: It was more streamlined.

Daughter: So it'd get better gas mileage, then.

Father: Yeah. Uh. Some of the other cars got fairly streamlined. In fact, that Cord over there. That was a fairly expensive car. (HF 30/9)

The dynamics of this interaction are interesting for several reasons. First, the girl tended to read labels as a device for beginning a conversational turn—thus prompting her father to expand—and for occasionally offering an interpretive comment herself ("so it'd get better gas mileage then"). Second, although the father and daughter seemed to be very comfortable together, they were still making an effort to engage one another in a slightly formal, didactic way. Third, this particular passage clearly shows the appropriateness of assigning to the entire group a single coding value that reflects the highest level of knowledge (or motivation) within a group.

In another family group, a father and son (touring with a mother and two other children who were not in this discussion) were engaged in a conversation that reflected high experiential knowledge. The father restored automobiles and worked in the automotive industry. He directed his son's attention to the finer points of the assembly of a car.

> *Father:* Pat, that's a flat-head engine on that frame. It's like my dad had in his '52 Ford, that I first rebuilt ever when I was a kid. It's a 6-cylinder flat-head.
>
> *Son:* [laughs] [watching a video showing the development of the Jeep]
>
> *Father:* It's a 1940 Oldsmobile chassis. See the side steps coming out, they look like steps? That's where the body attached. It would attach on those four points, and then there's two more points there in the middle—that's six, seven, eight—and then it would attach on the frame in the back behind the gas tank, and then it would also attach on the front clip, on the front of the frame, that's where the front clip is.
>
> *Son:* It's a small gas tank.
>
> *Father:* No, it looks like about a ten-gallon tank or maybe a fifteen-gallon one. [watch a video of car mass production] Carter, here's a V8 flat-head. Right here. That's a 6-cylinder flat-head; this one here is a V8 flat-head. [watching video and wandering past some cars] (HF 26/7)

In this example, the conversation reflects a distinctly different connection to subject matter knowledge relevant for an exhibition on cars than was present in the earlier father/daughter dyad. Whereas in the first example the father talked to his daughter about historical events and developments in car technology, in this example the father connected strongly to the details of the physical aspects of the cars and how they were put together. He closely analyzed the construction of the car and pointed out key elements to his son, revealing his experiential knowledge of engines and automotive construction. These two examples of background knowledge from conversations at the Henry Ford Museum also offer an interesting point of comparison in terms of how these fathers interacted with their children. In the first instance, the father built from his daughter's question and they had a conversation that revealed and supported the knowledge of each, with the father taking up the daughter's question about the meaning of hydromatic. In the second example, the father was more didactic, directing his son's attention to key physical details. His explanations of the car were highly specific and followed his own interests in cars. The son was not as engaged in the conversation with his father as was the daughter with hers, nor did the son make the same level of effort to keep the conversation with his father going.

In the following example, a family group of four (a mother, father, and teenage son and daughter) visits the *Aluminum by Design* exhibit. The group had high levels of experiential knowledge. The father had worked in manufacturing and had taught manufacturing processes. Throughout the visit, his detailed knowledge of the physical process of working with aluminum came out in explanations and supportive comments to his family. The excerpt provided below came from a part of their tour in which the family spent five minutes watching a video showing the steps involved in making an Emeco aluminum chair. Several of the finished chairs were displayed nearby.

Mother:	I think they're making this chair up. See? It can be brushed or polished.
Father:	Watch this, this is how they bend it. It has to go around that radius.
Son:	Oh. Jeez, he bends it really easily.
Father:	Press.
Son:	Wow. Why does it look like liquid?
Father:	Why does it look like what?
Son:	Why does it look like liquid?
Mother:	Because they've got water coming out at the same time.
Father:	Oh, yeah. That's coolant to blow away the chips and to keep the material on the tool cool. Otherwise they heat up and they wear out fast. Figured out what he's making yet?
Son:	A chair.
Father:	Yep.
Mother:	Think it's going to be one of these chairs here? I'm wondering about this guy in the background.
Father:	We had one of those at the plant too.
Son:	I think it's probably one of those. Oh, that's what it was.
Father:	Wow, this is like Mr. Rogers goes to the aluminum plant.
Mother:	No, there'd be music and talking.
Son:	It's kind of like Mr. Rogers for grown-ups.
Father:	It's showing you actually how much time goes into this. Do you know what breaking the corners means?
Son:	No.
Father:	It means just rounding them off so they aren't sharp.
Son:	Okay. Did you see the pile of scrap stuff that they did?
Father:	You'll see them stick a brush up there to get all the chips off. A bottle brush.
Mother:	Yeah, they did that already one time. Okay, final assembly we get to see what it is. Must be one of those.
Father:	Yeah. Oh, we missed the part where they made the seat, I guess.
Son:	Yep. Must be.

Father:	He's deburring the welds, taking all the flashing and stuff off.
Mother:	Yeah, it's that one right there.
Son:	All that for one chair.
Father:	Yeah, but he really doesn't have that much time in.
Mother:	Now what's he doing?
Father:	Um, salt.
Mother:	Why?
Father:	He may be cleaning it before they coat it, I don't know.
Mother:	Did it get hot in the salt bath?
Father:	It's usually hot. [sizzling noise of water bath]
Son:	Yeah, you're right. There isn't a lot of time that goes into that.
Mom:	Aging.
Father:	The one is an oxide coating on it. They brush it so it looks neat. Yeah, anodizing; but it's clear anodizing, not with a color in it. That just coats it so it won't corrode or anything like that. I know it doesn't rust but there are things that can attack the surface and you don't want that.
Mom:	Like pitting?
Father:	Yeah. It gets white and chalky. If you anodize it, it doesn't. [video shows the worker hammering a chair together]
Mom:	There you go! Ta da! Wow, look at this chair over here with painted flowers. (AL 01/55)

The lengthy conversation above involved a small family group juggling their attention between a video presentation and a set of objects (chairs) while questioning and discussing various points of the manufacturing process. The father, while following the video with evident interest, narrated the major aspects of the process being shown and introduced topics ahead of or in addition to the official narrator—bending, coolant use, Mr. Rogers, time, breaking corners, brushing, deburring, and anodizing. During the conversation, the mother and son introduced a smaller but equally engaged set of topics: liquid appearance, matching the chairs, pile of scrap produced, hot salt, and completion. The son clearly attempted to remain engaged while the father presented ideas such as time, which the son echoed by saying, "All that for one chair"; the father gently corrected him by saying, "Yeah, but he really doesn't have that much time in." From this comment, the son then understood that the earlier referent for time was the idea that time had been completely accounted for, not that it took a long time to produce the chair.

In each of the three sets of transcript excerpts above, one might have noticed that the knowledgeable member of the group, the father, was queried and responded to as he engaged with other members of the group and explained the history, details, and processes shown in the exhibit. It might be tempting to do a bit of gender analysis here, but gender is a highly complicated subject that will be explored thoroughly in a future study. For this study, the father in each example is treated simply as the knowledgeable member of the group, not as someone imposing his expertise. In other groups we have heard women talk about cars with similar expertise.

In the case of *Aluminum by Design*, as in other exhibitions that featured technology-based content, aspects of production as an activity and aspects related to theoretical, conceptual knowledge were both covered; thus it was difficult to classify whether high background knowledge of the content should be considered appreciative or experiential. In the next short quotation, the participants were classified as having high appreciative knowledge, although their knowledge was also grounded in practice. The threesome consisted of a female designer, a male architect, and a male builder who were business colleagues as well as friends. The conversation shown below took place primarily between the architect and the designer, while the builder remained on his own, occasionally floating into the conversation very briefly. The example provides evidence of background knowledge about design and designers, as the duo looked at a cupboard designed by Eileen Gray, a furniture designer who worked in Paris in the 1920s and who used a variety of materials in her designs, including aluminum, cork, glass, and wood.

Woman: Here's Eileen Gray, too.
Man: [inaudible] was big in that time.
Woman: I'd never heard of Eileen Grey until they started rereleasing her early furniture designs.
Man: Is it cork?
Woman: That's what it looks like. It looks like cork. Those are nice pivot hinges. I'll have to show those to Greg [the builder in the group]. (AL 20/31)

This brief example reveals a good deal about the background knowledge and interests of the group and the impact of the particular social roles of the group on resulting conversations. Unlike the first example of conversation in the *Aluminum* exhibition, where the family co-constructed, analyzed, and explained the process of making the chair, the work colleagues in this case rather obliquely dropped a few comments about what they were seeing. Although their comments were brief, they were key references that pointed toward a large body of shared knowledge and expertise. By dropping a name, or adding a small detail, the group was sharing a body of knowledge to which all three members could relate. In many cases, groups whose members shared a similar level of background knowledge with each other spoke in a similar kind of shorthand. This abbreviated talk meant that there was less in the way of extended explanation taking place in those groups than there was in family groups or in groups in which one participant with special knowledge was invited to be expert, to enlighten and explain concepts to the rest of the group.[19]

An additional form of background knowledge was the knowledge about museums themselves.[20] Visitors who frequent museums not only have a specific identity as museumgoers, but they may also learn the specifics of how to "do" a particular kind of museum or even how to contrast and compare objects or display characteristics among museums. Visitors' familiarity with the type of museum they were visiting, or perhaps with the particular museum itself, shapes the museum experience. The two examples below illustrate two different ways in which museum knowledge may surface in or support a museum visit. The first example is an excerpt from the opening moments of a couple's tour of the *Light!* exhibition. They oriented themselves to the show as regular and knowledgeable museumgoers. This lens shaped the couple's tour, as they constantly assessed whether or not, or where, they may have seen some of the objects in this exhibition before.

Husband:	[referring to their experience with audio guides, and looking at the layout map and guide to plan their visit] What was the one we took, when we were here last time, oh, at the International?
Wife:	"*At the Moulin Rouge.*" Where is it from, 36? [reading label] Does it say who it's on loan from? We saw this too! This is just too cool! I can't wait.
Husband:	"*The Deh-gah Interior.*" [reading label]
Wife:	Duh-gah, Duh-gah. There's no accent.
Husband:	"Monet, *Interior After Dinner.*" [reading label]
Wife:	Wait. Where are we?
Husband:	I told you it was Lautrec, *At the Moulin Rouge.*
Wife:	Well, I know, we saw that!
Husband:	Had to be at the d'Orsay. That's the only place I think I've seen Lautrec, or did we see it in London?
Wife:	Ooh, London's collection sucked, I don't remember too much.
Husband:	What?
Wife:	London's collection of Impressionists kind of sucked. I mean comparatively, of course, because it was much worse than the National Gallery's. (LT 16/11–12)

In the example above, the couple seemed so intent on identifying where they had seen various objects before that it almost seems as though they were not viewing them in the context of the *Light!* exhibition at all. The next example shows visitors (grandparents in the company of their grandchildren) who were very comfortable with the living history museum framework at *Prairietown*, having visited the museum many times before. The conversational excerpt provided below shows their comfort in the environment as they joked with the interpreter, Mrs. Curtis, and "played along" with her by entering the conversation as though they were genuine 1836 visitors to town.

Mrs. Curtis:	And I have a little boy Edward who's asleep upstairs. He woke up with an earache today.
Grandpa and Grandma:	Uh-oh, oh dear.
Mrs. Curtis:	So, I told him he had to stay in bed.
Grandma:	You might have to take him to Dr. Campbell.
Mrs. Curtis:	Ah, I'll try some sweet oil on a piece of wool first, ma'am. Dr. Campbell is expensive. Twenty-five cents for a house call.
Grandpa:	Oh, really. You didn't tell me he was expensive.
Mrs. Curtis:	You have to be frugal with your husband's money. You can't spend it foolishly.
Grandma:	Oh. No one ever told me that before. I've learned something today. I thought the object was to spend it as fast as you could.
Grandpa:	Maude, you should listen to this woman. This woman has some good advice. (CP 11/12)

The identity construct, as we are working with it, comprises roles, motivation, and an appreciative or experiential knowledge dimension. These are major components of what the visiting group brings to the interactions in the museum. Hands-on experience with and acquired appreciation of the content of an exhibition help visitors gain an entrée into the details of a show. In some senses, these knowledge components help to "problematize" the environment in that they support the visitors' inquiry and observation of specifics, which they can then engage with, talk about, and share with their companions. However, this background knowledge does more than that—it also prompts a level of sharing and reminiscence among the members of a group. The interactive behavior of personalizing objects in an exhibition is discussed more thoroughly in the chapter on explanatory engagement, but interaction with people and objects is also a reflection of background knowledge and experience; an example of this kind of interaction is provided next.

This final example of conversation reflecting visitors' personal connection to objects took place at the *Aluminum by Design* exhibition among a group of three women—two middle-aged women friends touring together and a third, a stranger, who became involved in their conversation. The two friends had been taking their time looking at the exhibition. The conversation excerpted below occurred at an area featuring household goods, including pots and pans and vacuum cleaners. Woman 1 was excited to see a vacuum cleaner that she remembered from her childhood. She started a story about it, but sensing that she was losing her audience, she engaged a stranger (woman 3) who was also taking notice of the vacuum cleaner. Woman 1 extended and elaborated the story to this passing woman—who supported what was now a retelling of the story by responding with an additional bit of information about the same object.

Woman 1:   Oh, am I ever going to have to harass my sister.

Woman 2:   One of those?

Woman 1:   We found one of those when we cleaned out my mother's house a couple of years ago.

Woman 2:   My mother used that all the time when I was growing up. An Electrolux. It smelled funny.

Woman 1:   Yeah! But I told my sister, "I think that could probably be a collector's item." And she goes, "It's trash day and we're putting it out." And that was the end of that!

Woman 2:   And here it is!

Woman 1:   I'm hoping that somebody had the sense to come by and pick it up before it ended up just gone.

Woman 2:   "1937." [reading label]

Woman 1:   I would be surprised if she hadn't *bought* it in 1937. You know what is funny? That is the year they got married, 1937.

Woman 2:   [chuckle] May be!

Woman 1:   It could have been the one she bought when she got married.

Woman 2:   Hmm.

Woman 1:   It's kind of neat to see that there's one saved.

Woman 2:   Yes.

Woman 1:   This is pretty shiny.

Woman 2:   That's a . . Wow. By golly . . . symbol. [mumbling and talking to a woman in background]

Woman 1:   "1940. Electrolux." Brings back a memory, doesn't it? [chuckling]

Woman 2:   Not that it's necessarily a good one.

Woman 3:   Oh really? I'd love to have it.

Woman 2:   Wow.

Woman 3:   Because I have slate floors.

Woman 1:   Oh, wow.

Woman 3:	And trying to find something that does not have a beater bar because it chips my slate. Right. It's like, you can't!
Woman 1:	Forget it. You've got to do that by hand, unfortunately.
Woman 3:	Yeah.
Woman 1:	That's what I was just saying, we cleaned out my mom's house a couple of years ago and there was one of those in the back in an old cupboard. And I told my sister that looks like something we ought to hang on to. She's one of these clean-sweeper people.
Woman 3:	Oh yeah, so is my sister.
Woman 1:	Gone!
Woman 3:	My aunt still uses hers. She has carpets now. I'm trying to talk her out of it.
Woman 2:	I'm sure my mother would still use hers if she was alive.
Woman 1:	Yeah.
Woman 3:	Mother had a Hoover, which we finally just couldn't fix any more.
Woman 1:	Yeah.
Woman 3:	The only reason it died—it probably wasn't aluminum! [laughs]
Woman 1:	Probably not. I remember that as having the Hoover name on it.
Woman 2:	This one says Kenmore. Look at the headlights! Looks like a car! It definitely looks like a car. Look, there's a rubber bumper on it. (AL 30/34)

There are many possible interpretations of this lengthy interaction, but we want to emphasize the way in which we saw identity reflected in the discourse. The women positioned themselves as knowers and owners—even if through their parents—of the object, and then moved on to seeing themselves as appreciators, either because of inherent value (as in the case of woman 1) or because of unique functionality (as in the case of woman 3). All three women were excited by their own recognition of and relationship to the object. They seemed to want to linger a bit and discuss its meaning, a meaning that went well beyond that of the exhibition's intention to show a simple example of aluminum's use in common household equipment. Interestingly, woman 1 accurately guessed that the stranger nearby, woman 3, would be just as interested in the object as she herself was.

Findings

This section is intended to give the flavor of how the rich, complex ideas that surround identity were enacted in the particular data the MLC gathered. We do this in two parts: First, we simply wanted to share the way different museums and exhibitions looked with respect to some of the identity constructs we explored—populations of visitors (in terms of the social roles or relationships within the group), the identity of visitors (in terms of their background knowledge and motivation), the same knowledge and motivation identity measures for all the exhibitions together in terms of specific populations (social groups, families, or couples), and, finally, whether visitors at each exhibition tended to be local or out-of-towners or a combination of both (see figs. 3.1 to 3.3). Second, we wanted to show how the global variables within identity related to learning.

Figure 3.1 shows the distribution of number and type of groups that participated in our study at each exhibition. With the exception of the *Alcoa Foundation Hall of American Indians*, we had approximately equal numbers of groups at each exhibition. In general, families with children visited the Exploratorium (*Behind the Screen*) and Conner Prairie (*Prairietown*) more than they did other exhibitions and more than other types of groups who came to those museums. Couples and social groups were the predominant visitor type at *Aluminum* and *Light!*, both held at the Carnegie Museum of Art. Thus, for example, 25% of the visiting groups at *Aluminum* and *Light!* were family groups, whereas 59% were family groups at Conner Prairie and the Exploratorium.

Given that different types of groups seemed to gravitate toward different museums exhibitions (although every type of group appeared at each museum), it is useful to examine the distribution of prior-knowledge and motivation ratings at each of the different museums. For this analysis the appreciative and experiential codes are combined and averaged. The two codes were merged because, although the two types

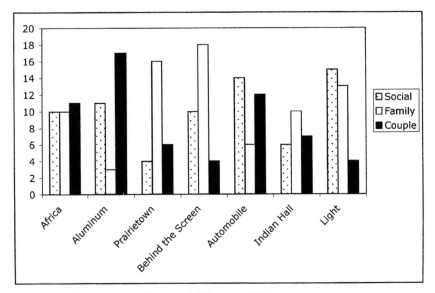

Figure 3.1.   Group types at different exhibitions (*n*=207).

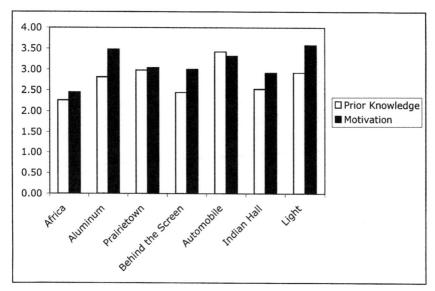

Figure 3.2.   Mean identity codes by exhibition (*n*=207).

of background knowledge could be reliably differentiated, it seemed that the codes for the two constructs generally moved together—high scores on appreciative knowledge were often accompanied by high scores on experiential knowledge, and they both related to other variables in the total model of learning in a similar fashion. In all future references, this dual identity element will be called "prior knowledge."

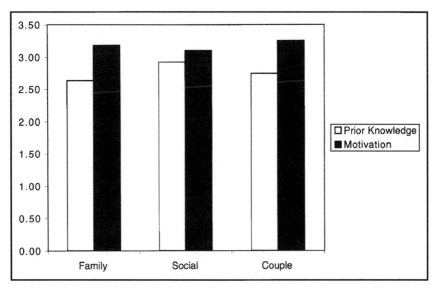

Figure 3.3.   Mean identity codes by visiting group (*n*=207).

In general, visitors to the *Automobile in American Life* exhibition at the Henry Ford Museum had the highest levels of knowledge about the show's content. Visitors to *Light!*, *Aluminum*, and *Prairietown* seemed to have considerable prior knowledge as well, whereas those to *Africa* and *Indian Hall* had the least prior knowledge and motivation for their visit.

A thorough discussion of the way the data from the identity codes emerged appears in the Results section of chapter 6. The discussion here is designed simply to give the flavor of how the information on identity related to other important ideas in the model. Table 3.1 below shows the correlations between the averaged appreciate and experience codes (prior knowledge) with the motivation and learning estimates. All correlations were significant. To read a correlation matrix, consider that the number in a cell may be either positive or negative and may range from zero to one. A positive number means that as one dimension in a pair increases, so too does the other. It should always be the case that a variable correlates perfectly (1.00) with itself. For these data, .19 or higher is significant at a probability of .01.

The correlation matrix in table 3.1 indicates that the two measures of identity (prior knowledge and motivation) are correlated but that each contributes some separate information. Both of these estimates of identity are positively related to our estimate of learning. Motivation appears to be more strongly related to our learning estimate than is prior knowledge.

Message

The message of this chapter is quite direct. First, visiting groups enter the museum with a rich sense of identity as families, couples, or friends; with a cluster of purposes that may gradually morph over the course of a visit from casually passing the time or getting in out of the rain to profound interest in learning or sharing some particular kind of knowledge; and with a set of background information that filters and colors the experiences that they have. Second, the intentions of the museum curatorial groups and designers may or may not align with the mission and knowledge of the visiting groups. Third, while we can easily demonstrate the effects of different background knowledge or different motivations on the kind of activity and language visitors used in a museum, deciding on ways to capture those aspects of identity is not trivial and, as with learning, involves serious trade-offs.

Table 3.1.   Correlation Matrix

	Prior Knowledge	*Motivation*	*Learning*
Prior knowledge	1.00		
Motivation	.38	1.00	
Learning	.30	.46	1.00

We focused our research on visiting groups in the museum because groups talk and share information in a public and traceable form. We also felt that, given our approach to studying learning, this focus on groups was one that would best reflect both the social and the cultural aspects of the environment. However, the use of groups poses a challenge for the concept of identity. Identity is most commonly associated with individuals or with highly defined organized groups such as ethnic groups. Nonetheless, the construct of identity has been a useful and usable one, albeit a temporary identity for our visitors. Identity was measured less by the demographics and more by the details of how the groups were enacting a particular visit, specifically by their level of interest, motivation, and curiosity, and by their appreciative and experiential knowledge. Because groups were the focus of this work, these experiences and values were considered to be things that could be easily shared if any one member of the group had access to them. Specifically, if one member of the group had worked in an aluminum design plant for twenty years, then the whole group was considered to be likely to have access to that experiential identity throughout the tour. This sense of group identity, then, is a sense of group resources for enjoyment and learning.

Questions

As we have thought about the visiting groups in our study, we sometimes felt that we should have known more than we found out by our simple self-administered interview. In one set of discussions among members of the research team we explored the idea of directly asking a visiting group such things as: In the context of your visit today, what roles are each of you playing? How would you describe yourself as a group—friends, family, dating, or some other description? What kinds of knowledge do you have that might be related to this exhibition? And we considered perhaps having members of a group describe each other and the roles they normally assume in such outings.

Consider, if you will, both your own answers to such questions the next time you visit a museum with someone else and how the answers relate to museum actions, discussions, and behaviors. In addition, consider how the combination of self-descriptions and activity might or might not impact learning. What kind of a study would you design to get at this? How might you analyze the information?

Notes

1. The idea of constraining how many aspects of identity can be considered has both a pragmatic and conceptual base. On the one hand, to tell a general story that is rooted in specific details, the set of details needs to be limited; this is the pragmatic problem of generalizing from data. On the other hand, in order to get to the activities associated with learning, we want to avoid becoming mired in the entire complex issue of Identity with a capital I; this is part of the conceptual difficulty of creating a model of learning.

2. Falk and Dierking 1992, 2000; Hein 1998; Hooper-Greenhill 2000; Roberts 1997; Silverman 1993.

3. See especially Rice 1995.

4. Falk and Dierking 1992.

5. Hein 1998.

6. Hooper-Greenhill 2000.

7. Silverman 1993.

8. Roberts 1997.

9. See, for example, Doering and Pekarik 1996; Koran, Koran, and Longino 1986; Hilke 1988; Hood 1983.

10. Brown 1975.

11. Chi and Roscoe 2002.

12. Lave and Wenger 1991.

13. Falk, Moussouri, and Coulson 1998; Hood 1983.

14. Doering and Pekarik 1996.

15. Graburn 1984.

16. Hein 1998; Roschelle 1995.

17. Leinhardt 2000.

18. Other researchers, such as Howard Gardner and others, have tried to account or test for different types of knowledge. For our purposes, in an environment that focuses primarily on the academic or verbal and visual modes of learning, and in a minimally invasive research design model, we needed a more general way to think about learning, but we did want to acknowledge hands-on learning, and non-academic kinds of learning, with our experiential measure of prior experiences.

19. See, for example, Fienberg and Leinhardt 2002.

20. Leinhardt, Tittle, and Knutson 2002.

Conversation   4

"Side chair." That's an interesting design.
I wonder how comfortable that is?
Cool chairs, we should get one. Hey, stop beating up on your
   sisters.

—VISITOR CONVERSATION AT THE *ALUMINUM BY DESIGN* EXHIBITION

Oh, I like that. Remember in the Harrisburg Museum, there
   was that heart you could kind of walk through? It's like on
   Pee Wee Herman—the talking chair.
Oh, I never watched Pee Wee Herman.
Your loss!

—VISITOR CONVERSATION AT THE *ALUMINUM BY DESIGN* EXHIBITION

The Problem

WE APPROACHED OUR STUDY with a particular image in mind. As we thought through the kinds of learning that might result from a group of people visiting a museum, we imagined the following scene: A small group had a lovely afternoon at a museum. They stopped at the end of the visit for a cup of coffee or a soda and began to mull over their experiences. After they left the museum and got into their car, they continued the discussion of the major objects and activities that had attracted their attention. They recounted the foibles of who got lost and who got confused and talked about the one cool thing they all liked.

The image of that scene was mixed in with, and confounded by, an image of visitors actually going through exhibitions, step by step, and talking as they were touring the exhibits in the shows they had chosen to see. The opening quotes of two different groups, a family and a young couple, looking at chairs in the *Aluminum by Design* exhibition illustrate the complexity of these conversations and the factors that influence the nature of talk in museums. Our questions about the scene inside the exhibitions were: What took place? What did people talk about? What were they seeing and doing?

In chapter 1 we presented a framework that rested on conversation and shared language as the basis for defining and estimating learning in the museum. In chapter 3, we examined the identity that visiting groups draw upon during a museum experience—including motivation and prior knowledge as key features. In this chapter, we look at the conversations that took place during the museum visit, and we connect these conversations to learning. Certainly, what visitors bring with them in terms of expectations and knowledge is a part of their museum experience and affects what they say and when they say it. The social relationships within a group impact these dimensions of conversation as well. A family may encourage or invite their least knowledgeable member to talk about and explore objects or ideas presented in an exhibition, and they may respond with somewhat exaggerated interest as the group practices the routine of being a family that visits museums. A small group of friends with a highly knowledgeable member may prod, cajole, or otherwise encourage that person to talk and share what he or she knows. A couple may take turns showing off knowledge and listening attentively to one another. The combination of the identity, the exhibits on display, the engagement with that set of displays, and language interact to influence learning.

As we thought about our specific picture of a lovely afternoon at the museum, considered the admonitions and advice from other museum researchers, and spent more time informally watching visitors at museums, we recognized three potential risks to using language in such a central role: confounding museum talk with group histories, possibly artificial talk, and destructive segmenting of the recorded talk. These risks needed to be carefully considered because they could pose serious problems for interpreting or using a coherent model of museum-based learning.

The first risk was one of confounding museum talk with group experience. Language does not occur independent of a group's history. Topic choice and even who gets to speak are activities that exist within a group before, during, and after a visit. As people talk during a visit they are reflecting their past and rehearsing both their own roles and the content of conversation that may continue after the visit is over. Just as visitors bring with them their personal identities and group identity in a way that shapes the activity of the visit, they also carry out with them the experience and conversations that took place during the visit. By considering learning through the lens of conversation, we are treating conversation as both process and result. Focusing on conversation in the museum as learning is to knowingly isolate and thereby distort a continuous process that begins before and continues afterward. We needed to use an analytic approach that reflected, to some extent, the group's past and future conversational trajectory, but we were also constrained by the need to sample conversations at a specific moment and in a specific locale.

The second risk in focusing on conversation is the possibility of "artificial talk." At the outset of our research, some colleagues wrote to tell us that in their experience people did not really speak during the museum visit; in truth, we knew that, on some occasions, we ourselves were not likely to speak during a museum visit either. Traditionally, museums, like libraries, are seen as places of quiet contemplation that inhibit conversation, where public behavior encourages silence or lowered voices. Other colleagues were concerned that what speech did occur would be artificial and produced for our benefit alone. Pilot work conducted in the first phase of our research showed that groups of visitors did, for the most part, talk to each other.[1] Although some visiting groups spent part of their visit examining objects in silence, or alone, visitors did tend to talk to the members of their group most of the time. As to the issue of provoked artificiality of speaking while wearing a microphone, there too we saw a few instances in which individuals spoke for our benefit or hushed each other because we were listening in; but most frequently (over 90% of the time), we saw behaviors and heard language in our pilot data that strongly suggested either that they had forgotten they were being audiotaped or that they had few or no inhibitions about it. Did people speak more, or more artificially, than they normally would have done?[2] Perhaps, but one cannot say what one does not know or know how to say. Visitors cannot discuss connections between an object and their personal world if the idea of doing so has never occurred to them or if they had no such connection. The challenge, then, was to capture speech that was authentic and to interpret it in a meaningful way.

We then focused on the third risk: that of destructive segmenting of the conversation that we did capture. How should the conversation be broken apart or segmented to examine it? The purpose of breaking apart conversations is to provide usable meaningful interpretation across different groups. We discuss more thoroughly in the appendix the general issue of segmenting visitor talk, but for the purposes of this chapter, we consider the issue of segmenting or organizing the talk in terms of the risk it poses to the intentions of the study. The risk inherent to the segmenting activity is that by breaking apart the stream of conversation, the speaker's intentions and meanings might be inadvertently distorted. We examined three options for artificially dissecting the authentically connected and interwoven conversations of our visitors. One option would be to break the conversation into equal sized time units (thirty to forty-five seconds). Segmenting by time in this way would create short chunks of visitor talk to which a clear and unambiguous set of codes could easily be assigned, and the true rate of talk to silence for each group could be accurately captured. If this time-based segmenting were used, we would be able to make statements such as: This group spent 25% of its time talking about objects in the show, 25% talking about family or personal matters, 40% discussing management of the visit, and 10% on other issues. Furthermore, the reliability of the segmenting itself could be easily measured and high reliability achieved by simply re-clocking the time. But the risk or trade-off in using time-based segmenting was that the artificiality of the boundaries of the isolated chunk of talk would make interpreting the meaning of the conversation as a whole nearly impossible. Standard time units do not correspond to the idea units of a conversation.

Alternatively, we could take the total stream of conversation and consider it one interconnected set of speech and then select themes—such as personal reminiscences, object responses, environmental discussions, visit management discussions—as the unit of focus. Several excellent and very useful computer software programs (such as Nud*ist) are available to support this kind of coding. The problem with that approach, however, is that it would emphasize the visitors' identity and conversational style over the dialogue with the museum objects, ideas, and design features. That approach would also make the task of drawing systematic formal connections to learning problematic.

Finally, we could choose to break the conversation up according to the physical movement and content discussions of the groups. We could follow the group as they moved from one exhibit station to another and as they began to notice a new object or display (or decided to leave the current station and seek another), and we could mark a segment of their conversation at that point. This type of segmenting is called *event-based*. This way of breaking the conversation up by a combination of actions and speech would highlight the specifics of the visitors' engagement with the objects in the exhibitions. Such an approach would make it possible to describe the proportion of engagement represented by each of several different forms and content of talk. With this approach, however, a brief stop at an exhibit station accompanied by abbreviated conversation would be weighted equal to those stops and conversational engagements that were longer and more extended. In terms of authenticity, there are both advantages and disadvantages to each way of breaking things apart. Fortunately, with the availability of complete audiotaped and observational records, all three approaches to segmenting the data can ultimately be undertaken.

The Concept

Conversation is a uniquely human enterprise. Conversation that is primarily devoted to expressions of appreciation, analytic responses, and meta-level commentary on the responses or behaviors of others as an end in itself is not only uniquely human but a relatively rare occurrence.[3] As linguists, philosophers, sociologists, and even film producers have noted, conversation has rules that govern not only what is permissible and expected but also the changes that may occur in response to different settings.[4] There are many important books and articles that describe different ways to consider the discourse among human beings; whether that discourse is a simple utterance or an extended exchange.[5] To date there are none that deal exclusively with the discursive practices of the museum.

In choosing to focus on conversation in the informal environment of the museum, we were choosing both a location that is unusual (in that most people spend most of their time at home, at work, shopping, or traveling) and a situation that is somewhat unusual (in that the goals are unspecified or underspecified and the roles for each group member are quite fluid). Although these features of unique setting and situation were likely to influence conversational content and activity, it was also likely that the museum-based conversations would reflect some general underlying commonalities with other conversational practices.

One approach to thinking about conversation is to consider the normal permissions and expectations that undergird this most human of activities. Grice has described a series of structures called *conversational implicatures*, which enclose the conversational space and suggest "rules" that govern expectations and responses among the speakers.[6] One value of Grice's contribution to discourse analysis is that he focuses on expectations among speakers that form a "cooperative principle." Among several implicatures that instantiate the cooperation principle, the ones most salient for our task are the ones that require that conversation be as *informative as required* but not *more informative than is required*.[7] This set of constraints means that if two people are both gazing at a painting, for example, one does not say to the other, "Oh, we are standing in front of this painting by Van Gogh called *Gauguin's Chair*, and I notice that you are noticing. . . ." Such talk would sound quite bizarre. However, the normal conversation at an exhibit station, with its absence of such markers to indicate the object of gaze or discussion, requires that researchers know more about the exchange than simply the content of the speech alone in order to interpret it. In thinking of conversation as having underlying principles, one assumption is that the speakers are operating in a shared goal system. For museum conversations this idea of a shared goal system may not always hold, however; in fact, one activity that is likely to emerge during the course of a visit is the process of establishing a set of goals for the visit of learning, experiencing, enjoying, and sharing. However, even if the visitors' goal system is hard to discern, the "cooperative principle" suggests that everyone in a group should "identify . . . with the transitory conversational interests of the other" and that the contributions should be "dovetailed [and] mutually dependent."[8] So, while museum conversations may "sound" fragmented, disjointed, and sometimes meandering, they can still be meeting the needs of the visitors because the situation—the museum environment—is supporting and supplying the information that allows the implicatures to hold true.

Taking a somewhat different view of language and its use than Grice, Clark emphasizes the social usefulness and shared coordination of language. Like Grice, Clark sees language, and conversation in particular, as a coordinated form of joint action. The particularities of the coordination depend in no small part on the setting and purposes of the conversation. Clark focuses on a number of settings in which language is used quite differently—for example, an *institutional setting* where a sermon is given as contrasted with a *mediated setting* in which one hears or makes a standard recording as on an answering machine.[9] Using Clark's framework, museum conversations take place in a *personal setting*—that is, a face-to-face setting in which there are no formal constraints on who may talk or what they say. There are moments in museum conversations, many of them, in which the visitors engage in what Clark refers to as *layered discourse* or *mediated discourse* by reading the label copy or interpreting what they think the curatorial or artistic team meant by something in the exhibition. There are also moments in which visitors say nothing or other times when they are quite literally talking about the weather. In our analysis of museum conversations, we are assuming that language is used in a social manner and that it is a system of joint actions that require some level of coordination. We assume that there are meanings, intentions, and layers in the conversation. The work of understanding museum conversations is well served by making use of a few critical features identified by theorists such as Grice and Clark.

As discussed in chapter 1, research has been done on visitor conversations, and the range of methods illustrates the complexity of the material being studied—natural language. Some work has focused primarily on discourse acts and looked at the ways in which conversations are structured. Did visitors summon, reply to, or prompt their conversational partners? Borun, for example, used similar kinds of structural categories, looking at "performance indicators" and examining whether visitors asked or answered questions, whether they read the label copy silently or aloud, and whether they described, interpreted, or applied the knowledge provided in the exhibits.[10] Crowley and his colleagues focused on small fragments of explanations found in museum conversations.[11] These fragments, which Crowley refers to as "explanatoids," are thought to form the basis of more extended understandings or appreciations that become "islands of expertise" for families. Others, such as Tunnicliffe, have focused on the content of visitors' utterances, a prospect that can result in numerous categories.[12] A unique aspect of this work is that it follows and connects language over time and place within the museum with respect to both aspects of structure and content.

In using visitor conversation as a window into learning in museums, the most salient features are those that concern the content of the museum and the visitors' responses to the local and more complexly layered features of an exhibition. One might focus on the substantive content of the talk itself, the affective import of the talk, the positional role the talk is designed to play, or the structural features of the talk. Museum conversations may be seen as a way in which groups can re-hearse particular roles, such as parents and children, friends, and lovers. Conversa-tion allows group members who are playing out different roles to express themselves quite differently. In the situation of the brief, one-hour visit, it seems most useful to focus on two dimensions of conversation: the *content* of the talk, es-pecially as it relates to the museum exhibits, and the *structure* of the conversational segments, because these structures shed light on how deeply the conversation re-flects visitors' engagement with aspects of the exhibition. Our approach to these two constructs of content and structure is consistent with the theoretical posi-tions of both Grice and Clark but does not derive from them. In our coding de-cisions, we assumed that members of a visiting group were in fact engaged in a socially shared task of meaning making and construction around the objects and activities of the museum.

Content

As described in chapter 2, we worked with the curators at each site and with the available exhibition literature to develop a set of five overarching themes unique to each exhibition. The themes reflected the content of the exhibitions and were used to help analyze the content of the conversations at each site.

As we studied the museum homes of the exhibitions, we realized that although we could not actually hope to capture all of the issues in the environment that vis-itors might talk about, progress could be made in several domains. Each exhibi-tion was structured around a core set of curatorial premises that helped define spaces, groupings, and activities. The number of themes and the levels of explic-itness for them varied from show to show. By walking through exhibition spaces with curators and studying the exhibition catalogues, we were able to identify *cu-ratorial themes*.

We used these curatorial themes to help guide the development of our own five *overarching themes*, which we briefly described in chapter 2. The curators had a central message to share, one big idea they hoped visitors would take away with them. Within the exhibition, the curators either explored their topic in increasing levels of detail or examined different aspects of the topic. The subdivisions were supported by variations in wall color, spacing, and lighting, as well as by large panel wall text, hands-on elements, and sometimes central explanatory videotapes. Curatorial themes tended to apply more closely to geographically defined sections of an exhibition or to specific sets of objects, whereas our themes were designed to be applicable to each object—that is, any object in the show could be seen through the lens of any theme. Table 4.1 shows the five themes that were developed for each show. These themes borrowed heavily from the curators' essential ideas and were confirmed in consultation with the curator at each site. The somewhat arbitrary decision to develop the same number of themes for each exhibition allowed later quantitative analysis to proceed in a more streamlined manner. When thematic talk occurred among visitors in response to objects or groups of objects and their specific markers, we included the thematic talk in the analysis of explanatory engagement. But we did not force conversations into those themes.

For each segment of conversation in which the content of the exhibition was described or discussed, that discussion was assigned a code that corresponded to the applicable theme for the exhibition. If, for example, a visiting group discussed the sheen and beauty of chrome or a particular color of paint on a car at Henry Ford's *The Automobile in American Life* exhibition, then that comment was considered to be about the aesthetics of cars. If color and sheen were discussed as a part of the manufacturing process in the *Aluminum by Design* exhibition, then that talk might be classified in the thematic category of problem solving and design, depending on other parts of the context in which they were speaking. Once the thematic content for each exhibition was established, all of the themes were treated as equal in terms of value or complexity.[13] The underlying concept for this analytic approach, then, is that each exhibition dealt with several ideas; that each object or at least most objects in the exhibition could be considered in light of any one of five core ideas; and that these thematic ideas were of roughly equal importance for connecting with the main message of the exhibition.

Structure

Thematic language was present or absent from the conversational segments depending on the way each conversational segment was structured. Building on phase I research, five types of conversational structure were identified, yielding structural codes for the conversational segments: *list, personal synthesis, analysis, synthesis,* and *explanation*. For segments of a museum visit where there was silence or talk that was totally unrelated to the content, two additional structural codes were established: *no talk* and *not applicable*. These codes allowed us to account for talk that was unrelated to the content of the exhibition, as well as for times when there were meaningful pauses but no conversation.

Table 4.1. Themes by Exhibition

Exhibition	Theme 1	2	3	4	5
Africa	Ecosystems and natural resources	Social groups and ways of living	Belief systems and practices	Crafts, skills, and technology	Africans around the world
Aluminum	Style and aesthetics	Problem solving in design	History (of discovery and use)	Transformation and recycling	Corporate presence
Prairietown	Social class and gender	Family economics	Values, religion, and attitudes	Sense of place, settlement, and migration	Training and education
Behind the Screen	History and the role of movies in popular culture	Technology of movie production	Assortment of job positions involved in making movies	Artistic and technical skills involved in the process	Layering of different elements to create an illusion of reality
Automobile	Engines and technology	Aesthetics	Automotive industry	Impact of cars on society	Personal experiences with cars
Indian Hall	Role of nature	Spirituality	Gender roles	Cultural influences—tradition and change	Skills and techniques
Light!	Science and technology	Art and artistic techniques	Spirituality	Work and the Industrial Revolution	Societal changes

List refers to simple identification or short-phrase evaluations. *Personal synthesis* refers to comments that connect an object or activity to a personal circumstance or possession. *Analysis* refers to language that examines one or more specific features within an object or activity. *Synthesis* refers to conversations that connect an object or idea to other objects or activities within the exhibition or to similar objects or ideas found elsewhere. *Explanation* refers to language that investigates some aspect of causality either with respect to how a specific object or particular effect was created or with respect to how a larger thematic idea progressed within an exhibition. Unlike the five thematic categories for each exhibition, these five structural features were considered hierarchical; therefore, in coding each segment we took the highest structural code available within a segment and assigned that as the code for the entire segment. In general, the higher-level code, such as explanation, usually incorporated language that would otherwise be considered list, personal synthesis, analysis, and synthesis; therefore, to count the lower-level code as well the higher one would inflate the results for the presence of lower-level structures in the overall tour conversation.

The following transcript excerpt illustrates the presence of multiple levels of structural talk in a single conversational segment. In this example, a family group consisting of grandparents and two grandsons were comparing the Tlinglit and the Hopi cultures while looking at a full-scale replica of a Hopi house that includes a place for visitors to grind corn in a traditional way.

INDIAN HALL, HOPI HOUSE: GRANDPARENTS AND TWO GRANDSONS

Grandmother:	Look, there are sheepskins on the floor. Is that meal?
Grandson 1:	Yeah.
Grandson 2:	Yeah.
Grandson 1:	It's where they were grinding.
Grandfather:	Isn't it amazing how humans, even though they're almost alike, how they adapted to different environments? It was so dry here they had to irrigate; the Tlingits had so much water they didn't have to worry about it. (IN 20/16)

The above segment could have been coded as list (had it stopped at the first line, "Is that meal?") or as analysis (had it stopped at the fourth line, "It's where they were grinding"), as the family group noticed and named the elements of the house and then analyzed how the sheepskins were used. It is when the grandfather added an *explanation* of adaptation by humans in response to different ecological environments that we assigned the segment an explanation code. This segment also carried a thematic code—the role of nature (theme I).

Thematic and structural codes are connected within the coding scheme. That is, the thematic code assigned to a segment corresponded to the same bounded segment receiving the structural code. We coded for themes in a segment of conversation only if the structure of that segment reflected talk at the level of analysis, synthesis, or explanation. We limited the assignment of thematic codes in this way because by definition lists could not include a thematic element and also by definition the most important part of a personal synthesis was the personal connection, not the thematically relevant aspect of the object being looked at.

Examples

Several examples of visitor talk from two different groups are provided below to illustrate the nature of a segment of conversation and to show how such segments were coded on both structural and thematic dimensions. One group went through the *Automobile in American Life* exhibition and one went through the *Light!* exhibition. These groups were chosen as examples because they displayed very high levels of conversation on the structural dimension.[14] The examples are not typical; rather they reflect situations that provide strong examples for each structural code.

In the two-column chart below, the left column shows the conversations of a group of three adults from Canada visiting the *Automobile in American Life* exhibition. The group included two professors and the wife of one of them. They were very knowledgeable about cars, and they shared stories about the history of the auto industry as well as personal anecdotes about the cars that were significant in their lives. The right column shows the conversation between two women friends, one of whom was an artist, as they visited the *Light!* exhibition. They spent a long time examining objects in the exhibition, and the artist explained to her friend at great length how to create different painterly effects at great length. Each column is headed by the exhibition title, the section of the exhibition where the talk occurred, and the specific exhibit station or stop where the visitors were actually located at that moment.

List

Automobile in American Life *Concept Cars: The Nucleon*	*Light!* *Gallery 2: Clouds, Constable*
Man 2: Oh it's electric. Woman: Yeah. Man 1: What is this? Woman: It's a Nucleon. (HF 15/15)	Woman 1: But they get grotesque if they're bigger. [pause] Woman 2: Beautiful. Woman 1: I like that. (LT 26/47)

In the left column, the man and woman identified one auto component as being electric and then looked at a car called a Nucleon. The simple abrupt discussion was considered to be a list-like identification and was coded as list. As the trio continued they made many personal connections to the exhibits, using the exhibition as a whole to exchange information about themselves. In the right column, the segment shows two women visitors at the *Light!* exhibition making a brief and passing evaluative comment about a painting by Constable that was likewise coded as list.

Personal Synthesis

In the next example, the two visitor groups can be heard using the museum visit as an opportunity to connect what they are seeing to their own lives, drawing upon experiences from their past.

Automobile in American Life *Chronological Spine: Boom Years*	*Light!* *Gallery 1: Lubin Projector*
Man 1: He's trying to get one of every model. Man 2: Does he have the one with, uhm, the little shifter? Man 1: No. The one in the dash you mean? Man 2: Yeah. Man 1: No. Man 2: Yep, well, that's the Corona. That's a Toyota actually. But those are good cars. Oh gee, an old Roadmaster. What's that one there? Man 1: Nash, I think. Isn't it? Man 2: Yeah. Man 1: Was it a Nash? I think so. [pause] So, another thing I want to do is restore a Ford flathead. Man 2: Oh, yeah. Well, see, there's the one I'd like to do. They were around.	Woman 1: Movie projector. Woman 2: Oh my. How old-fashioned. Woman 1: I have a couple of reels bigger than that. Woman 2: Do you? Movie reels like that? Woman 1: Yeah, bigger than that. 16 millimeter I guess. My dad had a theater when I was a kid, do you remember me telling you that? Woman 2: No. Woman 1: Oh, yeah. I guess that's where I first saw flickering light. Yeah, I went to the movies every Friday, Saturday, Sunday, and Monday, whether I wanted to or not. Of course I

continued

Automobile in American Life *Chronological Spine: Boom Years (continued)*	Light! *Gallery 1: Lubin Projector (continued)*
Man 1: What is that, a Kaiser?	loved it. And there
Man 2: An old Chevy or a Pontiac. These ones I never fit in to.	were all these musicals and good, good
Man 1: Really?	shows.
Man 2: Well, those ones I did fit in; it just wasn't as comfortable.	*Woman 2:* Did he own the theater?
Man 1: I had a '51 when I was in engineering school.	*Woman 1:* Yeah, he owned it. He ran the projector; my mother sold tickets.
Man 2: Chevy?	*Woman 2:* You're kidding.
Man 1: Yeah. It's the only car I had that would run at 30 below, 35 below. I was out one night going from the University of Mount Royal for some reason. It was 35 below. The wind was blowing. The only other car I saw on the road was another '51 Chev. And that was in 1983, I think. (HF 15/7)	*Woman 1:* No, wait a minute, my sister sold the tickets; my mother took the tickets. I got to go in first and sit in the front row.
	Woman 2: What did you do?
	Woman 1: I sat in the front row.
	Woman 2: Did you critique the shows?
	Woman 1: My eyes were always really bad; I couldn't see and this was excitement for me, because I got to be in the front row right in the middle. It, like, opened the world of sight to me, because I couldn't see; I didn't get glasses until I was in third grade.
	Woman 2: Aaah [with sympathy], I didn't know that.
	Woman 1: I got to see. These movies, it was big. (LT 26/26)

In the excerpt shown in the left column, the two male friends in this group used the presence of a few cars to allow them to discuss a third friend who collected cars. One member of the group also reminisced about a very cold, wintry drive in 1983. The tale of battling the wind and cold and of seeing only one other car, and one that was of the same make, clearly brought pleasure and a certain nostalgic bonding to these two friends. Notice that this brief personal narrative was preceded by a series of very short list-like identification phrases and labels. Similarly, in the right column, the two women began by identifying the target of their observations, a movie projector, and then one of the women seized the opportunity to share with her friend a bit of personal history. This personal narrative included recollections of visits to the movie house and the way her family worked together to run the establishment. Notice also woman I remembering, "that's where I first saw flickering light."

In both of these examples, the visitors used a particular object not only as a springboard to their personal lives but also as a permission to construct a short narrative of their earlier lives. The object was used to mediate a personal story. It is exactly this type of narrative that leads friends to know, and know about, each other, by pushing the time window of information out beyond the specific brackets of the immediate experience. These examples echo the example in chapter 3 in which the two women at the *Aluminum by Design* exhibition shared their vacuum cleaner histories.

Analysis

Returning to the two professors at the *Automobile in American Life* exhibition, another excerpt of their conversation shows them analyzing the composition of one of the materials used to make cars. The two men and the woman were engaged in a hands-on exhibit where visitors could lift and compare equal-sized bars of different materials (including wood, magnesium, aluminum, and steel) used in car manufacturing. A parallel excerpt of conversation from the two women in the *Light!* exhibition shows them analyzing an early photograph of lightning.

Automobile in American Life Designing the Automobile: Hands-on exhibit, Materials	Light! Gallery 1: Photograph of Lightning
Man 1: No, I never saw. Oh, it's a concept car. Man 2: There's the concept car for the Edsel. Man 1: Yep. Uh-huh. [pause— walking and looking]	Woman 2: This is an artist's lightning! [reading, laughs] Woman 1: "Real lightning. First photography to capture lightning on film."

continued

Automobile in American Life Designing the Automobile: Hands-on exhibit, Materials (coninued)	Light! Gallery 1: Photograph of Lightning (continued)
Man 2: [lifts metal bar] Whoa, look at that. Look at how heavy steel is compared to magnesium. It's just amazing, isn't it? Woman 1: Oh, wow! Is magnesium lighter than aluminum? Man 2: Yeah. Try that one out. Woman 1: But they don't use magnesium, do they? Man 2: No. (HF 15/17)	Woman 2: Oh, for pete's sake! Isn't that fascinating? Woman 1: Wow! Woman 2: "1885. Gelatin silver print." Ah, man! Woman 1: Yeah, it's like electrical current going out, not jagging down. Woman 2: It's so fast that you can't even get a mental image to draw it, to paint it. Woman 1: No, that's true. All you see is ziggy-zags. (LT 26/29)

In the left column, we see a small bit of role rehearsal as two men talked expertly, the woman asked a question, and one man answered, thereby displaying more of his knowledge of car manufacturing. This segment was coded as reflecting the theme of engines and technology because of the discussion of metals and their properties; the structural code of analysis was assigned because the visitors compared the weights of the metals and their use. In the right column, the two women were drawn to an early photograph of lightning shown next to an artist's sketch of lightning. Both women were fascinated by the photo, reading the details provided in the label and closely examining the photo, especially the shape of the lightning. Their talk reflected the theme of art and artistic techniques, emphasizing how difficult it is for an artist to capture or represent such an ephemeral phenomenon.

Synthesis

The next example features excerpts of museum conversation at the level of synthesis. In the left column, there is a rich combination of identification, analysis, personal synthesis, and synthesis. In the discussion between the two men, once again, man 1 took the opportunity to expound a bit, with both a personal connection and a rather abstract set of claims about handmade and hand-worked objects, producing the poetic phrase, "a kind of humanness of imperfection." He then made use of the "handmade" analytic feature that began his comments about car handles to discuss brass instruments and later bicycles. Synthesis occurred in this excerpt as he brought his knowledge of brass instruments to bear on his discussion of car handles. The thematic content of this excerpt reflected the issue of aesthetics. In a parallel example of museum talk at the level of synthesis, the two women in the *Light!* exhibition, as shown in the right column, examined a painting by Signac, comparing it to pointillism and the most famous example of that style, Seurat's *Sunday Afternoon on the Island of La Grand Jatte*. Thematically, this excerpt reflects art and artistic techniques. This particular example of conversation was interesting on other levels, as the women recalled seeing the Signac painting in advertising materials for the exhibition—also an indication of some planfulness with respect to their motivation to see the exhibition. Both women were familiar with the Seurat painting in Chicago, but only one had actually seen it. She recalled the sheer magnitude of the painting and the incredible use of small dots used to create it. The conversation was coded as an example of synthesis because the woman referred to the style of pointillism and compared the work on view by Signac with that of Seurat.

Automobile in American Life *Chronological Spine: Origins*	*Light!* *Gallery 2: Signac, Place des Lices, St. Tropez, 1893*
Man 1: Look at that thing. [pause] You know, to me, the thing I really miss is—I mean, you look at those handles and you know somebody took a lot of time and effort and care to make that thing.	*Woman 2:* This is the one they had in AAA. [referring to a picture in an advertisement for the exhibition in the Automobile Association newsletter]
Man 2: Yep.	*Woman 1:* Oh really. I didn't know that.
Man 1: And it's funny how you can take that exact same shape, better material; you can make it by machine a thousand times faster; but as soon as you hold onto it, you know it was not done by a human being. You know. It's funny, that's	*Woman 2:* Yeah. Pointillism, I guess.
	Woman 1: Uh huh.
	Woman 2: "Scientific ideas of perception." [reading]
	Woman 1: I guess it's Seurat, that one who painted that *Sunday Afternoon at Grand Jeté* [sic]. I'm thinking of him when I'm doing

continued

Automobile in American Life *Chronological Spine: Origins* *(continued)*	*Light!* *Gallery 2: Signac, Place des Lices,* *St. Tropez, 1893 (continued)*
what I am looking at. I'm trying to build French horns now because the whole idea of instrument making has gone the same route, where, "Oh we don't have to do that with a person anymore; we do it with a machine." And a musician will pick it up and say, "This isn't very good." And they say, "Oh, well, it's your imagination. It's perfect. I'll show you. I'll measure it for you." And you know, brass instruments have just started to go like this—where they're just at this constant level of mediocrity. And to find a really great horn— I mean, mine is worth— it was made in '64— there's people lined up around the block waiting for me to die so they can have this horn. It's worth probably $8,000 or $10,000 whereas you can buy one—a much better horn in some sense—for $4,000. But with my horn, it's all its	this park [referring to a painting she's working on].[15] I figure if he's doing dot by dot, who am I to complain? It's in Chicago.
	Woman 2: Oh, I've seen pictures of it, but I've never seen it.
	Woman 1: It's in Chicago. It's 8 by 15 feet.
	Woman 2: Oh, that big? I didn't realize. (LT 26/45)

continued

Automobile in American Life Chronological Spine: Origins (continued)	Light! Gallery 2: Signac, Place des Lices, St. Tropez, 1893 (continued)
imperfections that make it *fantastic*. I can make it go this way or this way, or make it play this way or that way. We are losing that whole idea of the sort of the humanness of imperfection. *Man 2:* Well, also, and the uniqueness that goes along with it because sometimes that's all we want. *Man 1:* Yeah. *Man 2:* God, look at the old bicycles. [pause] Just look at the workmanship on that second one there. *Man 1:* Yeah. Yeah. And even the way the ones, that brass whatever it is there, where it changes into the front fender. *Man 2:* Yeah. *Man 1:* You know, there is just this evidence from this distance of, you know, somebody's had their hands on it and you just know it. Man 2: Yeah. And they painted that stuff like it's a work of art. *Man 1:* Yep. (HF 15/13)	

Explanation

In the next set of examples, the conversational excerpts show museum talk at the level of explanation. In the left column, as the two men continued their tour they engaged with the theme of the automotive industry, reviewing the industry as a whole and at one point posing a query to themselves. Such queries and the subsequent attempts at constructing "answers" are the hallmark of explanations. In the right column, the women at *Light!* constructed an explanation during a discussion that involved using an object—a reflective lens—to bring prior knowledge to bear on the conversation. Interestingly, the next object they encountered after discussing this lens was the very object—a lacemaker's globe—that woman 2 had been trying to explain.

Automobile in American Life *Chronological Spine: Origins*	*Light!* *Gallery 1: Lacemaker's Globe*
Man 2: So the question is, why did it start in Detroit?	Woman 2: Oh, and I read this, that a lot of embroiderers
Man 1: It had to be the river.	and a lot of people who
Man 2: Why Detroit, and why was it not Ohio? Had to be the ore.	worked the lace would put a ball like this, a glass ball in front of a candle—
Man 1: Yeah, it had to be the ore. And they got to get it to here.	Woman 1: —so it would enhance the light!
Man 2: Coal so that you could heat it up.	Woman 2: And all the women around it could see it,
Man 1: Is there coal around here? I suppose. What river are we on? Where does that river go? Does that go—	and it would only be like one candle, with this ball of—
Man 2: Well—	Woman 1: —and it's showing through the sphere.
Man 1: —into the Great Lakes?	Woman 2: They could point it
Man 2: Yeah, it comes through. When we were at the Ford House they were saying that Henry Edsel Ford could see three-quarters of the shipping through the Great Lakes.	right down to where they were working.
	Woman 1: Okay. It would be like a spotlight on their work?
	Woman 2: Yeah, right.
	Woman 1: Just move the candle up or down.

continued

Automobile in American Life Chronological Spine: Origins (continued)	Light! Gallery 1: Lacemaker's Globe (continued)
It came right within a mile or two miles within his house at Grosse Point. Man 1: Because certainly for manufacturing in Alberta that's one of the big issues is you're so far away from both the supplier and the market. It's really hard to get it going. Man 2: You know, it's always cheaper to do things by sea or by water than it is by the rest. Man 1: And it's funny to listen to, you know, I take the students out and visit manufacturers around town and the students—I try to get them to—well, I set up two or three companies; and they watch all these companies work for three months and they give one of them sort of a critique. And, boy . . . (HF 15/13)	Woman 2: Oh, look. Here it is! "Lacemakers' globe, 1800-1850!" Woman 1: There you read it ahead of time. That's because you're so interested to know about lace. Woman 2: "Water-filled globe." I remember reading that. "Could serve as a lens to focus light. As with any lens, rays of light passing through are reversed so that the image projected is upside down." (LT 26/15)

In the *Automobile in American Life* example, note the linked set of questions the men posed as one hypothesis was replaced with another: Why did it start in Detroit? Why Detroit and not Ohio? (since both had rivers) Is there coal around here? (checking out the revised hypothesis) What river are we on? Where does that river go? In this excerpt these two friends brought their prior knowledge to bear on the topics of transportation, in general, and shipping in particular, while thinking about the origins of the automotive industry. They compared the Great Lakes region with their own province of Alberta and discussed the advantages of a water-based shipping system (to provide access to raw materials and to convey finished goods). Their discussion also incorporated knowledge from a previous museum visit (the Edsel and Eleanor Ford House).[16] As they were working out the explanation task they set for themselves, they wove in personal anecdotes and synthesized various elements from both their own experiences and other parts of the exhibition into their conversation. In the excerpt from the *Light!* exhibition, woman 2 introduced the idea of a water-filled globe that was used to focus light. She brought prior knowledge to bear on the subject of lenses, as the two women walked through an exhibit area filled with different kinds of lenses. Her language reflected the theme of work and the Industrial Revolution. The two friends subsequently encountered an actual lacemaker's globe after the discussion, a happy accident that reinforced the statements of woman 1 about the existence of such a tool. As with the other examples in this chapter provided for this particular group, the co-generation of conversation is apparent as the two constantly supported and added to one another's points, all while interrupting and talking over one another.

The previous section of conversational examples was organized by the structure of the talk; thematic information was embedded within those segments whose structure was at a level that supported thematic discussions (i.e., analysis, synthesis, and explanation). The language of thematic talk is addressed more directly in the next section on findings.

We expected that a visit to a museum would contribute to the elaboration of general conversation among members of a group in terms of details and interconnections about the substance of the exhibition as well as the overall experience of the museum visit. We assumed that these small fragments of ideas, anchored as they were with vivid experiences with objects and activities, would act as both placeholders in memory and practice episodes for more fully developed conversations that might take place afterward, "off-stage." We deliberately chose to segment the ribbon of conversation into elements that corresponded to visitors' stops along the route of their exhibition visit, both in terms of content and geographical location within the exhibition. In segmenting the talk in this manner, we recognize that we abandoned, in any analytic way, the ability to trace longer, overarching conversational development[17] in favor of an approach that emphasized the coordination taking place among visitors in a more focused way around the interpretation of objects and activities.

Findings

In this section we examine the research results to see how the structural codes were distributed across museums, how the structural codes related to each other, and how the different thematic codes for museum conversations were distributed across the different exhibitions. In the final section we show how the combined explanatory engagement conversations related to the other variables in the coding system. As noted earlier, there is more involved in the language and activities of the visitors than is captured by a segmented coding system. However, the codes do help us to focus on the coordinated social activity of people as they examine objects or engage in activities. We see the ways in which they relate to specific exhibition themes and the ways in which they identify and explain different aspects of the shows, and how they use these moments as occasions to share with the members of their groups little parts of their own histories.

Structure of the Talk

Along the horizontal axis, figure 4.1 displays the categories of structural language with each bar representing the mean number of instances (frequency) of talk per group at each exhibition. Specific numerical values associated with each bar on the graph are shown on the table below the chart. A first concern in any coding system is to be sure that the category for "other" (in our case, NA and NT) is well behaved, or at least not dominant. The first set of results in the figure shows that indeed the not applicable code (which refers to talk about the management of the museum visit and personal needs) is politely small (usually less than three instances per group). The second category refers to segments where there was silence (no talk). A segment of the transcript was coded NT if no talk occurred while visitors were clearly stopped at an exhibit station. Visitors may have been looking at arti-

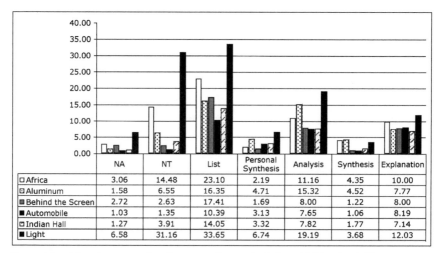

	NA	NT	List	Personal Synthesis	Analysis	Synthesis	Explanation
☐ Africa	3.06	14.48	23.10	2.19	11.16	4.35	10.00
▨ Aluminum	1.58	6.55	16.35	4.71	15.32	4.52	7.77
▨ Behind the Screen	2.72	2.63	17.41	1.69	8.00	1.22	8.00
■ Automobile	1.03	1.35	10.39	3.13	7.65	1.06	8.19
▨ Indian Hall	1.27	3.91	14.05	3.32	7.82	1.77	7.14
■ Light	6.58	31.16	33.65	6.74	19.19	3.68	12.03

Figure 4.1.   Mean instances of each structural type of talk by exhibition (n=178).

facts, reading silently, or watching a video without comment. This code suggests possible engagement but not conversation, and without conversation we cannot gauge what they were necessarily thinking about. The *Africa* and *Light!* exhibitions had the greatest frequency of NT codes, but these two exhibitions also showed a large amount of analytic and explanatory talk relative to the other exhibitions. The remaining structural codes have been described in detail earlier in the chapter.

Clearly, list-like behavior was the dominant mode of conversation for some groups, at some exhibitions taking up almost a half of the conversational segments. This finding suggests that visitors may need a certain amount of surface engagement with an exhibition before they are able to engage more deeply or that they need a break between periods of more engaged looking and talking about the exhibits. What is important to note here is that, just as with the examples provided above from the *Automobile in American Life* and *Light!* exhibitions, visitors who engaged in highly elaborated conversation also engaged in some of the quick, short, list-like behaviors as well. It is important to realize that in the presence of no talk and list-like behavior there is also a good deal of the conversation at all of the exhibitions that was what we considered meaningful and engaged. The data also seem to indicate that if a frequency count comparison alone was used then one might come to believe that most visitors did not talk substantively about content when visiting a museum.[18]

Since the structural conversational codes play a highly significant role in our model, it is worthwhile to examine how they correlate with each other and with the overall measure of learning. In the correlation matrix shown in table 4.2, several correlation values are worth discussing.

First, note that personal synthesis is negatively correlated with other kinds of talk except for list. This result indicates that the more a group discussed their personal connection to an object the less they were likely to pause and say anything else—to analyze, synthesize, or explain it. Consider a group that repeatedly saw and used objects to remind them of their past. Their conversations tended to move away from the object and toward their personal histories and values, rather than toward a more in-depth analysis or explanation of the details of the object or display in front of them. Second, there is a small but significant cluster of conversational behaviors—analysis, synthesis, and explanation—that are both correlated positively among themselves and, more important, with the learning measure. Because of this particular pattern in the data, we will combine these codes into a composite category called "explanatory engagement" and use that as our conversational variable in the overall analyses. Finally, it is important to note that the conversational moves of not talking, listing, and making personal connections do correlate positively with learning, but they do so at a much lower level than the acts of analysis, synthesis and explanation.

Table 4.2.   Correlations of Levels of Structural Talk and Learning

	No Talk	List	Personal	Analysis	Synthesis	Explanation	Learning
No talk	−1.00						
List	.39	1.00					
Personal	−.27	.39	−1.00				
Analysis	.19	.44	−.30	1.00			
Synthesis	.07	.30	−.22	56	1.00		
Explanation	−.04	.02	−.46	.33	.30	1.00	
Learning	.32	.31	.32	.58	.52	.43	1.00

Thematic Talk

For six of the exhibitions, we can look inside the conversations and compare the themes to see which seemed to predominate in the conversations there. Each of the next six figures shows bar graphs that represent the average amount of talk that incorporated a given theme at each exhibition. Each figure is followed by an example of thematic talk that is representative of the dominant theme for that exhibition. Remember that these are conservative estimates because themes were only counted once if the talk in a given segment was analytic, synthetic, or explanatory.

In the *Africa* exhibition, conversation was fairly evenly distributed across the five themes; but ecosystems and natural resources was the theme that dominated the talk of visiting groups (theme 1: 7.16), with talk on the theme of crafts, skills and technology following closely behind (theme 4: 6.00). The least used theme was belief systems and practices (theme 3: 3.29). (In these numbers, the first number is the theme number and the number following the colon is the average number of references to that theme.)

The following conversational excerpt comes from a college-aged dating couple at the *Africa* exhibition when they were at an exhibit station that focused on animals known as mega herbivores.

"Believe it or not, hippos are light eaters": College-aged dating couple
Theme: Ecosystem and Natural Resources
Structure: Analysis

Woman: Oh my God, what *is* that? Is that a hippo?
Man: What?
Woman: That's a hippo's face?
Man: Yeah.
Woman: Sick.
Man: There, those are his teeth right there.

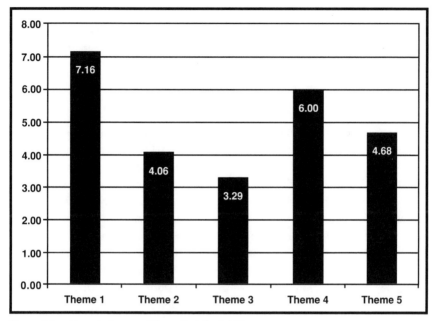

Figure 4.2.   Mean instances of thematic talk at *Africa*.

Woman:	That's so gross. It eats with its mouth nearly shut. Did you know that?
Man:	[reading] Look at his menu. [laughs] Fresh cut grass.
Woman:	They don't eat meat? Wow.
Man:	Fresh cut grass. I guess not.
Woman:	I didn't know that.
Man:	That sucks, he's missing out.
Woman:	Oh, that's a rhinoceros.
Man:	Yeah.
Woman:	He doesn't eat meat either. I didn't know that. [pause, reading] That's funny. What's that thing? Oh, a giraffe. How cute are giraffes? Woo.
Man:	Here's one right here.
Woman:	Oh, he's so cute. (AF 15/41)

Visitors bring their own style and substance to bear on their museum experience, and conversations that evolve there can contain both educational insight and personality. Here we see a young couple using the show as a backdrop for their social agenda. While they were obviously joking around and being a bit silly, they did utilize the content information provided for them. They dropped just enough of the content into their speech to have it connect to the exhibition and to the theme of ecosystem and natural resources. This particular exhibit, within a section that discussed wildlife and ecosystems, showed three herbivores: hippopotami, rhinoceroses, and giraffes. Animatronic heads of these animals were displayed with flip-up labels that generated noises, as well as displays of food and animal skulls. This example illustrates one of the varieties of types of conversations that take place in museums.

The *Aluminum by Design* exhibition showed a different pattern of thematic conversation, not at all evenly distributed. Nearly 90% of the conversation dealt with two themes, either style and aesthetics (theme 1: 10.42) or problem solving and design (theme 2: 11.58). While these were the major thematic categories of the exhibition from the perspective of the curator, another theme, corporate presence (theme 5: 1.68), was both important in the exhibition as an object of consideration and apparent to visitors who noticed that the sponsor of the exhibition was Alcoa. Some visitors to the exhibition were members of the local aluminum corporate culture, but this factor did not find its way into the thematic conversations of the visiting groups, and few groups addressed that theme during the post interview.

In the next example of thematic talk, which occurred at the level of analysis, two older women examine parts of the *Aluminum by Design* show in some detail.

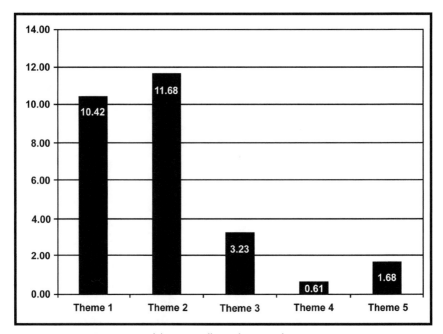

Figure 4.3.   Mean instances of thematic talk at *Aluminum by Design.*

Among other features, this example shows that although the thematic categories used by the MLC are distinct, their boundaries sometimes blur and blend into each other. This excerpt might have been coded as belonging to the theme of style and aesthetics except for the fact that what they analyzed was more closely associated with the inherent problem of making thread and a dress from aluminum and not simply the aesthetic qualities of the resulting item. The excerpt comes from a pair of older women friends while they were at an exhibit station showing promotional items from two aluminum companies.

Alcoa and Reynolds Promotional Items, including a Rug and Two-Piece Dress: Two
   older women friends
Theme: Problem Solving and Design
Structure: Analysis

Woman 1:	I think this is ugly, absolutely ugly.
Woman 2:	Look, isn't that absolutely beautiful.
Woman 1:	Now I like *that!* Oh, my!
Woman 2:	And such temptation to reach over and touch it.
Woman 2:	"Aluminum, jute, wool, and viscose." But you know what? My question is, how much of it is aluminum? You know, like, 1%? But isn't that beautiful?
Woman 1:	Uh-huh. Just enough to qualify for a show.
Woman 2:	Probably. Probably.
Woman 1:	What's this?
Woman 2:	It's a dress.
Woman 1:	A dress from what?
Woman 2:	It's a "Two-piece dress with belt, 1950. Aluminum thread and rhinestones."
Woman 1:	Oh no!
Woman 2:	See, you can see the threads.
Woman 1:	Yes.
Woman 2:	But you know what though? That's a design that's still good today, a basic shirt-dress.
Woman 1:	Absolutely.
Woman 2:	But wouldn't it be itchy?
Woman 1:	Yes. (AL 29/38)

This part of the exhibition introduced the idea of promotional programs undertaken by both Alcoa and Reynolds to expand the market for aluminum products after World War II. The two savvy women question the real role of aluminum in the products displayed and ponder its utility in the roles shown (would it be itchy?). They also note the enduring and timeless quality of the design of the dress and thereby connect the object on display to their own lives.

Behind the Screen presented still another portrait of thematic engagement by visitors. As figure 4.4 shows, by far the majority of the talk at this exhibition was concerned with the theme technology of movie production (theme 2: 8.97); we believe this was the case because the visitors were in a "hands-on" environment in which they were invited to model parts of the actual production activities. The coordinated discussions among members of a group focused heavily on how specific production techniques were done, and how to mimic effects that had been seen in other films. Discussions reflecting another theme, layering of effects to create an illusion of reality, were the second most common focus of talk at this exhibition (theme 5: 3.19), though considerably less frequent than the dominant theme.

In the following example of thematic conversation at *Behind the Screen*, a somewhat complex explanation was provided about the difference between tape and film, and this discussion was accompanied by a brief review of the time when the change from one format to the other was most noticeable in different television

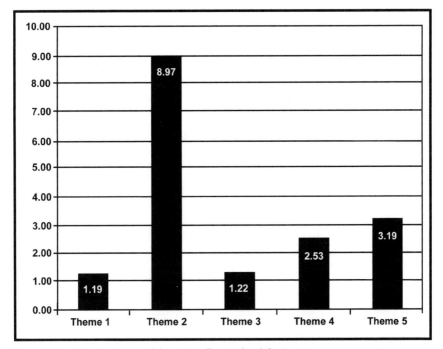

Figure 4.4.   Mean instances of thematic talk at *Behind the Screen*.

programs. The explanation occurred as the visitors examined a computer-based display on the two media. The group in this example consisted of two friends, a man and woman in their early thirties. As mentioned before, the museum setting seemed to provide a good place or opportunity for a certain style of role-based flirtation to occur. In this example, the woman mentions to the man that a mutual friend, who was not with them, had the remarkable capability to detect the film medium instantly. The man's response to the perceived challenge was to immediately demonstrate a comparable skill.

Computer station, How Cameras Work: Two thirty-something friends
Theme: Technology of Movie Production
Structure: Explanation

Woman: So this makes much more sense to me. But now I understand it, because you can't broadcast this stuff.

Man: No.

Woman: Okay. [pause]

Man: See, I don't know. Remember, this would be back in the late seventies, early eighties. And, you notice how some TV shows had that different kind of look to it? Because some, they were shot on film, and some were actually shot using a television camera and going right to videotape. Film gives you a kind of more realistic look and quality and feel to it than I guess videotape did. Way back.

Woman: Mmm-hmm.

Man: What were some of the shows that actually did this?

Woman: See Anthony can look at a television and say that's film.

Man: That's videotape, yeah. Videotape is cheaper than film, doing twenty-six shows a year; yes it's cheaper to use videotape but film looks better. They use one or another. Oh, remember when *ER* went live?

Woman: Yeah.

Man: And it, how it had that whole different look? (EX 07/07)

At the *Automobile in American Life* exhibition the pattern of thematic talk among visitors had one dominant and two secondary themes. The first theme, engines and technology (theme 1: 8.45), had by far the greatest amount of discussion. But the themes that ranked second and third—the automotive industry (theme 3: 3.26) and aesthetics (theme 2: 3.03)—received a considerable amount of attention from visitors. This finding again may well be an artifact of our coding structure. That is,

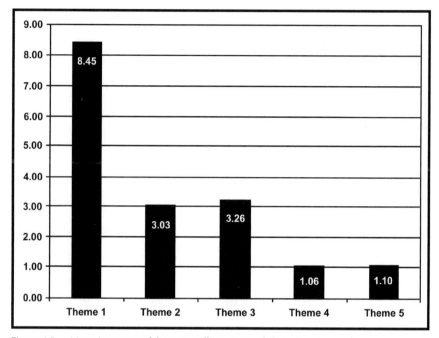

Figure 4.5.   Mean instances of thematic talk at *Automobile in American Life.*

if each segment of talk were coded with multiple thematic references instead of only the dominant one (associated with the appropriate structural code), we might have seen different patterns in the emphasis of one theme over another. Another confound in the coding was the presence of talk about engines (coded as engines and technology) that certainly bordered on a discussion of the aesthetics of the engineering and design of the machines.

The excerpt of conversation shown below comes from the *Automobile in American Life* exhibition where a married couple and a male friend were looking at an exhibition area that equated certain automobiles with different kinds of indicators of status or style. This conversation took place as they looked at a GTO, a muscle car that was linked to a sense of power.

Power, GTO: Married couple and male friend
Theme: Engines and Technology
Structure: Explanation

Man 1:   Later they were all, I think, orange.
Man 2:   Oh, alright. The GTO. Pontiac, though, it's not a Ford.

Man 1:   Yep. They like to call these the first muscle car, but they forget about the Chryslers.

Man 2:   Here's, here's your Chrysler design here.

Woman: That's a good photo. That's a DeSoto

Man 2:   It's a DeSoto—that's a Virgil Lexner design.

Woman: That's like Lee and Dad's car, isn't it? Yeah.

Man 2:   Yep. Well, theirs is one year earlier than that, though. That was just gorgeous, that '57.

Woman: That's a nice looking—

Man 1:   Yeah. A six-pack; I never figured out why they wanted a six-pack on an eight-cylinder engine. Why didn't they have, like, a four-pack?

Man 2:   Or an eight-pack?

Man 1:   Yeah. Because the cylinders don't draw at the same time, so it's just a matter of total capacity.

Man 2:   Yeah.

Woman: Oh, let's go to the diner.

Man 2:   Oh, you want to go to the diner? Okay. (HF 12/5)

The explanation above connects with the specific design features of the engine's cylinder arrangement, and although the topic is of clear interest to the two men, the woman found it difficult to break in to their conversation. She tried first with her comment, "good photo," then with an even less connected, "nice looking," and finally with a request to go to a different section of the exhibition. Although this example of conversation shows a stereotypical female response, it is important to note that conversations at this exhibition on cars were not in any way gender-exclusive. We did in fact see many women who were both interested in, and knowledgeable about, cars. In another group, for example, two older women were peeved that the car hoods were not raised in order to show the mechanics of some of the cars; and in another group the daughter of one male visitor was eager to both learn about and share her knowledge of cars (see *Automobile in American Life* examples in chapter 3). Another observation about this particular GTO example is that it demonstrated a common belief among visitors that the Henry Ford Museum would only display Fords, not Pontiacs, or the cars of other manufacturers ("The GTO. Pontiac, though, it's not a Ford").

In *Indian Hall*, two themes were noticeably more important than the other three. One was cultural influences, tradition, and change, and the other was skills and techniques (see fig. 4.6). Since the designers of the exhibit hall had hoped to create an atmosphere that celebrated contemporary American Indian culture alongside an examination of its longstanding roots and traditions, we think they

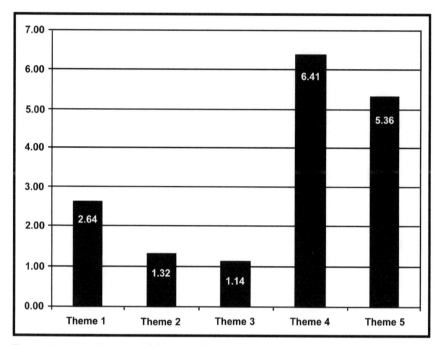

Figure 4.6.   Mean instances of thematic talk at *Indian Hall*.

would be happy to know that the language of visitors strongly reflected theme 4 (6.41). On the other hand, skill and techniques (theme 5: 5.36) represents a more generally predictable thematic aspect in an exhibition based so much on historical cultural artifacts (where visitors commonly ask things like, "How did they do that? It's so detailed"). Similarly, it was not surprising to see the third most frequently discussed theme, the role of nature (theme 1: 2.64), in an exhibition comparing cultures from different geographic regions.

The example of thematic talk from *Indian Hall*, which is provided below, is a segment of a conversation among three women who were discussing a display of photographs of contemporary American Indians. The tribal affiliations were listed below the photograph, and not only did the photographs not look like traditional stereotypical Indians, in their dress or facial coloring, but many photographs listed several cultural and racial mixtures, reflecting the melting pot notion of American culture.

Didactic Photos: "Do you know any?": Mother, daughter and woman friend
Theme: Cultural Influences, Tradition, and Change
Structure: Explanation

Mother: [reading] "Do you know any American Indians in your com-
             munity?" And it just shows everyday people.
Daughter: Where, here?
Mother: Well, [reading] "What does an American Indian person look
             like? What does a Black Indian look like? And a White Indian?
             If an Indian doesn't have the traditional Indian features, does
             that mean they're NOT Indian? These are the basic kinds of is-
             sues . . . begun to deal with, especially in the east."
Woman 2:   Yeah, because that's when we went to the, watchamacallems-
Mother: Went to who-whats?
Woman 2:   When Belinda and I went to the—
Daughter: Powwows—
Woman 2:   Yeah, some people looked like Indians but others don't.
Mother: Right.
Woman 2:   Like the little girl.
Mother: Yeah, that's what I'm saying.
Woman 2:   And that was a big issue.
Mother: Right, because if you were to meet this gal on the street, you
             wouldn't say that. It's not the traditional image of a Native
             American. But I just liked the way they show this. Because,
             yeah, the German she's got the blonde hair in there. "Mo-
             hawk." "Mohawk, German, Irish, and Croatian."
Woman 2:   Oh, really?
Mother: Yeah, it's a mix. See I would look at her and say she's Croatian.
Woman 2:   Any Apaches?
Mother: No. "Cherokee, Seneca, Croatian, German, Cherokee, African
             American." [reading label]
Woman 2:   This is cute.
Mother: I just liked this, when I was here before. (INI6/32)

One woman in this group, the mother, had visited the exhibition previously,
and a couple of times during this visit, she directed the group's attention to her
favorite exhibits. This collection of contemporary photos was one of her favorite
parts. A series of headshots of different-looking people were identified by their
ethnic makeup under the caption: "Do you know any?" As the group's discussion
shows, the exhibit highlights the fact that having Indian blood of some kind may
or may not mean that an individual looks stereotypically Indian. Some visitors in
our sample claimed American Indian heritage at the outset of their visit or informed friends of that heritage as they went through the exhibition. In this group,
the mother had been to the exhibition before and believed that her friend of

Apache background would find some level of identity in it. Their discussion related to the theme of cultural influences, tradition, and change.

In the *Light!* exhibition, two of the themes overwhelmed the thematic discussions, as figure 4.7 shows. The two dominant themes were science and technology (theme 2: 21.29) and art and artistic techniques (theme 1: 10.97). Given that these themes were also embedded in the very title of the show, this finding is not surprising. In this exhibition more than perhaps any other, it was extremely difficult for visitors to expand beyond the overarching thematic vision of the curatorial team. Thus, while the show had sections devoted to the themes of spirituality, work, and social change, and while one could in many cases relate a variety of objects to these themes, these were not what people came to see nor what they noticed or discussed.

In the following example of visitor conversation reflecting themes in the *Light!* exhibition a college-aged couple were looking at a painting by Ford Madox Brown that naturalistically depicted strong daylight falling on a girl standing in a field with sheep.

The Light of Nature, Daylight, Ford Madox Brown, Pretty Baa Lambs: College-aged couple
  Theme: Art and artistic techniques
  Structure: Synthesis

Man:	Now that, see it makes it *so* much more real when they have the shadows.
Woman:	Look at how vibrant the colors are.
Man:	I know! And you can tell the difference, that that's daylight.
Woman:	Yeah. Gosh.
Man:	And that's, like, some of those other pictures, remember that picture it was Middle Eastern; it was like, evening, well, I thought it was evening anyways.
Woman:	Middle Eastern?
Man:	Yeah, right over here. [They walk back over to the painting, *A Turkish School*, that they'd looked at a few moments prior]
Woman:	Oh yeah, yeah!
Man:	And look at the difference. Isn't it amazing?
Woman:	Yeah. It almost looks like it's going to storm, though, because the sky's kind of dark. You know how it gets. That's what it looks like, you know how right before it storms and the sun is really bright but the sky is really dark?
Man:	Yeah.
Woman:	That's what it looks like.
Man:	It does. "Pretty Baa Lambs." Ha ha.

Woman: "Pretty Baa Lambs," that's so cool. [pause] Wow.

Man: That's awesome. I want those two pictures right beside each other just so you can see the difference, you know what I mean?

Woman: Uh-hmm.

Man: Of course, I just look at everything from an educator's point of view. You have to compare and contrast. (LT 02/31)

The above segment took place in the second gallery of the exhibition, where visitors have just moved from a room full of scientific instruments and lenses to a room with paintings, including works by artists such as Monet and Corot, who were concerned with depicting light effects in their work. This conversation was what we had in our mind's ear when we thought of how synthesis might sound within an exhibition. The two participants were both students—the man in teacher's college, the woman, an art student—and they spent a long time carefully discussing the aesthetic features of works. In this example they compared the brilliant daylight shown in this painting by Ford Madox Brown with a painting by Decamps that showed light coming through a window. Throughout their tour, this couple evaluated paintings based on their naturalistic effects, and they frequently compared different paintings in the exhibition. They did not spend much time

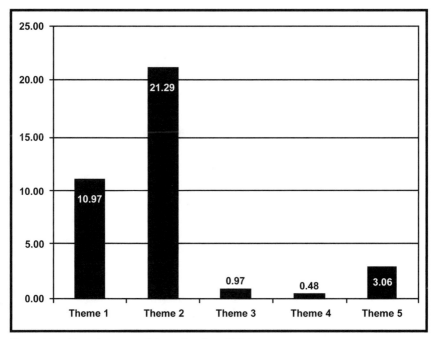

Figure 4.7.   Mean instances of thematic talk at *Light!*

studying the scientific advances explained in the exhibition, nor did they read much label copy.

In this section we have given examples of the thematic talk for each exhibition. We selected examples based on the most frequently accessed themes for each exhibition. While there are some similarities across themes in terms of broad categories such as history writ large, process by which the artifact was created, and universal cultural traditions, the thematic talk cannot be directly compared between exhibitions as the content distinctions across exhibitions are quite profound. If one rereads the thematic explanation exchanges from *Behind the Screen*, *The Automobile in American Life*, *Indian Hall*, and *Light!* the difference in content is pronounced. We believe it is the combination of content and structural forms of conversations that mark learning in museums. We will explore this notion more fully in chapter 6.

Message

Using visitor conversations as a means to examine learning in museums is a complex affair. In the previous chapters we discussed the way the exhibitions themselves and the identity features of the visitors shape the visitors' experiences. In this chapter we examined the resulting conversations and illustrated two of the ways in which we analyzed the data. There are other ways in which we might have attacked the problem, but we wanted to build procedures that would capture both the *ways* in which visitors attempted to approach the museum displays, and the *content* of those conversations. As the examples suggest, the conversational segments allow us to compile results that illustrate the roles of visitors' identity, background experience, and knowledge and to integrate these results with the specifics of the environment in which the conversations took place.

Structural coding provided a means to examine the level of engagement of visitors, to characterize the ways in which visitors most commonly used their prior knowledge to make sense of an exhibition and shared their insights with one another. Coding the structure of the conversations also allowed for some cross-museum comparisons. Thematic coding provided a reference point for the content of the exhibitions themselves. The themes offered insight into the ways in which content was presented to the public and the ways in which visitors were most likely to engage with the materials on view, providing a means to access the actual content learned.

Questions

Throughout this analysis of conversations we have indicated the varied ways in which research decisions were made that affected the framework, coding, and results of the study. One goal of that undertaking was to give you, the reader, an opportunity to examine the decision-making process involved and try your own hand at thinking about the design and use of a coding system. To further that goal, a sample transcript is provided—a transcript from a relatively short visit by a group of two men who went to see the *Automobile in American Life* exhibition. The transcript of their conversation includes breaks that indicate the stop names as well as breaks that show divisions of time spent. The solid lines mark the segmenting that we used. Solid lines indicate new stops or ninety-second intervals within a long track. For any segment lasting more than thirty seconds, a dashed line has also been inserted to indicate a thirty-second break. We invite readers to use this transcript to code the language of the visitors. Decide whether to segment or not, to use segments based on speaker turns or not, to use equal sized time-based segments or not, to choose structural or thematic codes or neither, and to try and imagine the best ways and the many different ways one might tell the story of this visit. Have fun!

Transcript of a tour conversation. This copy of the tour transcript does not include the pre- and postvisit interviews, nor the entrance/exit segments (where the microphones were being attached or returned).

Stop Name	Conversation
Fast Food	Man 1: Ah! '56 Chevy. Now there's a cool car. Man 2: You know, I think my mom had one just like that. Man 1: Oh yeah? A convertible? Man 2: No, I guess hers wasn't a convertible, but that color. Man 1: Oh, my folks had a—
Power Car	Man 2: I had a Tempest just sitting here, a '65 Tempest that was a convertible. Man 1: Hmm. Man 2: Not with tri-power though. That would— Man 1: Oh, yeah. Man 2: That'd be cool. Man 1: A friend of mine in Phoenix had an Olds 4-4-2 that he restored, and THAT was a pretty neat car. Man 2: Yeah. What was that, a 4-barrel, 4-speed dual exhaust?
Global	Man 1: I forget what the whole set-up on it was, but

continued

Stop Name (continued)	Conversation (continued)
	the, uh . . . [pause] [sound of narrator] The original Corvair!
	Man 2: Yeah. I forgot they made four-door Corvairs.
	Man 1: Yeah.
	Man 2: Weren't all the ones at that other museum two-doors?
	Man 1: Yeah. Of course, they mostly had the Mazda convertibles and stuff, but, uh . . .
	Man 2: Ahh.
Boom Years	Man 2: There's a nice Datsun.
	Man 1: Yeah.
	Man 2: I think we had one like that.
	Man, 1: Oh, it's a Toyota.
	Man 2: Oh, it is?
	Man 1: Yeah, Corona. Yeah.
	Man 2: Oh, they all come out of the same mold anyway.
	Man 1: Well . . . [pause]
	Man 2: Tucker with the Cyclops, uh . . . Boy, that's a nice one!
	Man 1: Yeah.
New Challenges	Man 2: Look at, uh, look at the shifter there. Looks like you do something with your thumb on the, uh—
	Man 1: [chuckle]
	Man 2: —on the column there?
	Man 1: I wonder what that was all about. Maybe like an electric clutch or something? [pause]
	Man 1: Hmm.
	[Sound of video narrator: "During the early 1930s, automobile production dropped by 75%. Most of the remaining small companies went bankrupt."]
	Man 2: That'd be good, amphibious Jeeps.
	Man 1: Yeah. I'd really like to have an old Jeep like this. [Narrator: . . . And even the low-priced V-8s couldn't reverse the effects of the Depression.

continued

Stop Name *(continued)*	Conversation *(continued)*
	Questions about seniority . . ."]
	Man 2: Oh, here they are at different stages of the model. [points to hanging chassis]
	Man 1: Mmm-hmm.
	Man 2: Looks like that propeller's a little small for that.
	Man 1: The propeller. Hah!
Big Three	Man 2: That's all metal there, huh?
	Man 1: Yeah.
	Man 2: I wonder when did they change from that? [Video narrator: "A 1923 sedan, with an all-steel body-frame, was safe and durable and could be manufactured more efficiently than wood-frame cars, like the Model T."]
	Man 1: Mmm. It says the mid-'20s they went to the all-steel bodies. [pause]
	Man 2: Huh. Cool.
	Man 1: Here's a Chevy.
	Man 2: I've never seen one that old. [Video narrator: Chrysler, a new company, made a strong showing with its sporty 1924 model"]
	Man 2: [pause, glancing across room to airplane exhibit] Hey, there's the airplanes! Oh! [laughs]
	Man 1: Hmm.
Industry Grows	Man 2: Really going back in time here. [pause]
	Man 1: When you look at the size of some of the wheels on some of these things, they look like wagon wheels, like the
	Cadillac there.
	Man 2: [laughs]
	Man 1: Really go cross-country.
Birth	Man 2: Transitioning from horse carriages to, uh . . .
	Man 1: Yeah.
	Man 2: powered carriages. Oh, look at that thing!
	Man 1: Yep.
	Man 2: Horizontally-imposed 6. [chuckles]

continued

Stop Name (continued)	*Conversation (continued)*
	Man 1: Yeah. Front wheel drive. Man 2: Direct drive too. Man 1: Yeah. Man 2: They just turned the thing sideways and drove the, uh,
	I wonder if they're just turning one wheel or there's some interconnect. Man 1: Oh, probably this drives the whole axel, because see, it steers the whole axel so it's . . . Man 2: Oh, yeah. Man 1: Ah. But it must have some kind of transition, shifting stuff there? Man 2: [chuckles] That looks dangerous! THAT can't be OSHA approved! Man 1: [laughs] Yeah. [pause]
	Man 2: Huh. Is that the Speedo? Man 1: Uhhh, probably is, because see, it comes right up here. That must be what it is, eh? Man 2: Brakes look highly effective! Man 1: [laughs] Man 2: [laughs] That must have been a bicycle manufacturer did that. Man 1: Yeah. Of course
	high speed was probably not your greatest fear anyway. Man 2: 1907, wow. [pause] What's that, a J3?
Origins	Man 1: Yeah. Man 2: [pause] Cool!
Dream Machines	Man 2: Mustang concept car, huh? Man 1: Yeah. I can remember seeing pictures of these when they were . . . Man 2: Was that fiberglass? Man 1: [pause] Probably, huh. Man 2: One hundred and nine horsepower. It just doesn't seem—

continued

Stop Name *(continued)*	Conversation *(continued)*
	Man 2: Hmph! Man 1: —like a
	Mustang should be that low on horsepower. Man 1: Boy! Talk about a Batmobile, eh? Man 2: [laughs] That thing is odd! [pause]
	Another malfunction by American Motors— Turbine! Man 1: Yeah. I remember when they brought these things out. They built, like, I don't know, like 100, 200 of them, something like that. Man 2: 130 horse at 36,000 RPM? Man 1: Yeah. Man 2: That doesn't sound like THAT'S going to be very efficient. [chuckles] Man 1: Well . . .
	Man 2: Sounds like a lot of fuel flow. Man 1: Yeah, I suspect that fuel economy is not their strong suit. Man 2: [chuckles] Man 1: I wonder what it sounded like. Man 2: A bad APU? Man 1: Yeah. Yeah, I could . . . Man 2: Did it use regular exhaust? Or . . . [pause]
	Oh, interesting. [kneeling by Turbine car] It's like ducts. Man 1: Oh, yeah. Man 2: Right by the springs there. Man 1: Yeah. Huh! Man 2: That's . . . Man 1: Yeah. Man 2: It's actually a halfway decent-looking car body— Man 1: Yeah. Man 2: —for a Chrysler back then.

continued

Stop Name *(continued)*	Conversation *(continued)*
Andretti Race Car	*Man 2:* Mario Andretti. Four cylinder. [pause] Now that's more like it: 400 horsepower— *Man 1:* Yeah. *Man 2:* —out of four cylinders, 252 cubes. *Man 1:* Hmm.
Designing the Auto	*Man 2:* Kind of like the pocket door, swing to the side. *Man 1:* Mmm-hmm. *Man 2:* Rear engine. [pause] *Man 1:* Now there we go! *Man 2:* Yeah. *Man 1:* A trike. *Man 2:* That thing looks like at about 120 it'd leave the freeway. *Man 1:* [laughs] Could see THAT in a big crosswind, huh? *Man 2:* [chuckles] Shhhg!
Lola Race Car	*Man 2:* [pause] Oh, it—
Designing the Auto	*Man 2:* —looks like, on that one, those are, uh, air-cooled cylinder heads or something there. *Man 1:* Huh! *Man 2:* Then they run the exhaust back. Oh, Mazda. Might be a rotary engine, huh? *Man 1:* Could be. Yeah.
Lola Race Car	*Man 2:* "Lola!" *Man 1:* 850 horse out of, what, 162 cubic inch? *Man 2:* Holy moley! [pause] Wow. [pause] That's brutal. 162 cubic
	inch! [pause, kneeling to look at back of car] Is that a variable geometry inlet fin, or is that just a strut that holds it in place? *Man 1:* [pause] I don't know. *Man 2:* Isn't that kind of wild?
	Man 1: Uh, it could just be just to keep, you know, stuff from the tire to keep that from sucking in there but, uh, . . .

continued

Stop Name *(continued)*	Conversation *(continued)*
	Man 2: Be interesting to see the wind-tunnel, uh— Man 1: Yeah. Man 2: —tests on that.
Custom Cars	(No talk) Man 1: See the shock absorbers on this thing? A little strap, wound around a— Man 2: Oh, really? Man 1: —kind of a brake-fixing, brake deal there? Man 1: Huh? Man 1: [pause] Ever been to the Dusenberg collection in Las Vegas? Man 2: No. Man 1: In one of the casinos up on about the fourth floor, there's a whole car museum on the third floor, and on the fourth floor there's a whole collection of Dusenbergs. There's about fifty of them. Man 2: Wow! Man 1: You know, like gangster cars and all kinds
	of just amazing automobiles. They've got cars that cost, like, 50,000 bucks, in 1932, you know, so . . . Man 2: Wow! Yeah, this one's only 8,500 bucks for the chassis. Man 1: Yeah. Man 2: Wow. It's kind of like the cars got pretty big— Man 1: Yeah. Man 2: —y'know, and then they . . .
	Everything I guess cycles, you know, from little carriages to big cars and then back down to smaller cars. [pause] Is that a foreign rig? [pause] Hmm. Built in Long Island, NY. Man 1: Ah. Man 2: I like the scabbard for the umbrella.
	Man 1: Yeah. The chauffeur gets to sit out in the rain, while— [chuckles]

continued

Stop Name *(continued)*	**Conversation** *(continued)*
	Man 2: I guess so! [chuckles] But he's handy with the umbrella for the occupants in the back. Man 1: Yeah! Man 2: I think this would be the rig—
Family Cars	Man 2: —to take to Africa. Man 1: [chuckles] You've got your little picnic basket right on the side there. I suppose that's a tool-box there with the little drawers, huh? Man 2: That would probably be appropriate. Good viewing of the savannah. Man 2: Mmm.
Lasalle	Man 2: Rumble seat on that dude. Man 1: Oh, yeah. [pause] Man 2: Huh! Cadillac. [pause]
	Pretty neat. Man 1: Hmm. Man 2: Yeah, it uses that same kind of spring system— Man 1: Oh, yeah. Man 2: —with the strap. Man 1: Yeah. [pause]
Taurus	Man 2: That was a popular car, that Ford Taurus. [long pause] Man 2: [pause] You know it's funny, I never really like, thought much of these cars, but if you bought one and just, like, threw it in your garage and kept it there for 20 years, it'd probably be worth a lot of money. [chuckles] Man 1: Hmm.
Eldorado/Buick	[No talk]
Buick	Man 2: I think of all the cars here except that GTO I'd have this Cadillac. Man 1: Mmm.
Eldorado	Man 1: I've got a son-in-law that's into Rivieras and he's got one that he's been working on in his spare time. But it's a later model than . . .

continued

Stop Name (continued)	Conversation (continued)
Buick/Eldorado	Man 2: They're front wheel drive aren't they? Man 1: Uh, no, I don't think so. The Toronado was— Man 2: Oh. Man 1: —front wheel drive but . . . [pause]
	[No talk, takes photo]
Buick	Man 2: [pause] You want to check out the airplanes? Man 1: Yeah. Yeah.

Notes

1. Fienberg and Leinhardt 2002.
2. See Allen 2002.
3. White 1995.
4. Grice 1989; Clark 1996; White 1995; Mische and White 1998.
5. Gee 1999; Linell 1998; Wells 1999.
6. Grice 1989.
7. Grice 1989, 26.
8. Grice 1989, 29.
9. Clark, 1996, 4.
10. Borun, Chambers, Dritsas, and Johnson 1997; Borun, Chambers, and Cleghorn 1996.
11. Crowley, Galco, Jacobs, and Russo 2000.
12. Tunnicliffe 1998. See also Allen 2002; Silverman 1990.
13. Stainton 2002; Leinhardt 2000.
14. The *Automobile in American Life* group had four times the amount of explanatory talk compared to the average group. The *Light!* group had more instances of analysis, synthesis, and explanation than other visitors. Both groups had very high motivation and knowledge scores.
15. By "doing this park," woman 1 was referring to a painting that she was working on that she had discussed earlier in their tour. This kind of context reflects a research design that allowed us to capture the whole visit; this context is a nice result of our time-consuming data collection process.
16. Susan Welch of the Edsel and Eleanor Ford House acknowledged that, while not part of signage or direct tour information, this fact about Ford and shipping may have been addressed by a docent to these visitors as a result of the high visibility of the shipping channel from the east windows of the house. While our study does not address the impact of museum visits in long-term memory, this brief excerpt demonstrates the potential of museum experiences to influence learning in the long term.
17. For an example of this overarching trace of visitor conversation, see Leinhardt 2000.
18. For reference, these two *Automobile in American Life* and *Light!* groups had the following scores: NA (1, 4), NT (8, 12), List (5, 22), Personal Synthesis (3, 11), Analysis (4, 23), Synthesis (0, 9), and Explanation (32, 43).

Learning Environment   5

Actually, we went the wrong way.
Did we really?
Oh, nice going, Mom.
Because here's the progression from the buggies, the horseless
carriages, and then down and around kind of.
Okay. Why don't we look at these while we are over here in this
section? It doesn't really matter anymore since we messed up.

—VISITOR CONVERSATION FROM THE AUTOMOBILE
IN AMERICAN LIFE EXHIBITION

Problem

THE PREVIOUS CHAPTERS EXAMINED the identity features (motivation and prior knowledge) that visiting groups brought to the exhibition and used during their visit as well as the conversational elaboration that occurred when visiting groups, with their shared identities, encountered the content of a particular exhibition. This chapter explores the exhibition itself and what the curators and design teams brought to the exhibition. Exhibitions are carefully crafted not only to highlight and display artifacts of value but also to provide and support learning about them. The challenge here is how to capture the elements of design in a grounded enough fashion to reflect the actual distinctive qualities of each exhibition, while also providing for a process of generalized cross-platform description. Unlike other museum research that takes place in a single museum or exhibition, this work was explicitly designed to examine learning across multiple and very distinct environments. Internally, for the MLC team, this created no small problem. In educational research enormous effort has been spent over the last decade to point out the profound differences in learning that exist among subject matter areas. Research has shown, for example, that a good question is not a good question independent of the subject matter under consideration.[1] Therefore, developing principled ways to discuss learning across extraordinarily diverse museum environments was challenging. How could the unique features of each exhibition (walking through a slave ship, watching explanatory videos, constructing one's own animation) be preserved, while still generalizing across them? How could we analyze, in comparable ways, displays that explicitly explain the processes and concepts of film production and editing and displays that implicitly connect objects of art and science through groupings and thematic links? The great concern in developing a cross-site analytic framework for examining the learning environment was that we might unintentionally seem to say: "hands-on manipulatives are good (or bad) and lead to learning (or not)," when in some environments this statement entirely misses the point of the unique experience offered.

The question of how to effectively examine the learning environment of a museum or exhibition remains problematic. The arrangement of objects, text, and hands-on elements within an exhibition space is conceptually designed with the layers of design, making it difficult to tease apart specific factors of the environment that affect learning. "Are visitors aware of the thematic subtext of wall color change, or does it go unnoticed?" "Do visitors read the labels or just notice the wall titles?" " Will visitors who miss the concept of refraction in gallery 1 be confused by the reintroduction of that concept in gallery 3?" "If we need to be redundant, how much is enough? How much is too much?" Curators and designers do not simply sequence and make room for groups of objects; they compose them according to complex classification or thematic orientations. Even more complex are the affective theatrical aspects of environmental design. Researchers have often avoided broad questions about the design of museum environments in favor of research that focuses on the minute and the measurable. These studies asked questions such as, "How much text will a visitor read?" or "What size font do visitors prefer?" We wanted to design a study that focuses on the larger aspects of the learning environment. But researchers can only see visitors' responses to the learning environment when design features are actively used or when they become a hindrance.

One approach to understanding the museum exhibition as a learning environment is the "design experiment."[2] In design experiments, elements of an exhibit are systematically changed over time and visitor response to each modification is studied.[3] These experiments include large-scale prototyping and conceptually driven didactic models employed most commonly by science museums.[4] While costly, the design experiment is effective.[5] As museums turn to more expensive technology-based exhibits, we are beginning to see more prototyping, front-end evaluation, and mock-up design tests.[6] Science museums, with their explicitly didactic mandate, lead the field in this regard, with most utilizing some kind of exhibit prototyping.[7] In most other museum contexts, prototyping is too time consuming and costly to consider on a regular, ongoing basis. Furthermore, in art museums, where artworks on loan often come for installation with their own security guards to monitor the installation, exhibitions cannot realistically go through this process.

Within our study, the learning environment was one strand of a more complex system of study. We did not conduct design experiments that evaluated the effectiveness of an environment but rather encountered exhibitions as faits accomplis. We were not expecting or expected to alter the installations in any way. Therefore, the impact of individual factors within a given exhibition's learning environment was not gauged. Features were measured in a flexible but consistent fashion to account for a group's specific use of that environment.

The Concept

The concept of the learning environment is partially restricted by the ways in which visitors engage with design elements, but the concept should be understood to include the full range of craft associated with display in a museum. Museum exhibitions are not meant to be "books on walls"; they are meant instead to operate on a visual level. Object placement and relationships are carefully thought out. Color choices, font style, lighting, and even ambient sounds are considered key parts of the exhibition design. All of these choices create a particular mood, an affective experience for visitors. Museums offer an immersive environmental experience. Think of the experience of walking through the cavernous, quiet halls of the Metropolitan Museum of Art versus the experience of looking at small prints in an intimate gallery setting; or consider the smell of wood smoke at an outdoor pioneer village versus the white noise and cool, air-conditioned, open spaces of a modern art museum. These three-dimensional, multisensory experiences remain somewhat elusive for the museum researcher, as visitors tend to remark on them most frequently when the environment is a hindrance.[8] When the environment functions in support of the message of the exhibition as intended, it seamlessly blends into the experience.

In the research literature some attention has been devoted to the examination of these more complex aspects of the environment. For example, Duncan and Wallach's classic study suggested that the architecture of the temple-style museum might impact visitor experience, create a pilgrimage-like ritualized approach to walking the long halls and gazing at iconic masterpieces.[9] Other studies examined the connections between styles of entranceways and museum missions.[10] Ideological studies of museums have examined the ways in which museums, through their systems of display, have supported and cemented the very structures of knowledge maintained by different cultures.[11] Researchers are beginning to look closely at the rhetorical systems present within exhibition narratives themselves.[12] In the humanities, researchers have realized that museums and exhibitions are key sites of cultural production and therefore merit closer attention.

Museum professionals are calling for more systematic methods of exhibition criticism as a way to move beyond personal opinion, or audience numbers, to look more closely at the workings of the exhibition as an experience.[13] Museum researchers are looking toward models from environmental psychology to assess the affective impact of exhibitions. Environmental psychology looks at issues such as, "How little personal space can a user tolerate before he or she feels the sensation of being crowded?" and "What details will create a sense of an eighteenth-century drawing room?"[14] Similarly, market-based research on shopping patterns, trends, and consumer preferences offer insights into visitor experiences with the museum environment:[15] "How long will a consumer wait in line for a cashier?" "Does the consumer tend to select items at eye level?" "How does a consumer orient herself to the space upon entering a shop?" The limitations to such studies lie in a potentially flawed mapping between commercial goals and leisure learning ones. The analysis of the exhibition as a conceptual whole and the psychology of environments have not yet made their way into more empirical discussions of visitor activity.

From a sociocultural perspective, the learning environment can be seen as offering affordances for the activity of meaning construction and interpretation or as creating obstacles to it. The learning environment supports the generation of new emerging goals among the active participants in a visiting group who are stimulated by small details of exhibit design and larger features of the overall environment.[16] Museum designers and curators focus on these multiple levels of design and detail, using changes in lighting, placement, and object groupings and isolation in order to point out significant ideas to visitors;[17] yet the problem of determining the contribution of the learning environment to visitor learning in museum research remains large, complex, and resistant to simple categorization and measurement. We chose to examine the learning environment in two ways: one that reflects physical features such as benches and resources, and one that reflects intellectual features such as large-scale, thematic text panels.

Physical Environment

Clearly, the physical features of a museum exhibition influence the learning environment. For example, the presence (or absence) of resource areas (tables and books) spaced throughout an exhibition communicates to the visitor not only expected activities but expected levels of involvement: "Sit down and read up. Explore this material." Or, perhaps, "Leaf through this catalogue for a moment before continuing with your tour." The presence (or absence) of physical guides and prompts for paths through a particular portion or all of an exhibition share with the visitor the curatorial team's ideas about both visitor needs and desires for guidance or independence. "Choose your own route through the exhibition, and here are some supports to assist you"; or "Follow the ideas in sequential order as we desire you to do." The presence or absence of benches or clear directions to the restrooms also communicates to the visitor how the museum values their comfort.[18] The presence or absence of comment books and feedback mechanisms indicates to visitors the value museums place on their opinions.[19] Engagement with these aspects of an exhibition are relatively easy for observers to capture; but, even in the case of simple feedback mechanisms, such engagement is not necessarily highly predictive of either total enjoyment or learning.

The physical environment may also work against the visitor. Some portions of an exhibition can be ambiguous and confusing, leaving the visitor puzzled with respect to his or her role and expected activity; or the visitor may find the path through an exhibition confusing, due to either a lack of guidance or confusing signals. Perhaps the lighting at a display throws a glare on the object or label that makes it difficult to see. Perhaps directions for using a hands-on exhibit are confusing, or the exhibit is temporarily out of order. Finally, the physical environment of the exhibition is influenced by the social context of the museum itself—the crowded presence of other visitors, or the isolated feeling of a quiet gallery; the shrill or calming voice of a docent; and the friendly or intimidating guard watching over the artifacts. The point is that not all of the physical aspects of an exhibition are supportive.

What to measure remained challenging. Specific behaviors such as sitting on a bench or pointing to a wayfinding device were simple to observe and to trace but occurred so rarely that they made little impact on the visit.[20] While features that influence ambiance, such as wall color, might well play a role, the effect of these design decisions on visitors could only be determined by visitors' commenting directly on those aspects, and that too was a rare event. Finally, mentioning the physical environment was most common when something proved to be an obstacle to visitors rather than support for their experience.

As chapter 2 described, there were many physical differences between exhibitions. To sense some of these differences, consider just the entrances to each of these exhibitions:

- Two glass doors separate the modern gallery space from the hallway. Opening the doors, the visitor is greeted with a cool breeze, which is augmented by cool blue walls, shiny aluminum objects, and a gently curling aluminum banner that leads the way through the galleries.

- Entering the galleries, visitors' eyes struggle momentarily to adjust to the low lighting levels and dark brown walls. Visitors are confronted by a case of shiny sparkling objects highlighted by boutique lighting, directly in their path. A brilliantly pure colored spectrum radiates from a prism overhead, directing the visitor to the right and into the show.
- In the depths of quiet exhibit halls in the natural history museum, visitors approach the vestibule for *Indian Hall.*
- A tightly compacted group of display cases filled the gallery, and visitors passed by a collection of marketing items, large-scale photos of African royalty from the turn of the century.
- At the very back of the cavernous high-ceilinged interior of the museum, past the children racing around the wind tunnel and shrieking at the soap bubble stations, just past the cafeteria and clunk-clunk of blocks at the bridge building station, temporary walls define the boundaries of the show.
- The *Automobile* exhibit is marked by an overhead highway sign, a carpet "road" with dotted yellow lines, and lots of neon road signs for motels, fast food, and advertising cars.
- After following a dusty winding dirt path through the trees, one emerges into a little village. Smoke curls from a small log cabin, and a brown cow lifts its head and bellows. Two women in long dresses and bonnets walk by arm in arm talking about Mrs. Whitaker's newest quilt.

As tangible as each exhibition was in terms of its actual atmosphere, entrance, sound, and layout, each exhibition also carried a unique set of intellectual communicative messages.

Intellectual Environment

In addition to the physical attributes of the learning environment, there are features that serve to support the curatorial messages of the exhibition. Labels and signposts help visitors to conceptually orient themselves within the exhibition story. Many museums use a system of layering to demarcate sections and subsections of an exhibition. The nature and number of layers vary from exhibition to exhibition and may change even within a single one in order to support the curatorial message. In the *Light!* exhibition, for example, there were five levels of intellectual signposting. Room-level divisions marked broad thematic areas: A Ray of Light, The Light of Nature, Makers of Light, Personal Lights, and Public Lighting. These room-level headings were the titles for text panels that included approximately 100 words of text. Within each of these areas there were second layers of signage. In the Makers of Light room, for example, four one-word titles—God,

Reason, The State, and Capitalism—indicated the subtopics. An addition level of distinction occurred with smaller group labels that discussed several objects, or a class of objects. In the area called "The State," for example, "Fairs" discussed the development of world fairs during the period from 1750 to 1900. The *Light!* exhibition had many levels of signposting, but not all exhibitions had these one-word section labels, subdivisions, or wall-panel texts, nor did each show necessarily have parallel levels of signage and labeling within each section. In the *Automobile in American Life* exhibition, for example, major sections were clearly marked with overhead signage, such as "Custom Design" or "Buggy to Roadster"; smaller signposts were used to provide an overview and orientation within the chronological story "spine" of the evolution of the automobile.

For coding and analyzing the intellectual aspect of the learning environment, we noted where visitors engaged with room-level, section-level, and group-level labels. We also included visitors' comments about the color scheme or other devices in the learning environment if visitors noted that these features were designed to assist in delivering the intellectual message. Conversation that featured specific reading of object-level labels was reserved for analysis within the explanatory engagement category of visitors' talk, as discussed in the previous chapter.

The next section provides examples of curatorial considerations of, and visitor responses to, the learning environment. Each example features a specific exhibit within a show, giving the combined voices of the curator, when he or she explained or planned for the exhibition, and those of the visitors when they were touring. The examples focus on language that describes the plans or responses to both the physical and the intellectual aspects of the learning environment. The section also includes a few examples when some other unintentional aspects of the museum environment became moments of concern or learning for the visitor. It is important to remember, however, as indicated throughout this chapter, that responses to the totality of the environment are complex and are carried by more than the verbal discussions of either the curator or the visitor.

Examples

The first set of examples focuses on physical aspects of the learning environment that were deliberately designed to communicate to visitors. More clear-cut examples of manipulation of the physical environment are presented first, followed by those that are more distinctly intellectual. The examples are drawn from all of the exhibitions.

In the *Light!* exhibition care was taken to create a layout that would encourage visitors to attend to the main issues and themes of the show. The curator wanted a very small but important still life, Chardin's *Glass of Water and Coffeepot* (ca. 1760), to illustrate the concepts of reflection and refraction. The painting had to compete with large and glittering objects in cases nearby. She talked of how the design of the exhibition was altered in order to help the Chardin painting stand out:

> You sort of have to put it off by itself and make a big fuss about it—it looks so humble—so people will get the point. So the bench and the lighting and the isolating space and even the dumb little acoustiguide symbol all tell people "it's important, guys, it's important." People will look at the acoustiguide picture even if they don't have the acoustiguide. So we have to tell them all that. (Louise Lippincott)

Visitors did not directly comment on the particular design features surrounding the Chardin painting; but they did, in fact, notice the painting, and many studied it closely. Twenty-seven out of the thirty-two groups stopped in front of this painting. One mother and her college-aged daughter were among the groups who noticed the painting and commented about the light effects that Chardin created:

> *Mother:* [pause] That's interesting. Look at that glass of water.
> *Daughter:* Uh-huh.
> *Mother:* And to paint that, and to paint that dense pot. I mean you get the idea of the depth and the water and the glass.
> *Daughter:* Let me tell you, drawing glass and water in a glass is one of the hardest things you could ever do.
> *Mother:* I bet.
> *Daughter:* We had to do it in, uh, back in freshman year. (LT 21/13)

In the *Aluminum by Design* exhibition the design details were very subtle but carefully thought out. The curator wanted visitors to feel they could make choices and construct their own route, but she also wanted some sense of guidance and direction. As she walked through the exhibition with us, she highlighted this issue at the beginning:

> The exhibition is laid out in four main sections. We very much wanted to layer everything. So the introductory panel here sort of tells you that there are four main sections, introduces you to the color-coding and all of that sort of thing. We worked with designers for the layout of the show. And we very much wanted not a linear tour. So that there's a certain amount of flexibility and freedom and the ribbon is actually meant to guide you through. (Sarah Nichols)

Many of the visitors noticed the aluminum ribbon snaking its way through the galleries high above the exhibits. They tended to perceive it as an added bit of artistry rather than primarily as a guide, but it worked very well. In the example below, a family notices both the ribbon and some aspects of its function—as a means of foreshadowing upcoming sections of the exhibition.

> Son: Hey! Look at that really, really, big sheet of it that's curling.
> Mother: Oh, yeah, it goes through this whole display. Did you see the map of it outside?
> Son: No I didn't.
> Mother: See, you read it: "The Modernist Ideal."
> Father: Yeah.
> Mother: It tells you what you're going to look at next. (AL 01/22)

As one might expect in a show on light, a considerable amount of effort was expended on the design of lighting for the *Light!* exhibition. Contrasts of dark spaces with spotlights and bright airy skylights predominated. In *Light!* the curator had an explicit goal of using lighting to jolt the visitor:

> This room, the purpose was to shake people up a bit, who were expecting to see a traditional art show are seeing two paintings, and a whole lot of other stuff. It's really a gallery to disorient and reorient until we move to the next room where we deal with more paintings. They love the drama of it. The darkness and the light. (Louise Lippincott)

Visitors responded to this manipulation fairly directly: "Wow, look at how bright this room is! Wow." Other visitors seemed to go even deeper to understand the complex and consistent manipulations within and between rooms.

> Boy: Oh, I figured this out now. This is daylight, and that's moonlight . . .
> Girl: Yeah.
> Son: . . . and so it changes every room you go into.
> Girl: Oh, yeah.
> Son: I finally get that now. (LT 27/48-49)

While it was clear as we watched visitors moving through the different galleries that they were aware of the lighting and responded to it, such direct comments were rare.

These examples focused on physical aspects of exhibition design and the responses to them. But other examples of physical design features were not as clearly constructed or responded to as physical supports. In some cases a physical feature such as a routing was intended to support a particular intellectual position. One instance of this involved the dividing highway line that marked the "spine" through the *Automobile in American Life* exhibition at the Henry Ford Museum. As a reviewer of the show noted, the timeline running down the middle was meant to cover two topics: the evolution of the automobile industry and the technological developments of cars. The spine was oriented so that visitors would start with the most recent and familiar cars (the first Honda made in the United States) and move back to the unfamiliar past.[21] The curator emphasized that this strategy was designed to take visitors from the current and familiar into the darker, less familiar, and presumably less accessible past. However, people tend to think of time as moving forward not backward; thus two ways of looking at time (as a present dictated by its past, or as a past evolving into its present) were in collision for visitors.

Woman:	I wonder why they have this arranged backwards, sort of; you go from the newest to oldest.
Man:	The D probably stands for something else, I don't know. [responding to an earlier unrelated query]
Woman:	Oh, there's a Hud mobile. Oh, duh. Made by Huds.
Man:	The Chalmers. I wonder if that's the same as the farm implement company.
Woman:	Oh, look at all the different insignias. Crossley.
Man:	I think we're going backwards, that's the problem.
Woman:	Well, that's what I said. Why was the exhibit set up this way? [pause] Maybe you start with the known and go to the unknown? (HF 22/2)

The couple was aware of the overall structure of the exhibition, while at the same time they were responding to a specific object on display. They seemed to feel that the exhibition was designed with a plan; yet they started out believing they were going backward and "that's the problem." The man assumed they were simply doing it wrong while the woman believed that the museum designed it wrong. However, she continued to search for underlying rationale and did come up with an explanation.

In other cases, there were features of the learning environment that were both more deliberately intellectual and more didactic. In all of the exhibitions there was some level of signage that either attempted to orient the visitor to the core ideas writ large (both literally and figuratively) or was designed to tie together some of the collections of items and to point out their central thematic features. In *Africa: One Continent, Many Worlds*, the introductory material was designed to shake up the visitor in a different way from the light changes in the *Light!* exhibition. *Africa* was near the very end of a long tour (five years). The curator explained the design:

The museum wanted to look at what Africa *really* is like and to combat the disinformation that Americans often have about it. And they wanted to connect it with people of African descent. . . . So the first step was to do audience research to find out what people actually know about Africa and what they want to find out. When you ask questions like these [pointing at exhibit]—"Can you name five African countries?"—most people could not; they started making up names, like "Zimwagbia." "What do Africans speak?" Well, you know, Africans all speak Swahili! "They speak African." Africa is often covered in the news in terms of negative media, crisis-oriented stuff, and people don't have any kind of background in which to contextualize that. It's not covered in general public school education at all. . . . So, there were a number of goals in doing this exhibition. (Deborah Mack)

As an introduction to the second room of the *Africa* exhibition, there was a set of displays that served to orient the visitor to demographic and geographic features of the continent and to raise specific questions that might address common misconceptions. The display itself was somewhat worn looking, but it attracted quite a few visitors. One of the groups who used the flip-label introductions was a couple who, as they worked through it, confronted their own misconceptions (e.g., forgetting that Egypt is in Africa).

Man:	Uh-oh.
Woman:	Islam. And some other stuff.
Man:	Well, I imagine Christianity is in there.
Woman:	"Islam, Christianity, belief systems that are retained in various African societies. Smaller number practice Hinduism, Judaism, and Bahai." [reading label answer] Bahai. "How far back does Africa's written history go?" [reading label question]
Man:	Probably pretty darn far back.
Woman:	"Hieroglyphic writing from Egypt." Duh.
Man:	Duh, that's right!
Woman:	Yeah. There you go.
Man:	That's right. You're totally correct—in my mind I totally divorced Egypt from Africa. [chuckles]
Woman:	Exactly! See?! It's not just me!
Man:	No.
Woman:	"6½ million people sailed across the Atlantic before 1776. How many of these people were African?" A whole hell of a lot!

Man:	Before 1776?
Woman:	Before 1776. Yes. There were a whole lot of slaves before 1776. [flipping label to show answer]
Man:	Wow!
Woman:	"5½ million people. 92% of those that crossed came from Africa." I had no idea! "Can you name the largest African cities?" No.
Man:	You're right.
Woman:	Cairo?
Man:	Uh . . .
Woman:	I only know two African cities, three maybe. [flipping label to show answer] "Cairo . . ."
Man:	You're wrong, Cairo's not on there. Oh, there it is.
Woman:	"Casablanca, Ivory Coast Ab-" I can't pronounce that. "How many people live in Africa?"
Man:	A lot more than in this country. [chuckles]
Woman:	"248 million, 239 thousand. 1 out of every 6 people in the world lives in Africa." "How many countries is Africa divided into?"
Man:	Oh, It's like 80, isn't it?
Woman and Man:	"54!"
Woman:	Oooo!
Man:	Two more than there are in deck of cards. (AF 26/49)

This example of conversation is probably the response desired by the curators as they envisioned the exhibition and its visitors. The man and woman asked each other questions, made guesses, however vague, and then were amazed by the correct answers provided. In this example we also see a willingness of visitors in our sample to do what they felt like doing in spite of being recorded. They did not appear to be inhibited by revealing a lack of knowledge. They were unable to answer any of the questions (except for Cairo) and yet they proceeded on with the discussion and activity.

The environment, writ large, also affects the visitors in ways that reflect neither the physical nor the intellectual intentions of the curatorial team. The environment is dynamic and changing, and other visitors, staff, guards, sights, and sounds all influence the experience. The experience of the museum's learning environment is shaped by the social context in which the experience takes place. In some cases, such as the Exploratorium's *Behind the Screen* exhibition, the social context was frequently one where the crowdedness of an exhibit station meant that people at the periphery who were not actually "working" the exhibit felt free to make comments and interject their opinions with members of another group.

In the following example, a teenage boy and his father approached the Music Supervision station. At that station, visitors could choose from a sampling of different movies and edit the sound in a scene by inserting different music. The exhibit illustrated the impact of music selection on the resulting mood of a film. In this case, the two visitors first watched another family group work on a movie. The two groups began to share in the experience, commenting back and forth as well as conversing within their original groups. The father and son then sat down to try their hand, while the first group watched this group's selections and choices.

Father:	That's the original scene; that's the original music from the scene.
Son:	What is it?
Father:	Hmm?
Son:	What is it?
Father:	*Twister.*
Son:	Oh, this is *Twister?*
Other Mother:	It's one of the more exciting scenes from the movie.
Man:	Ha. Well, they've *got* to be pretty exciting after this part!
Other Mother:	[to her kids] Just move the track ball. Go to *Vertigo.*
Man:	Oh, there's *Independence Day.* This is really neat, isn't it?
Son:	Yeah.
Father:	Did you see this? Didn't we rent this, *Vertigo?*
Son:	No, I've never seen it.
Father:	We never got *Vertigo;* we were going to rent it, weren't we?
Son:	We rented *Citizen Kane.*
Father:	No, but *Vertigo* is a Hitchcock movie.
Son:	A what?
Father:	Hitchcock, Alfred Hitchcock.
Son:	Oh.
Father:	So, without the music it's just . . . No big deal. But the music, the background just adds so much.
Other Mother:	We're not picking the most exciting scenes.
Father:	Nah.
Other Mother:	But it's a long scene.
Father:	Okay.
Other Mother:	Okay. Here's your choices. Opera. [opera music plays, then they choose spooky music, and spooky music plays]
Father:	So that makes it more mysterious, that kind of a scene. [music changes again]
Other Mother:	I think maybe the opera sounds better.

Son:	Yeah, that makes it mysterious.
Father:	Yeah, doesn't that add just a whole different feeling?
Son:	Feeling.
Father:	Yeah, you know something sinister is going to happen.
Son:	Yeah, wow.
Father:	Yeah, this is great! I mean this changes the whole feeling of the scene. [more spooky music playing] So the hair is the same.
Son:	Is that the real music?
Father:	No. The real music is this one down here.
Other Mother:	You want to play the real music so we can see what it looks like with the real music?
Other Son:	Yeah. This is the real music?
Father:	Yeah.
Other Mother:	Now hit "listen to selection." [music plays]
Father:	It's nice to be able to see the soundtrack isn't it, to be able to edit that?
Son:	Yeah, definitely.
Other Mother:	We'll have to get the movie and find out [responding to a query out of range; new music plays; conversation among doers continues]
Father:	So it's not as sinister. But there's still something . . . see I think this one's more sinister there, but there's still something mysterious going on here.
Other Mother:	It seems like for most of these there's a music selection that works better than the original.
Father:	Well, this was pretty good. I mean it made it even more sinister than it was.
Other Mother:	[to her kids] Okay, let this gentleman behind you do it.
Father:	You want to try one? Do you want to do one, or? Okay. Let's try, which one do you want to try? Do you want to try *Independence Day*? Watch the scene.
Other Mother:	This guy was in *Jurassic Park* also. [they stand behind now and watch the father and son do *Independence Day*]
Father:	Yeah. (EX 11/17)

These two groups developed a new set of goals momentarily as each became a part of the other's "learning environment," albeit one that the curatorial team could not have predicted. In some sense the jointly constructed responses affirmed both the significance of the activity with which the two groups were engaged and the sensibility of their interpretations. Also, of course, the cross-group interactions made the experience more fun.

At another level, there is the negative impact of crowds on the learning environment. The next example shows a couple reacting negatively to a sudden surge of people into the gallery. The couple had been gradually making their way out of the gallery, retracing their steps back to the main entrance of the *Light!* exhibition, revisiting their favorite paintings along the way. They were looking at a painting by Hunt called *Pretty Baa Lambs.*

Husband: Baa lambs.

Wife: What, as opposed to the non-baa lambs? [large noisy group walking through on docent tour]

Docent: I wanted to point these two out because . . .

Wife: Ah. We're in the middle of a tour group. A couple. Oh good, they're off the cathedrals. [they walk over to two cathedral paintings by Monet] [pause]

Husband: There were Rouen cathedrals in the d'Orsay.

Wife: I know, there were boatloads of them!

Husband: Oh, I know. I know.

Wife: There are so many. How many were there? Three or four?

Husband: Well, yeah.

Wife: Well, they were sequenced. But there weren't two morning effects; they were different sunlight.

Husband: No, right, there were morning and afternoon.

Wife: And, yeah, they weren't the same.

Husband: They were very distinct. [pause]

Wife: That's just too . . . I'd love to see a whole bunch of them together at the same time and sit for hours and stare. Oh! Forget it! I don't like those other pictures well enough to beat somebody up to go and see them. It's getting busy.

Husband: Yes.

Wife: Very busy.

Husband: All the tourists.

Wife: Did the bus stop out front or what? My gosh.

Husband: Like, a tour bus got off.

Wife: Yeah, that's what I said. Let me out of here. This is too much. I don't want to deal with this. It's like docent tours or something. [noise increases as they move through the incoming throngs of people] Help Help. Good Lord. Get me out! (LT 16/112)

These two visitors were sophisticated and experienced museumgoers. After looking at the entire exhibition they retraced their path back to pieces that they particularly enjoyed or wanted to examine more closely. The presence of huge crowds funneling through the galleries, coming toward them in the opposite direction and filling up a space that had been relatively quiet and calm, coupled with the very prominent presence of a docent with another large cluster of people, derailed their plan. While they may have been more vocal than most about their dislike of the situation, we certainly saw, and have experienced, similar situations where crowds or large group tours end a small group's visit prematurely.

We provided the two previous examples to explicate the way the learning environment is always shaped not only by the intended plans of curators and designers but also by the unintended actualities of a visit taking place on a particular day or at a particular time and place. Sometimes these environmental factors are facilitative of engagement, as when the two family groups merged; at other times, these actualities are disruptive, as when a large crowd suddenly filled a quiet space.

The final example shows an unexpected and unintended positive outcome of social context. In this case, two twenty-year-old women had come from West Virginia to Pittsburgh and had stopped by the CMNH to see the renowned dinosaurs. The CMNH was closed, so instead they wandered into the adjacent art museum (CMA) and found themselves at the *Light!* exhibition. Neither visitor had ever been to an art museum before, and they did not realize that they were not supposed to touch the objects. They walked up to the first painting that they saw in the exhibition and touched it, prompting the guard to come over and speak with them.

Woman 1: Oh my God, look at this. This is ancient. Who did this? Giovanni Batiste Pittoni. [she touches the painting]

Woman 2: You can't touch it!

Woman 1: Oh, you're not allowed to touch? [reading label] "It was an Italian, an allegorical monument to Isaac Newton." Oh my God, look at that! I wonder what it's worth.

Woman 2: They're busty women. They'd like me!

Woman 1: They were big women. That's what they were back then. You see like angels or cherubs or something.

Woman 2: Oh look, a prism. Oh gosh, that's how they did it. Can you imagine how much time it took to draw all this?!

Woman 2: Draw this? They painted it.

Woman 1: Look at the wings on that angel. That's a fat little angel there. What do you see in this picture? Do you see just different concepts of life, and different little . . . like right here, this dude's trying to paint something.

Guard:	You're too close!
Woman 1:	Oh really? Is there anything—I don't know anything about art. Do you know anything about the facts? Like about how much something like that is worth? Do they tell you?
Guard:	No. No.
Woman 1:	Can you imagine how long it took the guy to paint that?
Guard:	And how long ago it was done.
Woman 1:	*That painting* was done in 1727! No, Giovanni Battista did it in 1620 . . .
Guard:	Let's see, between 1727 and '30.
Woman 1:	Oh my *God!* He painted that *then?* That's unbelievable.
Guard:	And look at what good condition it's in. That's because nobody's allowed to touch it.
Woman 2:	And your hand was over the line. You'll get arrested.
Guard:	You're not even allowed to touch the frames. (LT 15/4)

As many researchers have noted, the first and most salient contact that many visitors have in a museum is with the museum guards. In the quiet space of an art gallery or museum an admonition by a guard, no matter how quietly and politely done, can be quite a humiliating experience for most people. But in this interaction, the guard made a lovely educational move, showing the visitors how very old the painting is and then, with a clever segue to her own goal, she explained that the painting looks so good in spite of its age because no one has touched it. This interaction with the guard left the visitors informed but presumably not feeling chastised.

Findings

Different museums may attract different kinds of visitors with different intentions, and the same visitors may have different expectations at different venues. The hushed stately pace of the art museum invites an examination of the entire environment. The cacophony of the science museum both visually and auditorily tends to press visitors into a close manipulation of the object at hand—literally. The learning environment is reflective of both design and visitor actions. In measuring the learning environment aspect of our model, we focused only on the interactions with intentional design features.

This section presents the measure of the learning environment that was used in our study. The measure's relationship to the various museum exhibitions and to the other measures of learning in the museum is likewise described. The measure of the learning environment is the number of segments in which the visitors commented on the environmental designs or read large-scale text panels. Just as with the construct of identity, there is more in the learning environment that we saw, and even more that existed, than what is captured by any one set of measures. Why? First, the curators and designers of an exhibition may craft many aspects of the total setting, but in order for an environmental feature to be used as a measure, researchers must connect aspects of that crafting to the actual behaviors and discourse of the visitors. Thus, if a visiting group seemed to respond to some environmental aspect but neither spoke about it nor stopped and read about it, then there was no record of it. Second, since we studied visitors' activities and not the exhibits themselves, codes had to be linked to visitors' behavior. For more details about the coding and the results see the appendix on methodology.

Figure 5.1 displays the mean scores on the measure of learning environment (LE) by exhibition. The scores represent the average LE score for a group visiting the particular exhibition. In both the *Light!* and *Aluminum by Design* exhibitions visitors were likely to comment four times or more about aspects of the learning environment, whereas in the *Behind the Screen* and *The Automobile in American Life* exhibitions visitors commented less than once a visit on average. The measures are probably very accurate with respect to the frequency of noticing environmental features (they saw a feature, commented on it, and it was recorded) but less precise with respect to the lack of notice (that is, they may have noticed a feature, not

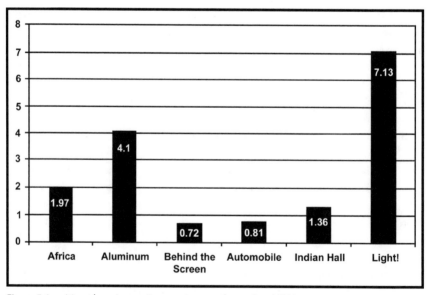

Figure 5.1.   Mean learning environment scores for each exhibition.

Table 5.1.   Correlation Matrix

	Learning Environment	Identity	Conversation	Learning
Learning environment	1.00			
Identity	.28	1.00		
Conversation	.47	.41	1.00	
Learning	.55	.44	.66	1.00

commented on it and thus it was not recorded OR they did not notice the feature and did not comment on it.)

We now turn to the simple correlations between the measure of learning environment use and comment and the other measures shown in table 5.1. The table displays the zero-order correlations among the measures. The identity of the visiting group is what visitors bring with them, and the learning environment is what the curatorial and design teams leave for them; thus, one would not expect to see a large association between LE and the measure of identity, and we do not (.28). However, one would expect to see a stronger association between what people discuss in a meaningful way about an exhibition and what they notice about the learning environment. There is indeed a stronger association between LE and conversation (our combined measure of analysis, synthesis, and explanation) (.47). Finally, the learning environment should affect learning that went on in the exhibition, and it does (.55). The correlation matrix shows that the learning environment, identity, and conversation all support learning.

Message

Of the three central dimensions of our model (identity, conversation, and environment) we struggled most with the role of the environment. This is where museums can enhance their effects, and so it is critically important. However, it is also the case that the environment is designed to do a great many things as well as to influence the level of learning and the feeling and disposition toward the exhibition itself. At some level the environment is composed of specific items, such as benches or flip labels, which can be moved, added, subtracted, and essentially tested for their impact. The learning environment is where the curatorial voice is spoken, and the measure of engagement with higher-level text panels is our estimate of whether that voice was heard. Initially, the physical cues and their responses were analyzed separately from the intellectual ones, but this was in some sense an inappropriate separation; thus in the end the two features were combined.

An intervention study would be necessary to study the learning environment more thoroughly. What kind of intervention might be best? Explicit questions about whether people noticed the environment or how they might change it might be useful. Also, a variety of short studies could be done with virtual tours before or after a group visit. In these computer simulations, certain features such as wall color or clustering of displays can easily be manipulated and examined for their effects. Reactions to virtual tours could be compared directly with real visitor experiences. For example, suppose that one wanted to understand the impact of the strong difference in wall color from gallery to gallery. One could design a study in which the virtual reality mimicked the actual one and see how visitors responded in both the real world and virtual environments. Then one could manipulate the colors, eliminating the contrast in the virtual world but leaving it in the physical one, and so forth. Differences in memory and in commentary would help elucidate the impact of that single manipulation. Third, one could use more long-term tools such as follow-up phone calls and even visitor diaries in which the overall impression of a visit is as likely to be recorded as is the response to any particular object.[22]

Questions

Museum learning is a complex issue. We invite you to turn back to chapter 2 and decide which aspects you would choose as the focus of your own queries in an examination of museum learning environments. How might you design a study to examine more fully the features of a museum learning environment? What trade-offs do you envision? What would you ask in an interview, and when would you ask your questions? How could you document the use of the learning environment? What unique and innovative tools, such as computer simulations, physical mock-ups, or diaries, might you use? How might you think about the overall and holistic atmosphere of these environments? If you were to design a set of studies that focused solely on the impact of the learning environment, what might that study or set of studies look like?

Notes

1. Stodolsky 1988.
2. Brown 1992.
3. See, for example, Schauble et al. 2002.
4. Allen 1997.
5. Another kind of experiment has been used extensively in the field of visitor studies in which visitors' behavior is measured in response to changes in the layout, context, or labels of exhibition.
6. Examples of different approaches to this research can be found in Bitgood et al. 1987; Serrell 1997; Korn 1988; Allen 1997.

7. Schauble et al. 2002; Crowley and Galco 2001.

8. Falk 2002; Bitgood and Loomis 1993.

9. Duncan 1995.

10. Yanow 1998.

11. Hooper-Greenhill 1992; Bennett 1995.

12. Greenberg, Ferguson, and Nairne 1996; Roberts 1997.

13. Falk and Dierking 1992; Serrell 2001.

14. Dean 1996; McLean 1993.

15. Underhill 2000.

16. Schauble et al., 2002.

17. Knutson 2002.

18. Hood 1993.

19. Worts 1995.

20. We are aware that our method of collecting data might have influenced visitors not to sit down or stop. While a few groups did stop and sit, most continued on with their tours, perhaps aware of the researcher's time.

21. Pursell 1992, 241.

22. Leinhardt, Tittle, and Knutson 2002.

Results 6

Problem

AS THE END OF THE STORY DRAWS NEAR there is one last problem: Do we try to squeeze in all of the details, the twists and turns, and the interpretive layers that we have left aside? Do we tell a clean, straightforward quantitative tale? Is it better to construct a lively qualitative story? Should we try to elaborate on the way sociocultural theory informed us as we engaged in this effort, or perhaps should we consider how we might add to the theory itself? In some ways, like a "Choose Your Own Adventure" book, this book offers you the tools to draw upon the rich data set to construct your own path. There are diverse and varied stories within the data set, and thus the difficult task is choosing a route through the rich and complex information. There are multiple parts of the story to share—the quantitative and qualitative, the pieces that link tightly to the data, what was "found," and the speculative aspects of what might be. To provide the quantitative story alone would leave many feeling the story was detached, impersonal, and simply a strange set of numbers. But to tell the qualitative side of the story alone would provide merely anecdotal instances, detached from either basic theory or the model's underlying quantitative strength.

The Concept

The challenge then is to provide insight into several aspects of the story. Qualitative discussion helps to build meaning around what the numbers represent, and the quantitative discussion both helps in understanding the patterns that go beyond the individual cases and serves to anchor the discussion of the specifics of those cases.

To begin, let us review the general framework with which we started. We assumed that learning is a socially constructed activity. One principal tool for learning, especially in an informal environment, is the coordinated activity of conversation. Learning in museums can be fruitfully thought of as (1) the short-term progress of a group toward having more elaborated and engaged conversations about the material and concepts in a museum and (2) as the continuation of those conversations after the group has left the museum and our hearing. The conversations that take place in a museum are mediated by the environments developed and constructed by museum staff. The content and focus of those conversations are strongly influenced by environment, the objects, and the identity of the group. The group's identity influences what the group develops as its goal in visiting the museum, as well as what the group chooses to share and bring to the experience of the exhibition. Museums are cultural institutions, and the learning that takes place in them is both dialogic and voluntary. The dialogic, voluntary nature of learning in museums contrasts sharply with the learning that takes place in the context of predefined formal instruction. The museum setting, as George Herbert Mead would have recognized, is a place where visitors are in dialogue with themselves; with each other, as Harrison White reminds us; and with the traces of the curatorial premises.[1]

Findings

Themes

In chapter 4, structural and thematic ways of considering conversation were discussed. Recall that we developed five thematic ideas for each exhibition after considering the curatorially stated themes, the wall text, and the various catalogues available to us. The themes were uniquely developed for each show; thematic talk among visitors varied according to individual group interests. Although a comparison of visitors' responses to themes cannot be made across exhibitions, it is possible to examine the patterns of thematic talk during the visit and in the visitors' posttour discussion (see fig. 4.1 for a listing of all themes). How did the pattern of thematic talk during the visit compare with the thematic talk that occurred at the end of the visit during the prompted, posttour discussion? Recall that the posttour discussion consisted of the group jointly looking at a series of cards that had questions or statements and pictures on them. Each theme for an exhibition was represented on a card by a picture with a statement to prompt discussion. For example, in the posttour discussion for the *Aluminum by Design* exhibition, the theme of aesthetics was prompted by a card that showed a photo of the shiny aluminum façade of the *Die Zeit* building with a caption saying "The Way It Looks."

Although the prompts were designed to elicit comments connected to a particular theme, responses were scored according to whatever thematic emphasis existed in the visitors' discussion. Thus, if the picture and statement focused on aesthetics but the ensuing discussion focused on issues of corrosion then the response would be coded in the thematic category of problem solving and design.

We envisioned that the thematic posttour discussions might reflect two different perspectives on learning. On the one hand, a group might spend considerable time and effort discussing a particular set of themes during their visit and thus, because they built up language and interest in those themes, might tend to discuss them again in the posttour conversation. This finding would support the idea that the ongoing conversations were both processes of learning and outcomes of learning. On the other hand, a visiting group might have exhausted all they had to say on some themes during their visit and might take the opportunity to discuss other aspects of the exhibition in the posttour conversation. This finding would support the idea that visitors are not talking very completely during the visit about what they are learning but rather are talking about what they already know and are leaving some very important ideas unsaid.

One measure of the consistency of the thematic emphasis between visitors' tour talk and their posttour conversations is to compare the content of thematic use in their visit conversation with that in the posttour conversation. We found that there was an 80% agreement between the tour talk and posttour conversation. This correlation held true even if different objects evoked the same themes. This finding lends support to the idea that there is both an extension and a rehearsal of ideas that propagate through the group as they engage with parts of an exhibition.

So what exactly does that sound like? Let's listen.

Examples

This section provides excerpts of conversations that correspond thematically, as an example of how thematic talk evolved within a group over the visit. We return to the group that shared the story of the vacuum cleaner in chapter 3. Two middle-aged women friends who were also members of the museum came specifically to see the *Aluminum by Design* exhibition. They spent over ninety minutes looking at the exhibition and planned to have lunch together afterward. They were interested in reading the labels to identify the dates for objects, and they made comments about the way things looked and their specific design features. They also talked about how one of the women might incorporate recycling into her own art-making activities. We selected this group because it had relatively high learning scores. We went back into their tour to examine what they looked at and what they talked about; we then compared the group's performance with the average activity of other groups that toured the *Aluminum by Design* exhibition. Here we provide excerpts of their visit conversation as they discuss two themes: problem solving and design, and aesthetics.

In the first example we hear the two visitors sharing their aesthetic opinions about a wild-looking chaise longue resting on a carpet, both of which are constructed from small squares of printed aluminum cut from pop cans. The piece was visually stunning, with intricate patterns of pop can labels. The women analyze the design and aesthetic decisions that the artist made:

Woman 2:   Don't tell me, it's made out of pop cans.

Woman 1:   It looks certainly like it is.

Woman 2:   And you're . . . [chuckles]

Woman 1:   What a dance floor, huh?

Woman 2:   It really looks neat! Cutting little squares out of cans.

Woman 1:   It's interesting. They have it so perfectly put together that this whole rim is all [reading labels on pop cans] "light, light, light, light, light."

Woman 2:   Yes. Serpentine shapes. [pause] Carpet. The thing is to stand here and pick out how many brands of beverages.

Woman 1:   [chuckles] That might take a while.

Woman 2:   Yeah, I don't think I'd want to do it.

Woman 1:   This looks kind of like a four-leaf clover down there. It looks interesting. I wonder what can that is, that has such a neat . . . Here's one closer. My God, but it's upside down. It's miniature or something. I never realized how much artwork was on these cans. (AL 30/60)

In the next example the two women were examining problem solving and design properties of items in a case with assorted objets d'art made from aluminum, including a violin made of aluminum and a statue of Venus de Milo cast in aluminum. Together they worked to construct an *explanation* about the different properties of aluminum:

Woman 1:   I wonder how they made these statues. How they [reading] . . . "Casting." I guess just like any other metal. [pause] I just realized how little I know about aluminum! Like, does it conduct electricity? It must. I'm thinking, like would it be safer—

Woman 2:   Yes, it does. No, it's not.

Woman 1:   It takes more aluminum than copper, I think.

Woman 2:   Aluminum wire is thicker than the same grade of copper wire.

Woman 1:   If you're sitting in your chair on the front porch and it's steel
             or if it's aluminum, which one has the higher probability of
             getting struck by lightning? [laughs]
Woman 2:   I can't answer that! [laughs]
Woman 1:   Because I was out on the front porch one day . . . (AL 30/14)

In the final example of thematic talk during the visit, the two women examined a corner of the exhibition that included beautiful machine-made airplane
parts. There was a modern Brancusi-like shiny propeller blade, its sleek design
highlighted by the blue walls behind it and the blue wooden plinth supporting it.
Large-scale, wall-mounted, black-and-white photographs of a man working inside
the wing of an airplane, and another photograph of a zeppelin structure, also surrounded the propeller blade. A section of a zeppelin girder mounted on the wall
was included in the display corner. In the following segment the two women analyzed the aesthetics of the objects.

Woman 1:   Is this part of a bridge maybe?
Woman 2:   "Pole of the Akron air ship."
Woman 1:   "Girder from a zeppelin." I thought maybe it was part of a
             bridge. Oh wow. [pause]
Woman 2:   They had a lot of interior, didn't it, structure. Looks like it's
             under construction.
Woman 1:   I don't think I'd ever have the courage to go up in a blimp. They
             are pretty though. [pause] This I like! It's an airscrew blade for
             a Douglas DC3.
Woman 2:   A what blade? Oh, propeller. I get it.
Woman 1:   You've got all your flying experience. I just thought of it as a
             great big feather!
Woman 2:   It certainly looks like it, doesn't it?
Woman 1:   A feather without the feathering. It's pretty, though. I like that.
             There's just something . . . (AL 30/26)

The preceding three examples of thematic discussion came from the tour.
What we want to show next is the posttour prompted conversation where echoes
of the tour can be easily detected. We provide the entire transcript of the group's
posttour conversation. Remember that this conversation is prompted by a flip
book of cards containing questions and photo prompts, but the conversation is
not led by an interviewer or researcher. The words in italics represent the questions
or parts of questions that appeared on the cards; phrases that were coded for the
two different themes exemplified above appear in bold.

Woman 1:   *How did you enjoy your visit?* Well, I thought it was really great.

Woman 2:   Yeah, I enjoyed a lot.

Woman 1:   *Did anything in particular surprise you in this exhibit?*

Woman 2:   Well, some of the clothing. [chuckles]

Woman 1:   I was surprised at how long aluminum has been used. I didn't think it was back in the 1800s.

Woman 2:   Yeah, and also the carpet made out of aluminum cans, that was kind of "Wow!"

Woman 1:   *Can you think of two or three things you saw that were particularly interesting to you? Why did they catch your interest?*

Woman 2:   Well, the clothing and the carpet, and the chair made of the aluminum can pieces, too, because they were just so different.

Woman 1:   Yeah. One of things that fascinated me in the beginning was the aluminum playing cards, Christmas cards, and postcards. I've never seen anything quite like that. And more towards the middle—the woman, the sculpture of the woman that was flying in the air, that was made out of aluminum, that was really fascinating too. There were tons of things. I liked a lot of things.

Woman 2:   **Yeah. I did too. I liked, right at the end, those chairs, where one of them was uncut, and the others were kind of, well, after you make the cutouts you've got a chair of this other shape. The one looked like a kid's pond.** [*Problem Solving and Design*]

Woman 1:   Oh, yeah, yeah, I remember those. Anything else?

Woman 2:   The basket made out of woven aluminum cans. I guess I liked the used aluminum can stuff. I also liked the film.

Woman 1:   Very good. *Discuss anything in the exhibit that challenged you, made you change your mind, or with which you disagreed.*

Woman 2:   Whoa. A propeller as a piece of sculpture, that was different.

Woman 1:   Uh-hmm.

Woman 2:   Challenged me, made me change my mind, or with which I disagree? I didn't particularly like the aluminum cars, especially those advanced sports-utility family van things, sedan things, toward the end. Actually, don't think I liked any of them, even the one at the beginning.

Woman 1:   Yeah.

Woman 2:   They were kind of crappy. What else?

Woman 1:   One of the things that challenged me, that had nothing to do with the actual aluminum, was that I'm not a real fast reader and there was a lot to read. I feel like if I wanted to read every-thing I would be here all day. So the next time I'll probably use the audio that's available. I didn't think of that, didn't know it was available at the beginning.

Woman 2:   Yeah. I think that would've been a good idea.

Woman 2:   *Here are some pictures related to the aluminum show. Please look at each pic-ture and talk about it.* [they flip the card and laugh] Back in those days [*photo of aluminum lawn chair*]. Like I said, I can still buy that chair at K-Mart I'm sure.

Woman 1:   I've got some downstairs.

Woman 2:   They sit on the porch in summertime.

Woman 1:   **They bring back lots of memories from when I was growing up and when my kids were growing up. I used to throw them in the backseat when my kids were on baseball teams and things. They were great for picnics or sitting in the yard and upon occasion if you had too many people in your house for the furniture you had, they could always be hauled out of the basement for extra seating.** [*Problem Solving and Design*]

Woman 2:   **The thing I remember is what a relief it was to have aluminum-framed chairs because my mother always made me carry her chair to the beach and it was two blocks and it was made out of wood.** [chuckle] **I was about eight years old and the chair was too heavy for me. Because I had a sand pail and bucket or something like that and I was going to dig but she wanted her chair down at the beach for when she got there. Agh! Maybe I was ten. But at any rate, those old wooden chairs were so heavy, that when we finally got aluminum chairs I was already fifteen or sixteen. It didn't make that much difference, but boy I wished they'd had them a few years earlier.** [*Problem Solving and Design*]

Woman 1:   **Yeah, I also remember the webs are replaceable, so when they wore out the aluminum lived on. They were invincible chairs.** [*Problem Solving and Design*] The way it looks [*photo of Die Zeit building façade*]

Woman 2:   Now that was something I didn't know before, that they had building fronts.

Woman 1:   I don't know how to pronounce it. Dye Zeet? "The way it looks."

Woman 2:   It was the front for the newspaper in Germany in 1930, or maybe it was even earlier.

Woman 1:   Mmm-hmm. Well, I enjoyed looking at it, but I didn't read the blurb about it.

Woman 2:   I remember what it was. I looked at it and I thought it looks art deco and the date was earlier than I thought art deco was, but I don't remember what the date was. 1906 or so?

Woman 1:   I don't know.

Woman 2:   I can't remember.

Woman 1:   Okay, the next one, *The way it works* [*photo of Chrysler Prowler car*]. It looks like a racecar. I don't actually remember seeing that specific car, unless that was the one at the very end in the last room.

Woman 2:   I don't remember that one either.

Woman 1:   So, if it is the one I'm thinking of, I remember seeing the back of it being a Plymouth something and thinking it was really pretty, but—

Woman 2:   Yeah, we never did go around to the front of that car. [chuckle] We went around the edges. But that's the—

Woman 1:   *Transformation and recycling* [*photo of Serpentine Chaise Longue made of pop cans*].

Woman 2:   That's the one I loved. That's the one I wanted to count all the different brands of soda pop and beer.

Woman 1:   **It amazed me, number one, that the design of the chair was so meticulous that the word "light" was all around on the outer edge. Light-light-light-light. It was kind of neat that someone went to all that time to get that pattern so it was so exact. And also I never realized how much beautiful artwork there is on cans, besides the advertising there's some little beautiful artwork.** [*Aesthetics*]

Woman 2:   Little details. Yeah.

Woman 1:   Anything else? Ah, *Community, nation and corporation* [*photo of airplane propellers*].

Woman 2:   The propellers. I don't know—propellers as sculpture is what I see.

Woman 1:   Yeah. We both really enjoyed that one.

Woman 2:   Yeah.

Woman 1:   **Behind, the blue wall behind the propeller it was rather incredible. You got the feeling it was like a whole new use of a propeller, you didn't even recognize it as a propeller. But the blue reminded me of the sky once I knew what it was. Yeah, so it was great.** [*Aesthetics*]

Woman 2:   **Just a beautifully sculptural shape, and yet it's such a practical shape.** [*Aesthetics; Problem Solving and Design*]

Woman 1:   Yeah. Community, nation, and corporation. I remember talking when we were there something about cooperation [sic], but I can't remember what that was now. It's a lost thought. *Are there any ways that what you saw in the Aluminum show connected with you personally?*

Woman 2:   Aluminum chairs, the lawn chairs. Yeah. Um. Yeah, some of those office furniture things I've used, things like them or things of the same shape, or maybe the same kind of thing.

Woman 1:   Yeah, the thing I thought about was, like, although I do some recycling there's other ways I could probably recycle. And even if you listen to the tape, I was talking I don't know if it came through or not, but our community does recycling and yet in their public spaces they don't necessarily have bins for recycling. So I think I'm going to talk with the government people about what more we can do to do that. Yeah. I never thought of all the different ways you can use it, there's probably like, like I like to tinker with art, so maybe there's some way I could incorporate aluminum into my art. But I'm not sure how to do that yet. I'll have to do some learning!

Woman 2:   **Figure out how to shred it, weave baskets.**

Woman 1:   **Yeah, or color it. I never knew you could seal it by putting it in boiling water.[2] That was pretty interesting.** [*Problem Solving and Design*]

Woman 2:   What do you start with, though?

Woman 1:   I don't know. It's a whole new field to look into.

Woman 2:   Yeah.

Woman 1:   *Has your experience with work, travel, or hobbies connected you with what you saw in the Aluminum show?*

Woman 2:   I drive past the Alcoa building. [chuckles]

Woman 1:   Yeah, think it's just kind of a repeat of what I've already said, like with art. When I was up in Alaska I saw a couple of those aluminum trailers and I thought it was interesting that they were even in Alaska.

Woman 2:   **I thought the pictures of the airships were kind of neat. I mean I always knew they were big, but I didn't realize what their structural members looked like. And there was all this insides of airships. That was kind of fascinating.** [*Problem Solving and Design*] (AL 30/22)

The purpose of sharing these visitors' responses to the exhibition and their posttour discussion is to demonstrate the ways in which the two sets of conversations were thematically aligned. Not only did the two women notice the cans and rug, the propeller, and the chairs as they were visiting but also they analyzed and explained these objects and speculated beyond the information given in the label copy in terms of future uses for aluminum in their own lives and in terms of general understanding. After their long visit, they patiently spent another eleven minutes summing up what they had seen and thought about, returning to some of the same objects of focus: the rug, the chairs, the propeller, thematically discussing them in terms of their aesthetic and design features. As friends, they were able to both expound for one another and also to prompt one another to solve the small tasks they set for themselves. (Note, for example, the discussion of shredding the aluminum in order to weave it.) In the small excerpts from their conversation one can see the ideas forming and then being revoiced later. We imagine that parts of these ideas will be carried forward into future conversations between the two friends and into conversations with other friends and family when the exhibition, aluminum, or folding garden chairs are discussed.

As we transition from the description of one group visiting *Aluminum by Design* to the full set of information from this study, let us consider for just a moment how these two women look in comparison with other visitors to *Aluminum by Design*. The average motivation score for visitors to *Aluminum by Design* was 3.5 out of 5. These two visitors had a motivation score of 4. The average appreciative and experiential (prior) knowledge score was 2.8 out of 5, whereas these two visitors had a score of 3. The average overall identity score for the exhibition was 3.1 while these two had a score of 4. Thus, the measures of identity for our two visitors suggest they were just a little more motivated and a little more knowledgeable than the typical visitors we encountered at the exhibition. The average number of segments in which comments or behaviors indicated connection to the learning environment was 4.1 on an open scale; these two visitors connected 9 times to specific aspects of the learning environment during their visit. That is, they responded more than twice as frequently to the designed features of the museum as did their fellow visitors. The average number of segments in which the conversation reflected explanatory engagement (either analyzing, synthesizing, or explaining) was 27.6, whereas these two visitors talked in that way 50 times. These two women connected in deep and meaningful ways through their conversations to the exhibition almost twice as often as other visitors to the exhibition. And how did their learning compare? The average learning score at *Aluminum by Design* was 116.8, and these two visitors had 219. They knew a little more, they were a little more motivated, but most significantly they engaged about twice as deeply as the average visiting group and they learned almost twice as much as other visitors.

We showed one group visiting one exhibition and described how their specific backgrounds and behaviors related to what they seemed to be building from the visit; we turn now to a description of what all of the visitors to all of the exhibits seemed to learn. Table 6.1 displays the means and standard deviations and correlations for each of the major constructs and learning for 178 visiting groups.

Starting with the first two columns, means and standard deviations, the first row (pre-score) represents the knowledge visitors had about the show before their visit. The pre-score reflects thematic references that occurred anywhere during the pre-visit conversation. Identity reflects why the visitors came, what their agenda was, and what they hoped to get from the visit combined with what they already knew or understood to impact the learning experience. (The identity variable is made up of a rating from 1 to 5. The fact that one set of numbers ranges from 1 to 5, while another ranges from 10 to 30, and still another ranges from 50 to 200, does not affect the way the measures relate to each other.) Learning environment combines both the physical and intellectual support provided by the curatorial design and reflects the visitors' response to them. Although there was substantial difference across exhibition venues, there was even greater difference in how these curatorially designed affordances were actually used by the visitors. The fact that, on average, visitors used the design elements only two or three times each visit suggests that many visitors did not attend to these features. The construct of explanatory engagement shows that visitors conversed in ways that engaged with the thematic content of the show by analyzing, synthesizing, or explaining for an average of twenty-three segments out of the average of sixty segments per visit. When we think of visitors moving through a space, surrounded by 200 or more objects and activities, the fact that they connected with and discussed more than a third of them (and either stood in silence, related personal memories, or simply identified others) is impressive.[3] Finally, the measure of learning is a combination of the number of thematic references made in the post-interview (times ten) and the amount of time spent in the visit. What the value of 110 on table 6.1 indicates is that visitors spent about one and a half hours and made about ten thematic references in the post interview.

Returning to table 6.1, to the right of the two columns of means and standard deviations is the correlation matrix. The correlation matrix shows how the central variables related to each other. For example, as the level of learning environment use went up, so did the level of conversational explanatory engagement. This relationship is shown on the table by the positive correlation of .47. The values displayed along the bottom row indicate that all of the core variables were positively associated with the measure of learning—and significantly so. Attributes of the group that reflect their identity affected learning. Design aspects of the exhibition mediated learning. The more the museum designers made available

Table 6.1. Means, Standard Deviations, and Correlations for Measures in the Model (n= 178)

	Mean	Standard Deviation	Pre-Score	Identity	Learning Environment	Explanatory Engagement	Learning
Pre-score							
Identity	2.91	1.10	.20	1.00			
Learning environment	2.74	3.61	.13	.28	1.00		
Explanatory engagement	23.44	14.94	.13	.40	.47	1.00	
Learning	110.88	50.38	.37	.44	.55	.65	1.00

intellectual and physical supports for the core ideas of the exhibition and the more they were used, the more there was evidence of learning. Conversation was a cognitive tool for learning. When groups coordinated explanatory conversation that reflected the contents and themes of a particular exhibition, the more that a group discussed the contents in a exhibition by analyzing its components, comparing or contrasting objects to other objects in the show or elsewhere, or explaining some feature of the objects or activities, the more they seemed to learn. (It should be noted that the measures that go into the estimate of learning are not measured anywhere else in the rest of the model.) Conversational activity as measured by explanatory engagement was the most influential factor in learning (correlation=.65). But all of the components matter. Furthermore, the learning environment and identity factors also influenced the probability that a group would engage in explanatory conversation in a positive way.

We can express these relationships in a quantitative fashion. Equation 1 and 2 below are the formal expressions of the regression analysis of the learning model.

$$\text{Equation 1}$$
$$\textbf{Learning} = 27.7 + \textbf{7.9 Pre-Score} + \textbf{3.6 Identity} + \textbf{3.8 LE}$$
$$+ \textbf{1.5 Explanatory Engagement}$$
$$R^2 = .58$$

$$\text{Equation 2}$$
$$\textbf{Explanatory Engagement} = 4.9 + .15 \text{ Pre-Score} + \textbf{2.4 Identity} + \textbf{1.6 LE}$$
$$R^2 = .30$$

So what do these innocent-looking equations mean? At the general level they mean that figure 6.1 is an accurate representation of learning in a museum as we investigated it. Equation 1 means that we can predict the average learning of a group by considering their preinterview measure, their identity, their learning environment behavior, and their conversation. The variables in bold are significant predictors in the regression, significant meaning that these results were unlikely to occur by chance. Explanatory engagement as conversation can also be predicted, and that is shown in equation 2. In this case, identity and learning environment both influence the conversational explanatory engagement, but pre-tour scores do not. Both regressions are highly significant ($p < .0001$), meaning that we would be likely to see these results occurring by random chance one in ten thousand times.

At one level our model is a conceptual framework that reflects critical aspects of sociocultural theory, namely, that the identity and past histories of individuals, the environmental mediators, and the human activity that people

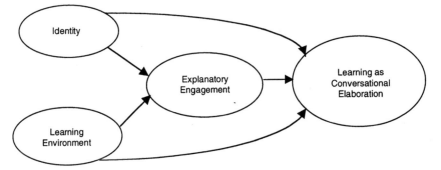

Figure 6.1.   Model of learning in the museum.

engage in provide an important context that shapes learning. At the same time, it is a rigorous and testable quantitative statement. The ovals in the model (fig. 6.1) were given values based on observational measures associated with each construct. The lines with arrows represent assumed causal influence. In a non-experimental research study of this type, causality cannot be proved; however, the correlations, the regression analyses, and the underlying theoretical coherence are consistent with the idea that learning in a museum is a result of explanatory engagement, the learning environment, and identity. The model also helps to support the idea that explanatory engagement itself is facilitated by both identity and responses to the learning environment. This embedded layer of causality is shown by the arrows that go from identity to explanatory engagement, and from identity to learning (as well as from learning environment). However, responding to the learning environment is not totally dependant on the identity of the group, and this is shown by the lack of a connection between these constructs.

This effort can act as the beginning of a conversation about model-driven analyses of museum activity. The important role of personal filters and tools are reified in the model and the findings. With this finding we are continuing the evidence from Doering's work on entrance narrative and Falk's work on personal background that claims that what visitors bring with them to the museum matters.[4] We hope we helped to extend these ideas by providing qualitative and quantitative evidence in a variety of settings. The model-driven analysis also supports the concept that the activity of conversation in museums mediates meaning constructions and revision. This concept grows out of the sociocultural construct of conversationally mediated activity and the centrality of conversation in learning. Finally, this particular model of activity and learning in museum works at one level of resolution—that of the visiting group, for one or two hours, at an exhibition. Other researchers have contributed to different levels. The work of Crowley examines individual or family groupings for a few seconds or a minute at an exhibit.[5] The work of Ash, Ellenbogen, and Falk and Dierking examine larger groupings, for several hours or days, at an entire museum.[6] It will be important to understand how such a model of learning will need to be modified as the level of resolution changes either to be more fine-grained or more broadly encompassing.

Message

What has been learned from listening in on museum conversations? Two messages emerge—one related to what was learned in a conceptual sense from the research, and a second related to what we think museum educators and staff might find most valuable from the findings.

What Was Learned

Individuals and small groups of friends and family members visit museums. When small groups engage in the activity of visiting museums we have an opportunity, by listening in on their conversations, to observe them sharing their available cultural and intellectual resources and building new ones together. Within the space of the conversational environment there is evidence that combined knowledge leads to more extensive kinds of discussion and elaboration. In the taped conversations, we heard fathers explaining ideas to sons and wives; we heard sons explaining ideas to mothers; and mothers explaining to sons. We heard friends jointly building up understandings and jointly setting new goals for the learning agenda. We also heard friends sharing bits and pieces of their past with each other, telling an anecdote or two around a car, a vacuum cleaner, or a chair. The cognitive tool for learning was conversation as it was constructed online, during the museum visit. A mediating factor was the learning environment that provided support for ideas through emphasis and direction to objects and their context.

We learned that what a group talks about, it thinks about; that talking is a tool for socially constructed thought, not just evidence of it; and that talk supports the gradual alteration and development of goals during the course of a visit. What groups talk about in engaged ways and think about, they remember. These memories become connected again through mutually self-referencing discussions to other ideas, activities, and objects. What is remembered is learned. When groups talk about a specific object, an idea connected to that object, and a thematic interpretation of it, they are building up shared meanings surrounding that object or concept. After the visit they are likely to remember both the object and thematic ideas surrounding it.

The Message for Museums

Throughout this book we have emphasized the role of visitors' identity, knowledge, and activity in constructing the learning experience. While museum curators and staff examine their own activity and decisions, there is considerably more to visitor learning than just those things that are under curatorial control. But the design of the learning environment is vital. It is, after all, the learning environment that is under the control of the museum. And if the learning environment is the aspect that museum professionals can really control or shape in the learning equation, how can curators make the most of it?

If the goal is to provoke, nurture, and support conversation in the museum environment, there is a need to have meaningful information for visitors, information that answers their questions. Visitors need to find information that addresses issues. Visitors seem to be interested in knowing the stance and role of curatorial interpretation. An aware public may misinterpret or find a particular interpretation not to their taste, and the ensuing controversy between visitor beliefs, agendas, and curatorial premises can threaten public support of museums. Yet to dumb-down material, neutralize a stance, or whitewash controversial aspects of the interpretation is not the answer. To the contrary, in cases where controversy of interpretation or controversy of content was put forward by the museum, we repeatedly saw visitor engagement and discussion.

In our observations we saw visitors upset by ambiguity in signage but nonetheless engaged by it. In cases where information was incomplete or visually difficult to read, they were distressed and not engaged. We sense that the ongoing move to lift the veil on the professional effort that goes on behind the scenes is a fruitful and meaningful path to follow. Visitors seem prepared to move to an understanding of the purpose of an object, the very act of deciding to show this object rather than another, and to emphasize one idea over another. Visitors also seem prepared to take on controversial content, not just controversy over content. Museums can and should capitalize on that willingness. We saw this willingness most clearly in the *Alcoa Foundation Hall of American Indians*, and *Africa: One Continent, Many Worlds* exhibitions. We also saw this willingness in the *Automobile in American Life* exhibition in conversations that ranged from Ralph Nader, to the Ford company, to unionization.

Sometimes museums introduced controversial interpretations of information— for example, the discussion of ill-formed amphibians at the Exploratorium,[7] the invitation to think about who should be considered an Indian in the modern context at the CMNH, or displaying the collision of expectations surrounding art and science at the *Light!* exhibition. Controversy and query are two of several ways to engage visitors in connections to the learning environment. In pressing for new ways of engaging the visitor we do not want to suggest abandoning the fundamental and critical power of authentic, powerful, exquisite, and valued objects to provoke and support learning conversations.

Museums are fascinating places; people who visit museums engage in fascinating conversations and activities. We want to encourage museums to make use of the theatrical, the unexpected, and the awe-inspiring to highlight the power of objects to arouse us to thought and engagement. But we also want to encourage museums to be clear and not to fear the inclusion of more information or the use of multiple means of presenting information to visitors. We hope museums continue to design exhibitions that inspire and challenge us and to pose questions that do not always have easy answers. We would encourage museums to explore more extensively the boundaries of what is considered "useful information" for visitors and researchers to explore museums as unique forums in which to study language, action, and thought among informally constructed groups of people, people unconstrained by formal objectives for learning.

Notes

1. Mead 1934; White 1995; .
2. The woman was referring to anodized aluminum jewelry by Jane Adam. The label copy indicated that the artist anodizes aluminum by dipping the piece in acid, then layering color with felt pens and sealing the surface with boiling water.
3. This compares with Beverly Serrell's findings (Serrell 1998).
4. Falk and Dierking 1992; Doering and Pekarik 1996.
5. Galco and Crowley 2001.
6. Ash 2002; Ellenbogen 2002; Falk and Dierking 2000.
7. Allen 2002.

Appendix

Problem and Context

METHODOLOGY REFERS TO THE TOOLS and rules of doing research. In examining reactions to the many different kinds of research conducted in museums, it sometimes seems as though it is the "rules" rather than the "tools" that have peppered methodological discussions. These discussions were sophisticated but often produced obstacles to the conduct of informative and interesting museum research. We include this appendix, then, not as a how-to manual but rather as an invitation to more confident, and we hope flexible, discussions about methodology.

The core problem for any methodology is how to select and then capture the important and valued information in a manner that is credible, reliable, and valid. Methodology is often cast in terms of protecting against threats to informational credibility, reliability, and validity. In the extreme, approaching a visitor and explaining with a smile that you personally put the exhibition together, are extremely enthusiastic about it, and really hope they are too, then saying you would like to ask some questions (and perhaps even adding, let us say, that this is your mother standing next to you) would render visitor responses highly suspect. The MLC needed to try and ensure the most objective conditions for data collection. The problem, then, is not how to do this "by the book" but how to best use the rich array of tools at our disposal to gather unique and important information. How can the reality of the situation best be captured with the tools at hand? This appendix is organized differently than the chapters in the book, in that the general procedure is presented first and then methodological issues for each chapter are discussed.

Informed Consent

In the world of research in museum learning, there is a rich variety of techniques and assumptions about what constitutes valid data. For example, museum researchers favor "naturalness" over experimentation, including the idea that the visitor should be minimally aware, if at all, of the researcher's presence. More important, research has historically been conducted in museums without the informed consent of the visitors themselves. (Indeed, in both the initial MLC proposal and early presentations of research from it, protests were raised over the requirement of informed consent.) The argument has been as follows:

> This is a public space owned privately. Therefore, what people do in a public space can be recorded without informing them about the collection of the data. By not informing people that data is being collected we can be reasonably assured that the information is accurate in that they have not "changed" their behavior.

In the past this might have been a completely justifiable position. However, over the past five to ten years, as concern for privacy has become more pronounced and the availability of "linked and linkable" data more common, universities have drastically changed their rules for collecting data from and about human beings— it is no longer enough to assure someone that names will not be used. The common practice for hospitals and universities engaged in any sort of human-subject research is that when data are collected, people are informed and their permission is secured (this is now a legal requirement in most areas). Many museums now do this as well. Does this change how people act? Yes. Does it change it so much that we cannot make sense of our results? No. Are the changes in behavior consistent with the underlying behavior patterns and beliefs of the individuals involved? Most probably. Thus, our argument for informed consent sounds like this:

> People cannot easily change certain fundamental features of their behavior—the reasons why they came to the museum in the first place, the personal historical connections to the material in the exhibition, their own formal and informal knowledge base, or the interpersonal dynamics of the group. Nor can they suddenly increase or alter their own vocabularies or sensitivity to objects and display issues. They can and do engage in more extensive and public conversations; they may censor their commentary with respect to hostile criticism and strong language. The effects of being aware of being observed are probably pretty consistent for the visitor population as a whole.

In this study we did offer group members a small gift (such as a museum logo pencil, a collection of exhibition-related postcards, a small toy, or candy) but only after they had agreed to participate and after they had completed their tour. Thus, visitors were not persuaded to participate because of the gift.

Sampling

A second feature of the museum research available six years ago was either an over-adherence to unweighted random sampling of people or, conversely, a complete avoidance of random sampling. Basically the sampling issue is the following: If one is trying to figure out what people are doing and thinking at a museum, in an exhibition, or in front of an object, one need not try to capture every single person who comes into contact with the target environment; rather, one may select a "sample." The questions are: Does the researcher sample knowingly or unknowingly? How many people are sampled? When? The correct answer is that we all determine the size of the sample based on a percentage of the total possible group of potential participants and/or the budget (almost always the constraining factor), and then individuals from that total are selected at random.[1] In the case of museums, where individuals are not distributed over a geographic space at a given moment in time (as is the case in a presidential poll), sampling is done across a longer time period that is randomly segmented into identifiable chunks. Thus, if an exhibition lasts ten days long and one believes that each day is like the next, and, further, if observation for all of the days is possible, then random sampling of chunks of time within each day would be appropriate (with similar actions if each part of a day or each season were presumed to be alike). However, many museum professionals do not believe that one day is like the next nor that time of day or season of the year is irrelevant.[2] The number of visitors to a museum is affected by rainy days, free admission evenings, and summer vacations. To be precise, one must sample proportionately according to the density and types of visitors usually involved at a given museum or exhibition. What should not be done is to collect data on Tuesday because it is convenient. NEVER! Well, hardly ever. The fact of the matter is that we all compromise on this issue. We do the best we can in combining the resources at hand with a desire to have some variety in the types of visitor responses obtained. (For example, if we picked the rainiest, coldest Saturday in November, then the reason for a given visitor's visit may be closely allied to that of another visitor simply because they both came to the museum to do something on a rainy, cold Saturday).

So what did the MLC do about selecting, informing, and sampling people? Because our study was about the conversations among small, informal groups of people as they visited a museum, we did not solicit participation from the following: school groups, large tour groups traveling intact, docent-led groups, groups of more than five or six, groups that did not speak English, and groups that had a member who required a substantial amount of attention from other members of a group (crying infants, dementia patients, or severely mentally handicapped individuals who needed close monitoring). We approached all other groups in a two-stage manner. First, we introduced ourselves and gave a short description of our work. If the group was willing to hear more, we then described the study and its participation requirements in greater depth. If the group was still willing to participate we gave them an informed consent form and had them sign it. The form assured the visitors that their information and conversations would remain confidential and that they could stop their participation at any time. There was considerable variation by museum concerning the refusal rate (50 to 10%); refusal seemed to depend on visitors' time constraints. For example, at the Henry Ford Museum, it was difficult to recruit people after 2:00 P.M. because most people had a long trip ahead of them when leaving.

How did we sample? We chose a block of time to visit an exhibition that ranged from ten days to two weeks; we distributed our data collection time within that block to include both weekdays and weekends; and we set a target number of groups that we hoped to sample for the block (across morning, afternoon, and early evening time slots). In some cases, sparse attendance at certain exhibitions impacted our target numbers; so an optimization strategy was adopted, where we concentrated our resources on the time periods and days when visitors were most likely to attend (e.g., Saturday afternoon). We avoided the first few days of a blockbuster show because of both sampling concerns and the simple impracticality of working in and among large crowds. We collected data from approximately thirty groups of visitors at each exhibition; thus our overall data set does not represent the true "draw"—the weighted average of attendance figures—for each of the exhibitions. To weight the attendance would have required that a series of days and times for data collection be selected at each site in advance; and if no visitors came during those times, then that exhibition would not be represented in the data—that lack would be compensated for by collecting/using more units at a very popular exhibition.

Recording

Different systems exist for collecting data from visitors, from short-form interviews to eavesdropping on groups and repeating their conversations verbatim into a tape recorder. The issue of what method to use for collecting the conversational data is, again, one of unobtrusiveness weighed against the collection of fine-grained data. The MLC used a combined approach. Small groups of visitors were audiotaped as they toured. Two visitors in each group were wired with very small wireless microphones connected to a small transmitter on their belts. The microphones transmitted conversations to a small, portable audio receiver unit that was connected to a recorder, both of which were carried by a researcher who trailed the group at a discreet distance.

A digital minidisc recorder was the device used by researchers to collect the data. The machines provided digital timing information and allowed researchers to insert track marks onto the recording. This timing and tracking capability meant that visitors' movement to a different exhibit station could be indicated precisely. Data collectors also indicated visitors' moves on a layout map of the exhibition in the order that the group traveled from one spot to another. Cordless microphones attached to two visitors' lapels allowed researchers to remain at a distance; a simple y-adapter connecting the two receiver units to the digital recorder carried by the researcher allowed for stereo recording—headphones worn by the researcher brought sound from one microphone (attached to one visitor) to the left ear, and sound from the other microphone came to the right ear. Microphones were sufficiently strong that conversation by surrounding group members was captured as well. The system provided easy and accurate access to timing information and location information and ready access to any part of the recording, simply by advancing to the desired track number. This easy access to any spot in the conversation allowed us to minimize transcription, as we could easily return to a specific track for verification of visitor talk. (See figs. A.1 and A.2.)

Pre- and Posttour Conversations

After two people in each group were selected to wear the cordless microphones, but before beginning their tour, the entire group was asked to have a conversation together as they looked at cards with questions on them, including some with photos. They were first asked why they came to the exhibition and what they expected to see. They then looked at five cards with pictures and captions related to the exhibition's content and were asked to discuss them. After they finished their visit, a similar set of questions and parallel pictures with captions were used to stimulate a posttour discussion. See figure A.3 for an example of a discussion-prompting card related to an exhibition theme—this one for the *Aluminum by Design* exhibition.

Specific Methodological Issues

Each of the following sections addresses specific methodological issues that pertain to each chapter in the book.

Chapter 1: Learning

The fundamental methodological issue posed by the issues surrounding learning was the need to develop an adequate measure of learning for each of the tour groups. There were essentially three sets of potential measures: the net number of usable tracks or stops, the total amount of engaged time, and a score of the

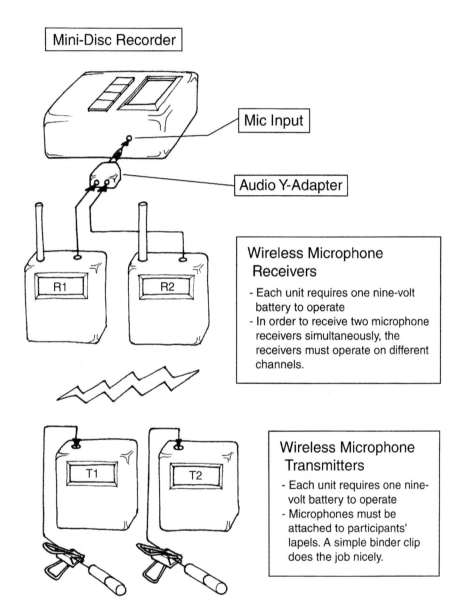

Figure A.1.   Equipment used to record conversations. (Drawing by Joshua Space.)

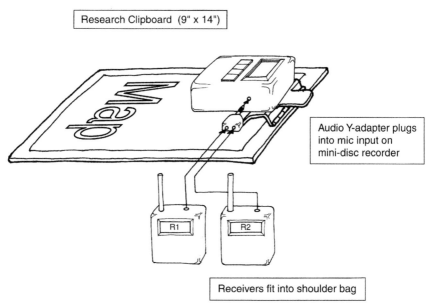

Research Clipboard (9" x 14")

Audio Y-adapter plugs into mic input on mini-disc recorder

Receivers fit into shoulder bag

Figure A.2.   Configuration of equipment. (Drawing by Joshua Space.)

Back in those days

Figure A.3.   Example of interview card with photograph and caption:
      History (discovery and use) thematic card posttour *Aluminum by Design* exhibition.

posttour conversations. The number of stops made by a group was considered to be an indication of the amount of effort and connection the visitors made during the tour; and it could be argued that the more stops a group made, the greater their chance to learn. True, but it could also be argued that a group might select fewer stops, spend a longer time at each one, and study those objects or groupings of objects very carefully; such a group might learn more than groups with a higher number of stops. We therefore decided not to use the number of tour stops or usable tracks.

The second candidate for a measure of learning was some estimate of time— average time per object or per track, total engaged time, or some other time estimate. Here again the argument was that if a group spent more engaged time at an exhibit or more average time per object, then the members of that group were likely to be learning, discussing, engaging more deeply.[3] This also is true, but time is constrained by other planned behaviors; although time is a useful indicator, it does not provide the entire picture. We had more information available than just the time the visitors spent in the exhibition: We knew what people were doing and talking about while they were visiting and afterward.

The third candidate involved using the conversations that occurred in the postvisit conversations. Recall that, in these conversations, each theme covered in the exhibition was prompted by a selected photograph or drawing of an object in the show and a phrase or question about it. We coded the entire postvisit conversation for thematic talk of all types, just as we had coded the tour talk for thematic references. For the measure of learning, the total number of detailed thematic references could be used. However, we noticed that on several occasions, especially for families with children, the posttour conversation was more limited than the conversation during the visit had been. This discrepancy meant that a thematic count alone would probably underestimate the kinds of learning from elaborated discussions that had been developed by such a group during the visit. In other situations, people who had seemed less than engaged during the visit or who talked less were quite verbal with respect to thematic ideas as they looked at various pictures after their visit. This meant that estimates of learning for these visitors might be overestimated. Under these conditions, it seemed as though thematic talk needed to be anchored to an additional estimate of effort or engagement in the museum visit.

After examining the actual values of total engaged time, thematic conversation, other discussions in the postvisit conversation, and the intercorrelations among them, we constructed the following measure: the total number of thematic mentions multiplied by 10 plus the total engaged tour time. Why times 10? We noticed that the average value for the number of thematic mentions was an order of magnitude smaller than the total time in minutes. To make the thematic measure and the time measure have equal weight in the constructed measure, the time measure would need to be divided by 10 or the thematic measure multiplied by 10. This was done because it is desirable to have one unit of increase in themes be approximately equal to an increase of a minute in a tour. The learning measure, thus, reflects both time and content. The combined theme/time measure had a reasonable distribution of high and low scores and seemed to best capture the sense of a group's engaged effort and expressed understanding. For the skeptic, we do want to point out that the "results" (in terms of correlations and regressions) did not look terribly different if we used themes alone or time alone; the patterns remain essentially the same.

Chapter 2: Exhibitions

One methodological issue apparently not discussed in the literature on museum learning and visitor studies concerns the manner in which the exhibition itself is captured or represented in the study. Most audience research adopts a transmission model approach as a communication model, looking only at the messages as received or responded to by visitors. Instead of focusing solely on the stated objectives for an exhibition, the MLC explored the intentions expressed by designers and curators as to the sequencing, layout, and layering of ideas and experiences they were providing for visitors. We went to considerable lengths to capture the curatorial intent and the core meanings of each exhibition. To do this, three sources were used: a videotaped and audiotaped curatorial discussion and walk-through, the exhibition catalogue when available, and the label-copy documentation or equivalent when available. A map of the entire space was developed and keyed to both location and label copy. These sources were used to build the thematically designed, self-administered interviews that probed visitors' background knowledge and to construct detailed maps of each exhibition for researchers to use to trace a group's moves through an exhibition.

Chapter 3: Identity

The problem to be addressed in order to establish a system of measures for identity was the need to incorporate the following dimensions: to use the type of group and the group's membership based on external characteristics as identity; to use an estimate of the motivation or reasons for the visit as identity; and to understand the connections between the visiting group and the content of the exhibition in terms of visitors' background knowledge, either experiential or appreciative. Each of these dimensions is discussed below.

EXTERNAL CHARACTERISTICS. After signed consent had been obtained from a group, the data collector filled out a brief data sheet, noting the number of people in the group, the approximate ages of the members, the genders, the ethnicity if obvious, the apparent structural roles (to be confirmed later in the visit), and the specific group members (if there were more than two) who were wearing the microphones. At the same time as the researcher attended to this task, the visiting group took a bound set of cards on which were printed the pre-visit discussion questions and went to a seating area to talk together in response to the cards. The researcher waited nearby until the group finished its discussion.

For the most part, establishing the external characteristics of a group was straightforward; however, the initial information was updated and adjusted based on the conversations that emerged during the rest of the tour. For example, visitors' ages were initially estimated by decade, but occasionally group members would provide specific clues about their age information during their tour (saying something like, "Oh, that was made in 1969; that's the year I was born"), which would either confirm or correct the initial age assumptions. More significant adjustments needed to be made about the social roles within the group. The use of family role names during the tour (such as, "Mom," or "Aunt") or when business colleagues talked about their shared work helped us to determine the presumed social roles with greater confidence. Families and married couples were the easiest types of groups to determine; all other types were presumed to be social groups unless a pair displayed obvious couple-like behaviors, either by speech (saying "Hon," or "Babe") or physical contact (such as holding hands or kissing). Finally, very rarely, a group's category type was changed in the records based on a change that took place during the visit. For example, if a group was initially identified as a family but the children soon went off on their own, leaving the mother and her friend to complete the tour, and if these two adults also participated in the end-of-tour discussion as a duo, the group was reclassified as a friendship group.

MOTIVATION. The pre-visit discussion was used to establish an initial estimate of a group's motivation—that is, the group's desire and reason for coming to a particular exhibition. The specific questions in the bound set of cards that related most directly to motivation were "Why did you come to see the XXX exhibition at the YYY museum today?" and "What do you expect to see or do at the XXX exhibition?" The answers to these questions were considered in light of the group's behaviors during the tour and whether the visitors had made a special trip to see the show. A motivation rating scale from 1 to 5 was established. As described in chapter 3, the scale was anchored to four factors. If the visiting group was low on all four factors, then it received a 1; if the group had a high rating on at least three of the four factors, then they received a 5. The four factors used in the rating were intentionality or planfulness, frequency of museum going, topical familiarity, and overcoming obstacles. Reliability using a conservative estimate was 72%, although 100% agreement would have been obtained if raters were considered to be in agreement when they were within one point. The value used to rate a group's motivation was an average of the scores assigned by three raters.

PRIOR KNOWLEDGE. We treated knowledge as a resource for the entire group and identified two distinct sources: Knowledge could come from the experience of working with or constructing objects like those in the exhibition; or it could come from study, collection, and deep appreciation. We did not give individuals or the groups a test, nor did we treat their tour as a test. Rather, we looked at their answers to relevant pre-tour and posttour discussion questions ("Are there any ways in which the exhibition connected with you personally?" "Are there any ways in which work, travel, or hobbies connected you with the exhibition?"). We also looked throughout the museum visit conversations for evidence of visitors' relevant background knowledge and experience ("I worked at the Ford plant for forty years," "I restore cars for a living," "I wrote my Master's thesis on lighting in the eighteenth-century French operas").

We created rating scales from 1 to 5 for both of the knowledge domains (experiential and appreciative). Interobserver reliability on a 25% sample of the data was 100% for ratings that were within one-half a point. As discussed in chapter 3, low ratings were given to groups with little connection to the content of an exhibition ("I don't really know anything about Africa" or "We studied the Sahara in elementary school"). Moderate ratings were given to groups that had what we considered to be an average level of knowledge of the content area. And the highest ratings were given to those who had professional-level connections to content related to the exhibition. Initially, the two forms of prior knowledge were treated separately; however, there was a high correlation between the two measures (.62) and, more important, the two measures seemed to relate to other variables in a similar fashion. Therefore, we combined the two by taking a simple sum and dividing by 2. The measure for identity, then, consisted of individual demographic characteristics of group members (available to do separate analyses), a group-type assignment (family, social, couple), the combination of a five-point motivation rating, and a five-point prior-knowledge rating.

Chapter 4: Conversation

SEGMENTING AND UNITIZING. In order to analyze the rich record of conversation, label reading, and movement through an exhibition, it was necessary to move from an unedited audio stream to some type of parsed or segmented document. The issues for parsing are the same whether one is working from videotapes, audiotapes, or written transcripts.

Essentially, the underlying question for parsing or segmenting the data is the following: What constitutes a codable chunk or instance? There are at least four types of segmenting systems. First, there is *instance* counting, the most common analytic process in computer-supported analysis systems. Basically, instance counting involves examining the data and marking whenever a looked-for statement or behavior occurs; everything else remains unmarked. This process can be considered as a special case of what is often referred to as *event* coding. The advantage of instance counting is that one only counts what one is interested in. The disadvantage of this approach is that one can easily overcount instances in multiple ways and one may precisely count things that actually occur quite rarely, although the reader has no way of knowing that. When one uses instance coding, one can talk about the quantity of an observed behavior.

The second type of coding is *event* coding, in which boundaries are placed around a piece of conversation or action based on a set of predetermined rules, for example, moving from one object to another, or a change in the topic of conversation from one object or station to another. In event coding, visits of the same length, say ninety minutes, may have quite different numbers of segments in them; some may be forty segments long and others seventy. In addition to the variability in number of segments, each segment can vary in its length. The advantage to using event coding is that it corresponds to a natural process for parsing—it feels right. The disadvantage to event coding is that disagreements among coders can easily occur about the boundary situation: Had the group moved on? Are they still talking about the vase even though they are now walking? The major benefit of using event segmenting is that it allows researchers to describe the proportion of talk devoted to one or another topic or the proportion of talk that occurred in one or another form.

Time-based segmenting is the most clear-cut and error-free system. Under time segmenting, the full audiotape is chopped up into equal time units—thirty to sixty seconds long, for example. Each time unit is then coded in response to the underlying query: What is going on in this unit at this time? The advantage to time-based segmenting is that there is little or no disagreement as to the segment boundaries, and it allows researchers to talk about the proportion of time spent discussing or doing a particular activity. The disadvantage is that the resulting segments are very unnatural—the breaks cut through topics and idea units with abandon.

Finally, a very common way of segmenting discourse in the linguistic tradition is by *turns*. Turns occur in conversation when the speaker changes. This form of segmenting is usually easy to do, and there is little disagreement as to when a turn has or has not taken place, although overlapping talk can create some difficulties in the segmenting process. Some researchers combine turns with topic-like content so that a grouping of turns is considered to form a single segment. But in all cases, the change of speaker is considered a notable circumstance. Using turn-based segmenting allows researchers to report on what proportion of the talk of a certain type was done by one or another person and how the talk was coordinated.

As described in chapter 4, the MLC used event-based segmenting. We preselected the segments by carefully identifying logical and discrete "stops" along the full route through an exhibition. Each stop, which visitors could make in any order, was noted by the researcher in the field who was watching and listening to the groups and who entered a new track mark on the audio disc every time a group moved to a new object, case, or station and changed topic. After the audiotapes were partially transcribed, we reassessed the track segments for each group and eliminated irrelevant segments (e.g., for trips out of the exhibition, mistaken marks when the researcher thought the group was moving on but they did not) or added segments for instances when a researcher failed to capture a move that did occur.

This system of segmenting worked extremely well. Out of 197 visits there were a total of 10,000 segments averaging 50 segments per visit. But the system was not perfect. The most serious problem occurred when a group stopped at an exhibit for a long time and had an extended discussion there. This occurrence was most common in the *Behind the Screen* exhibition at the Exploratorium, where visitors typically had long waits in line and tended to have lengthy interactions once they had access to the exhibits. Upon reading carefully through one transcript that had a nine-minute stop filled with detailed discussions, we knew we had to make an adjustment in order to account for the true amount of engagement at such stops. After examining all the transcripts, we decided to break any segment that lasted more than two minutes and to do so in ninety-second increments. The reasoning for this decision was as follows: Since the average segment for all the transcripts was about one minute long and the standard deviation was also close to one minute, stops that lasted more than two minutes were unusually long. However, if we were to select two minutes as both the resegmenting and the new chunk size, then there would be a large number of five- or ten-second "bits" left over; thus, we chose to resegment in the time chunk associated with approximately one half of a standard deviation from the mean—at ninety seconds. This combined system of segmenting by time and event seemed to work quite well.

CODING. Given a segmented transcript, the next step is to code the segments. The MLC spent a great deal of effort considering codes before we had transcripts in hand. The language that visitors use in the museum is rich and nuanced. It could be used to show how groups supported and worked together in the benign environment of the museum. It could be used to show how low-status members of a small group gradually were given or acquired more power in the group. It could be used to trace the entry into or avoidance of a particular discourse community, such as the aesthetic appreciation. In other words, the language could be considered from multiple vantage points, and we hope that in the fullness of time we can do just that.

The MLC's earlier work, reported in *Learning Conversations in Museums*,[4] indicated that two useful ways to consider the content of the segments were structurally and thematically based. There were at least five discernable types of conversational structure. We had observed that a good deal of the language of the visitors consisted of some sort of noticing and evaluating behavior. Talk consisting primarily of brief labels and evaluations of objects or stations was very common. Sometimes these brief mentions were simply partial label readings. We called these abbreviated kinds of conversations *lists*. Another structural conversational move involved the visiting group identifying and linking the object or experience to something personal, as in, "Aunt Sally had one of those in her living room," or "I remember when my Dad bought one of those Fords and really fixed it up in the backyard." This kind of personally relevant comment about something in an exhibition synthesized the visible object with a remembered experience; we called these comments *personal synthesis*. Another structural conversational move involved one or more members of the group looking quite closely at an object or interactive exhibit and talking about specific parts of it and their effects. These kinds of conversational moves tended to show a greater engagement with the object itself on the part of the speakers and seemed often to include an invitation to others in the group to either find a like instance or offer a different one, as in, "I love the way that green in the sky works to make it sort of pop out even though the sky still seems blue"; "Yeah, I like the dappled purple in the shadows—it is so unexpected." These segments of conversation in which an object or idea was pulled apart and its attributes focused upon were called *analysis*, because the conversational move was highly focused and directed toward a kind of analysis of effect, method, material, or intention. A fourth kind of conversational move involved the group selecting one or more dimensions of an object or set of objects in a display and relating them to the same dimension of a different object in the exhibition or perhaps to something seen at another venue. We called these kinds of structural moves *synthesis*. Finally, the conversation might reflect an answer to an explicit or implicit question about intent, purpose, mechanism, or some other aspect of an exhibit or display that described how or why something looked the way it did or happened the way it did and often used language that suggested causality. These language segments were considered *explanation*. For each segment, one and only one of these structural codes was assigned. The structural code that was assigned to a segment was the highest level of talk actually used in that segment if more than one level was present. Hierarchically, the codes were ranked such that explanation was the highest, synthesis the next, analysis the next, personal synthesis the next, and lists the lowest.

For segments that were coded at the three highest levels—analysis, synthesis, or explanation—the content of the talk was also assigned a thematic code. One theme was coded for each segment even if multiple themes were discussed. In cases where more than one thematic idea was discussed in a given segment, the chosen theme was selected based on its predominance and its connection to the structural code used. Thus, for example, if a group noticed an object, commented on it by analyzing some feature, and then explained that feature's function, the thematic code would be the theme referenced in the explanatory portion of the discussion. Themes were coded only once for each segment and only if some contributed idea was present. Themes were not coded simply because a word was mentioned or labeled. Themes were coded independently by three coders and agreement was reached by discussion. The total value for each code in a transcript was open-ended—that is, each theme could obtain a value from zero to infinity depending on how many segments were coded with that theme in a group's transcript.

Chapter 5: Learning Environment

Whereas the identity of a visiting group represents the dispositions of the visitors coming into an exhibition, the learning environment represents the aspects of the exhibition that were deliberately, asynchronously designed into the show to develop and portray the curatorial message. Developing measures of the learning environment was one of the most challenging sets of methodological issues with which we had to come to grips.

The problems in designing measures of the learning environment were the following. First, there are a host of design decisions that curators make in anticipation of the visitor, which may or may not be used. The visitor may simply not go to a certain area or take note of a particular feature; thus, it would be impossible for researchers to determine if a particular feature did or did not support learning. In response to this issue we made an early decision to consider as a part of the learning environment only those designed aspects that were actually used by members of a visiting group and to count those instances of use only when they were used by the target group. This approach meant that large environmental features of an exhibition were actually assigned to groups, not to the exhibit. There are statistical techniques that permit multiple layers of codes (hierarchical cluster analysis, for example); but using these techniques requires a larger number of exhibitions (around one hundred) to make generalities about design features alone, unattached to visiting groups.

A second issue was how to separate language or actions that reflected learning environment interactions from those that reflected conversational engagement or dialogical connection. We made an arbitrary decision to consider responses to such features as higher-level signage, guide marks, and floor layout to be responses to the learning environment, whereas responses to specific object- or case-level label copy or to specific displays within the exhibition were considered to be included in the conversational codes for explanatory engagement (thematic and structural talk).

A final problem for the design of learning environment measures was how to consider the issues of physical manipulations of features of an exhibition in contrast to intellectual manipulations—for example, painting adjacent walls of a gallery distinctive and message-bearing colors or deliberately designing a way-finding cue (such as a suspended metallic ribbon) as opposed to using intellectual support of the learning environment in the form of large, superordinate explanatory text panels. We examined each exhibition and the label copy for it. We developed a detailed map of the floor of the show and marked every location in which a learning environment feature might be coded. Thus, for the intellectual aspect of the learning environment, we noted all signage above the object level. If a group stopped and read part or all of the sign, then that stop was marked in a special way on the map that researchers used to traced their tour. Later, when the partial transcription of the tour was produced, those segments for which there was a learning environment stop were noted and then the number of such instances was summed to obtain a total for the visit. The value for the code was open-ended and could range from 0 to over 20.

For the physical elements supporting the learning environment, we included the following: chairs, benches, lighting, wall color, museum-provided maps and guides, flip charts, or hands-on feedback materials. Responses to these elements were counted only if the visitors made a comment about them or if the visitors actively used the guides or sat on the benches. Thus, a comment such as, "I love when they have questions and answers on flip charts" got a point, but visitors simply using such a device did not. Why? We decided on this restrictive use of the physical learning environment because otherwise the so-called measures would simply be a proxy for the museum itself. For example, *Aluminum by Design* did not have flip charts, so the presence or absence of them could not be determined as useful or not useful. Likewise, the majority of the exhibits at *Behind the Screen* were interactive, so there was no within-museum variation possible among groups to that exhibition. It turned out that visitors' responses to the physical elements were relatively rare; thus we ultimately combined the physical codes with the intellectual ones. The possible value for the learning environment code was open-ended, consisting of a simple frequency count.

Chapter 6: Results

In chapter 6 we reported both qualitative and quantitative results. We explained qualitative findings only when we felt they were supported by the quantitative ones. The fundamental methodology was simple linear regressions (using StatView). It is more common for the museum community to use ANOVA. The main substantive difference in approach (one can get mathematically from one to the other) is the form of the question. ANOVAs ask questions about the differences between one group or treatment and another while regressions ask about prediction of a variable (in this case learning) by a family of other variables.

This is also the place where we need to specify the limitations and boundaries of the study as we see them. We have not tried to identify specific practices that lead to learning because the data were not designed to do that nor could it have been within the bounds of the study, and we discussed that issue in chapter 5. Instead this was a study of clusters of phenomenon that taken together produced more or less learning on the part of groups of people who chose to visit a museum on a particular day and at a particular time. By the very nature of our selection and notification process, certain groups would not appear in this data set. For example, a group transiting between one part of the museum and another or a group who just wanted to stop in for a couple of minutes to see one or two items in a show would most probably not have agreed to stop and be wired up and have a pre-tour conversation. Groups who, at the other extreme, wanted to spend an extended and perhaps private time might likewise have not agreed to participate. On average one group refused to participate for every group that agreed. In combination, not having the very fast or the very slow probably evened itself out, but it may also account for the longer than average tour times and the frequency with which our groups stopped and engaged deeply with quite a few objects or stations. As to the other concern that might be raised, namely, that we altered the visit, we have tried to address that throughout the body of the book. We believe that most people realized that they were being taped for most of their visit; but on many occasions people clearly forgot or were tremendously uninhibited. But mostly we feel, as we mentioned previously, that people cannot suddenly reinvent themselves. They might have talked a little more, they might have stayed a little longer, or they might have left a little more abruptly; but the groups were engaged in a visit to the museum first and participants in a study second.

We opened this chapter with a concern that methodology be seen as a system of tools, not as a rulebook. In this study we think that we stayed within the boundary lines of acceptable research practices, but we tried to be creative and flexible in the construction of measures, in the coding and collecting of data, and in its interpretation. Most of all, we have tried to be open and public enough and to provide enough information so that both the critic and the curious can examine our choices and then decide to try the study in their way. We hope that this book will serve as a starting point for a continuing dialogue with other museum professionals and researchers about the nature of learning of museums and about the nature of studying learning in museums.

Notes

1. See Doering and Pekarik 1996, for a formal discussion of this material.
2. Hood and Roberts 1994.
3. Serrell 1995.
4. Leinhardt, Crowley, and Knutson 2002.

References

Abu-Shumays, M., and G. Leinhardt. 2002. Two docents, three museums: Central and peripheral participation. In *Learning Conversations in Museums*, edited by G. Leinhardt, K. Crowley, and K. Knutson, 45–80. Mahwah, NJ: Lawrence Erlbaum Associates.

Africa: One Continent, Many Worlds. Museum exhibition curated by the Field Museum of Natural History, Chicago, and available online at http://www.nhm.org/africa/home.html.

Allen, S. 1997. Using scientific inquiry activities in exhibit explanations. *Science Education (Informal Science Education—Special Issue)* 81(6): 715–734.

———. 2002. Looking for learning in visitor talk: A methodological exploration. In *Learning Conversations in Museums*, edited by G. Leinhardt, K. Crowley, and K. Knutson, 259–303. Mahwah, NJ: Lawrence Erlbaum Associates.

Ames, M. 1992. *Cannibal Tours and Glass Boxes: The Anthropology of Museums.* Vancouver, BC: University of British Columbia Press.

Ash, D. 2002. Negotiations of thematic conversations about biology. In *Learning Conversations in Museums*, edited by G. Leinhardt, K. Crowley, and K. Knutson, 357–400. Mahwah, NJ: Lawrence Erlbaum Associates.

Becker, J., D. MacAndrew, and J. Fiez. 1999. A comment on the functional localization of the phonological storage subsystem of working memory. *Brain and Cognition* 41: 27–38.

Behind the Screen: Making Motion Pictures and Television. Museum exhibition curated by the American Museum of the Moving Image, Astoria, New York, and available online at http://www.ammi.org/site/online/index.html.

Bennett, T. 1995. *The Birth of the Museum: History, Theory, Politics.* London: Routledge.

Bitgood, S., and R. Loomis. 1993. Introduction: Environmental design and evaluation in museums. *Environment and Behavior (Special Issue)* 25(6): 683–697.

Bitgood, S., M. Pierce, M. Nichols, and D. Patterson. 1987. Formative evaluation of a cave exhibit. *Curator* 30(1): 31–39.

Bliihm, A., and L. Lippincott. 2000. *Light! The Industrial Age 1750–1900, Art & Science, Technology & Society.* London: Thames and Hudson.

Borun, M., M. Chambers, and A. Cleghorn. 1996. Families are learning in science museums. *Curator* 39(2): 124–138.

Borun, M., M. Chambers, J. Dritsas, and J. Johnson. 1997. Enhancing family learning through exhibits. *Curator* 40(4): 279–295.

Brown, A. 1975. The development of memory: Knowing, knowing about knowing, and knowing how to know. In *Advances in Child Development and Behavior*, vol. 10, edited by H. W. Resse, 103–152. New York: Academic Press.

———. 1992. Design experiments: Theoretical and methodological challenges in creating complex interventions in classroom settings. *Journal of the Learning Sciences* 2: 141–178.

Carroll, J. 1963. A model of school learning. *Teachers College Record* 64(8): 723–733.

Chi, M., and R. Roscoe. 2002. The processes and challenges of conceptual change. In *Reconsidering Conceptual Change: Issues in Theory and Practice*, edited by M. Limón and L. Mason, 3–27. Dordrecht, Netherlands: Kluwer Academic Publishers.

Clark, H. 1996. *Using Language*. Cambridge: Cambridge University Press.

Crowley, K., J. Galco, M. Jacobs, and S. Russo. 2000. Explanatoids, fossils, and family conversations. American Educational Research Association, New Orleans, LA.

Crowley, K., and J. Galco. 2001. Everyday activity and the development of scientific thinking. In *Designing for Science: Implications from Everyday, Classroom, and Professional Science*, edited by K. Crowley, C. Schunn, and T. Okada. Mahwah, NJ: Lawrence Erlbaum Associates.

Crowley, K., and M. Jacobs. 2002. Building islands of expertise in everyday family activity. In *Learning Conversations in Museums*, edited by G. Leinhardt, K. Crowley, and K. Knutson, 333–356. Mahwah, NJ: Lawrence Erlbaum Associates

Dean, D. 1996. *Museum Exhibition*. New York: Routledge.

Doering, Z., and A. Pekarik. 1996. Questioning the entrance narrative. *Journal of Museum Education* 21(3): 20–22.

Duncan, C. 1995. *Civilizing Rituals: Inside Public Art Museums*. New York: Routledge.

Ellenbogen, K. 2002. Museums in family life: An ethnographic case study. In *Learning Conversations in Museums*, edited by G. Leinhardt, K. Crowley, and K. Knutson, 81–102. Mahwah, NJ: Lawrence Erlbaum Associates.

Falk, J. 1983. Time and behavior as predictors of learning. *Science Education* 67(2): 267–276.

———. 2002. Taking an environmental psychology perspective in museums. Paper presented at annual meeting of the American Educational Research Association, New Orleans, LA.

Falk, J., and L. Dierking. 1990. The effect of visitation frequency on long-term recollections. In *Proceedings of the Third Annual Visitor Studies Conference*, edited by S. Bitgood, 94–104. Jacksonville, AL: Center for Social Design.

———. 1992. *The Museum Experience*. Washington, DC: Whalesback Books.

———. 2000. *Learning from Museums: Visitor Experiences and the Making of Meaning*. Walnut Creek, CA: AltaMira Press.

Falk, J., T. Moussouri, and D. Coulson. 1998. The effect of visitors' agendas on museum learning. *Curator* 41(2): 107–120.

Fienberg, J., and G. Leinhardt. 2002. Looking through the glass: Reflections of identity in conversations at a history museum. In *Learning Conversations in Museums*, edited by G. Leinhardt, K. Crowley, and K. Knutson, 167–212. Mahwah, NJ: Lawrence Erlbaum Associates.

Fiez, J. 2001. Bridging the gap between neuroimaging and neuropsychology: Challenges and potential benefits. *Journal of Clinical and Experimental Neuropsychiatry* 23: 19–31.

Fisher, C., and D. Berliner. 1985. *Perspectives on Instructional Time*. New York. Longman.

Ford Motor Company. 2002. Africa: One Continent, Many Worlds. Press release available online at http://www.ford.com/en/ourCompany/corporateCitizenship/artsAndHumanities/africaOneContinentManyWorlds.htm.

Fosnot, C. 1993. Revisiting science education: A defense of Piagetian constructivism. *Journal for Research in Science Teaching* 30(9): 1189–1201.

Galco, J., and K. Crowley. 2001. How mundane parent explanation changes what children learn from everyday scientific thinking. Unpublished manuscript, Learning Research and Development Center, University of Pittsburgh, Pittsburgh, PA.

Gardner, H. 1983. *Frames of Mind: The Theory of Multiple Intelligences*. New York: Poseidon.

———. 1993. *Multiple Intelligences: The Theory in Practice*. New York: Basic Books.

Gee, P. 1999. *An Introduction to Discourse Analysis: Theory and Method*. New York: Routledge.

Graburn, N. 1984. The museum and the visitor experience. In *Museum Education Anthology: 1973–1983*, edited by S. Nichols, M. Alexander, and K. Yellis, 177–182. Washington, DC: Museum Education Roundtable.

Greenberg, R., B. Ferguson, and S. Nairne, eds. 1996. *Thinking about Exhibitions*. London: Routledge.

Greeno, J. 1998. Where is teaching? *Issues in Education* 4(1): 111–119.

Grice, P. 1989. *Studies in the Way of Words*. Cambridge, MA: Harvard University Press.

Hein, G. 1998. *Learning in the Museum*. London: Routledge.

Hilke, D. 1988. Strategies for family learning in museums. In *Visitor Studies 1988: Theory, Research and Practice*, vol. I, edited by S. Bitgood, J. Roper, and A. Benefield, 120–134. Jacksonville, AL: Center for Social Design.

Hood, M. 1983. Staying away: Why people choose to not visit museums. *Museum News* 61(4): 50–57.

———. 1993. Comfort and caring: Two essential environmental factors. *Environment and Behavior* 25(6): 710–724.

Hood, M., and L. Roberts. 1994. Neither too young or too old: A comparison of visitor characteristics. *Curator* 37(1): 36–45.

Hooper-Greenhill, E. 1992. *Museums and the Shaping of Knowledge*. New York: Routledge.

———. 2000. *Museums and the Interpretation of Visual Culture*. New York: Routledge.

Housen, A. 1992. Validating a measure of aesthetic development for museums and schools. *IVLS Review* 2(2): 213–237.

Karp, I., and S. Lavine, eds. 1991. *Exhibiting Cultures: The Poetics and Politics of Museum Display*. Washington, DC: Smithsonian Institution Press.

Kindler, A. 1997. Aesthetic development and learning in art museums: A challenge to enjoy. *Journal of Museum Education* 22(2 & 3): 12–16.

Knutson, K. 2002. Creating a space for learning: Curators, educators and the implied audience. In *Learning Conversations in Museums*, edited by G. Leinhardt, K. Crowley, and K. Knutson, 5–44. Mahwah, NJ: Lawrence Erlbaum Associates.

Koran, J., M. Koran, and S. Longino. 1986. The relationship of age, sex, attention, and holding power with two types of science exhibits. *Curator* 29(3): 227–235.

Korn, R. 1988. Self-guiding brochures: An evaluation. *Curator* 31(1): 9–19.

Lave, J., and E. Wenger. 1991. *Situated Learning: Legitimate Peripheral Participation*. Cambridge: Cambridge University Press.

Leinhardt, G. 2000. Lessons on teaching and learning in history from Paul's pen. In *Knowing, Teaching and Learning History*, edited by P. Stearns, P. Seixas, and S. Wineburg, 223–245. New York: New York University Press.

Leinhardt, G., and K. Crowley. 2002. Objects of learning, objects of talk: Changing minds in museums. In *Multiple Perspectives on Object-Centered Learning*, edited by S. Paris, 301–324. Mahwah, NJ: Lawrence Erlbaum Associates.

Leinhardt, G., K. Crowley, and K. Knutson, eds. 2002. *Learning Conversations in Museums*. Mahwah, NJ: Lawrence Erlbaum Associates

Leinhardt, G., K. Knutson, J. Fienberg, and C. Stainton. 2002. Museum Learning Collaborative Research Manual. Unpublished manuscript, University of Pittsburgh, Pittsburgh, PA.

Leinhardt, G., C. Tittle, and K. Knutson. 2002. Talking to oneself: Diary studies of museum visits. In *Learning Conversations in Museums*, edited by G. Leinhardt, K. Crowley, and K. Knutson, 103–132. Mahwah, NJ: Lawrence Erlbaum Associates.

Linell, P. 1998. *Approaching Dialogue: Talk, Interaction and Contexts in Dialogical Perspectives*. Amsterdam, NL: John Benjamins.

Madden, J. [1985] 1992. To realize our museums' full potential. In *Patterns in Practice: Selections from the Journal of Museum Education*, edited by S. K. Nichols, 118–122. Washington, DC: Museum Education Roundtable.

Matusov, E., and B. Rogoff. 1995. Evidence of development from people's participation in communities of learners. In *Public Institutions for Personal Learning*, edited by J. Falk and L. Dierking, 97–104. Washington, DC: American Association of Museums.

McLean, K. 1993. *Planning for People in Museum Exhibitions*. Washington, DC: Association of Science Technology Centers.

McManus, P. 1993. Memories as indicators of the impact of museum visits. *Museum Management and Curatorship* 12: 367–380.

Mead, G. H. 1934. *Mind, Self and Society from the Standpoint of a Social Behaviorist*. Chicago: University of Chicago Press.

Mische, A., and H. White. 1998. Between conversation and situation: Public switching dynamics across network domains. *Social Research* 65(3): 695–724.

Montessori, M. 1964. *The Montessori Method*, translated from the Italian by A. George. New York: Schocken Books.

Mohr, J. 1994. Soldiers, mothers, tramps, and others: Discourse roles in the 1907 New York City Charity Directory. *Poetics* 22: 327–357.

Perry, D., L. Roberts, K. Morrissey, and L. Silverman. 1997. Listening outside and within. *Journal of Museum Education* 21(3): 26–27.

Piaget, J. 1955. *The Language and Thought of the Child*, translated by M. Gabain. Preface by E. Claparède. London: Routledge and K. Paul.

————. 1967. *Biologie et connaissance; Essai sur les relations entre les régulations organiques et les processus cognitifs.* Paris: Gallimard.

Poundstone, W. 2000. *Carl Sagan: A Life in the Cosmos.* New York: Henry Holt.

Prairietown. Living history museum exhibition at Conner Prairie, Fishers, IN, and available online at http://www.connerprairie.org/explore/prairietown.html.

Pursell, C. 1992. Telling a story: "The Automobile in American Life." In *Ideas and Images: Developing Interpretive History Exhibits,* edited by K. Ames, B. Franco, and L. Frye, 233–252. Nashville, TN: American Association for State and Local History.

Rice, D. 1995. Museum education embracing uncertainty. *Art Bulletin* 77(1): 15–20.

Roberts, L. 1997. *From Knowledge to Narrative: Educators and the Changing Museum.* Washington, DC: Smithsonian Institution Press.

Roschelle, J. 1995. Learning in interactive environments: Prior knowledge and new experience. In *Public Institutions for Personal Learning,* edited by J. Falk and L. Dierking, 37–51. Washington, DC: American Association of Museums.

Rosenthal, E., and J. Blankman-Hetrick. 2002. Conversations across time: Family learning in a living history museum. In *Learning Conversations in Museums,* edited by G. Leinhardt, K. Crowley, and K. Knutson, 305–329. Mahwah, NJ: Lawrence Erlbaum Associates.

Schauble, L., et al. 2002. Supporting science learning in museums. In *Learning Conversations in Museums,* edited by G. Leinhardt, K. Crowley, and K. Knutson, 425–454. Mahwah, NJ: Lawrence Erlbaum Associates.

Schleier, C. 1998. Stephen Jay Gould: Was it survival of the luckiest? *Biography Magazine,* March 1998. Available online at http://www.biography.com.

Serrell, B. 1995. The 51% solution research project: A meta-analysis of visitor time/use in museum exhibitions. *Visitor Behavior* 10(3): 5–9.

————. 1997. Paying attention: The duration and allocation of visitors' time in museum exhibitions. *Curator* 40(2): 108–125.

————. 1998. *Paying Attention. Visitors and Museum Exhibitions.* Washington, DC: AAM.

————. 2001. A tool for judging excellence in museum exhibitions. *The Exhibitionist* (Spring). Available online at http://www.excellentjudges.org.

Sfard, A. 1998. On two metaphors for learning and on the dangers of choosing just one. *Educational Researcher* 27(2): 4–13.

Silverman, L. 1990. Of us and other "things": The content and functions of talk by adult visitor pairs in an art and a history museum. Ph.D. diss., University of Pennsylvania, Philadelphia.

————. 1993. Making meaning together: Lessons from the field of American history. *Journal of Museum Education* 18(3): 7–11.

————. 1995. Visitor meaning-making in museums for a new age. *Curator* 38: 161–170.

Sinatra, G., I. Beck, and M. McKeown. 1992. A longitudinal characterization of young students' knowledge of their country's government. *American Educational Research Journal* 29(3): 633–661.

Stainton, C. 2002. Voices and images: Making connections between identity and art. In *Learning Conversations in Museums,* edited by G. Leinhardt, K. Crowley, and K. Knutson, 213–257. Mahwah, NJ: Lawrence Erlbaum Associates.

Stevenson, J. 1991. The long-term impact of interactive exhibits. *International Journal of Science Education* 13(5): 521–531.

Stodolsky, S. 1988. *The Subject Matters: Classroom Activity in Math and Social Studies.* Chicago: University of Chicago Press.

Tunnicliffe, S. 1998. Boy talk/girl talk: Is it the same at animal exhibits? *International Journal of Science Education* 20(7): 795–811.

Underhill, P. 2000. *Why We Buy: The Science of Shopping.* New York: Touchstone Books.

Vygotsky, L. 1978. *Mind in Society: The Development of Higher Psychological Processes.* Cambridge, MA: Harvard University Press.

Weil, S. 2002. Museums: Can and do they make a difference? In *Making Museums Matter.* Washington, DC: Smithsonian Institution Press.

Wells, G. 1999. *Dialogic Inquiry: Towards a Sociocultural Practice and Theory of Education.* New York: Cambridge University Press.

White, H. 1995. Where do languages come from? Switching talk. Unpublished manuscript, Columbia University, New York.

Worts, D. 1995. Extending the frame: Forging a new partnership with the public. In *Art in Museums,* edited by S. Pearce. London: Athlone Press.

Wertsch, J. 1991. *Voices of the Mind: A Sociocultural Approach to Mediated Action.* Cambridge, MA: Harvard University Press.

Yanow, D. 1998. Space stories: Studying buildings as organizational spaces while reflecting on interpretive methods and their narration. *Journal of Management Inquiry* 7(3): 215–239.

Index

About the Authors

Gaea Leinhardt, senior scientist at LRDC (the Learning Research and Development Center) and professor of education at the University of Pittsburgh, was the principal investigator of the Museum Learning Collaborative. In addition to learning in museums, her research has dealt with the teaching and learning of history, mathematics, and geography with special attention to the nature, purposes, and consequences of explanations. She is currently involved in the study of online education at the college level, the development of enriched and deep history lessons for teachers, and the study of teachers' use of new instructional tools in their classrooms.

Karen Knutson was project manager of the Museum Learning Collaborative. She works at LRDC as senior researcher, where her research focuses on communication processes, interpretation, and learning in museums, with a particular interest in the study of art museums. She is currently conducting an ethnographic study of an expansion of the Children's Museum of Pittsburgh examining the design of exhibits and programs, administration and organizational structures, and visitor experience. She is also interested in community-based art education and provides consulting services for museums.